NON SANS DROICT.

William Shakespeare

The History of
HENRY IV
[PART ONE]

EDITED BY MAYNARD MACK

THE SIGNET CLASSIC SHAKESPEARE
GENERAL EDITOR: SYLVAN BARNET

𝒞

A SIGNET CLASSIC from
NEW AMERICAN LIBRARY
TIMES MIRROR
New York and Scarborough, Ontario
The New English Library Limited, London

SIGNET, SIGNET CLASSICS, MENTOR, PLUME AND MERIDIAN BOOKS
are published *in the United States* by
The New American Library, Inc.,
1301 Avenue of the Americas, New York, New York 10019,
in Canada by The New American Library of Canada Limited,
81 Mack Avenue, Scarborough, 704, Ontario,
in the United Kingdom by The New English Library Limited,
Barnard's Inn, Holborn, London, E.C. 1, England

10 11 12 13 14 15 16 17

PRINTED IN THE UNITED STATES OF AMERICA

Contents

Shakespeare: Prefatory Remarks

Between the record of his baptism in Stratford on 26 April 1564 and the record of his burial in Stratford on 25 April 1616, some forty documents name Shakespeare, and many others name his parents, his children, and his grandchildren. More facts are known about William Shakespeare than about any other playwright of the period except Ben Jonson. The facts should, however, be distinguished from the legends. The latter, inevitably more engaging and better known, tell us that the Stratford boy killed a calf in high style, poached deer and rabbits, and was forced to flee to London, where he held horses outside a playhouse. These traditions are only traditions; they may be true, but no evidence supports them, and it is well to stick to the facts.

Mary Arden, the dramatist's mother, was the daughter of a substantial landowner; about 1557 she married John Shakespeare, who was a glove-maker and trader in various farm commodities. In 1557 John Shakespeare was a member of the Council (the governing body of Stratford), in 1558 a constable of the borough, in 1561 one of the two town chamberlains, in 1565 an alderman (entitling him to the appellation "Mr."), in 1568 high bailiff—the town's highest political office, equivalent to mayor. After 1577, for an unknown reason he drops out of local politics. The birthday of William Shakespeare, the eldest son of this locally prominent man, is unrecorded; but the Stratford parish register records that the infant was baptized on 26 April 1564. (It is quite possible that he was born on 23

April, but this date has probably been assigned by tradition because it is the date on which, fifty-two years later, he died.) The attendance records of the Stratford grammar school of the period are not extant, but it is reasonable to assume that the son of a local official attended the school and received substantial training in Latin. The masters of the school from Shakespeare's seventh to fifteenth years held Oxford degrees; the Elizabethan curriculum excluded mathematics and the natural sciences but taught a good deal of Latin rhetoric, logic, and literature. On 27 November 1582 a marriage license was issued to Shakespeare and Anne Hathaway, eight years his senior. The couple had a child in May, 1583. Perhaps the marriage was necessary, but perhaps the couple had earlier engaged in a formal "troth plight" which would render their children legitimate even if no further ceremony were performed. In 1585 Anne Hathaway bore Shakespeare twins.

That Shakespeare was born is excellent; that he married and had children is pleasant; but that we know nothing about his departure from Stratford to London, or about the beginning of his theatrical career, is lamentable and must be admitted. We would gladly sacrifice details about his children's baptism for details about his earliest days on the stage. Perhaps the poaching episode is true (but it is first reported almost a century after Shakespeare's death), or perhaps he first left Stratford to be a schoolteacher, as another tradition holds; perhaps he was moved by

> Such wind as scatters young men through the world,
> To seek their fortunes further than at home
> Where small experience grows.

In 1592, thanks to the cantankerousness of Robert Greene, a rival playwright and a pamphleteer, we have our first reference, a snarling one, to Shakespeare as an actor and playwright. Greene warns those of his own educated friends who wrote for the theater against an actor who has presumed to turn playwright:

> There is an upstart crow, beautified with our feathers, that with his *tiger's heart wrapped in a player's hide* supposes he is as well able to bombast out a blank verse as the best of you, and being an absolute Johannes-factotum is in his own conceit the only Shake-scene in a country.

The reference to the player, as well as the allusion to Aesop's crow (who strutted in borrowed plumage, as an actor struts in fine words not his own), makes it clear that by this date Shakespeare had both acted and written. That Shakespeare is meant is indicated not only by "Shake-scene" but by the parody of a line from one of Shakespeare's plays, *3 Henry VI:* "O, tiger's heart wrapped in a woman's hide." If Shakespeare in 1592 was prominent enough to be attacked by an envious dramatist, he probably had served an apprenticeship in the theater for at least a few years.

In any case, by 1592 Shakespeare had acted and written, and there are a number of subsequent references to him as an actor: documents indicate that in 1598 he is a "principal comedian," in 1603 a "principal tragedian," in 1608 he is one of the "men players." The profession of actor was not for a gentleman, and it occasionally drew the scorn of university men who resented writing speeches for persons less educated than themselves, but it was respectable enough: players, if prosperous, were in effect members of the bourgeoisie, and there is nothing to suggest that Stratford considered William Shakespeare less than a solid citizen. When, in 1596, the Shakespeares were granted a coat of arms, the grant was made to Shakespeare's father, but probably William Shakespeare (who the next year bought the second-largest house in town) had arranged the matter on his own behalf. In subsequent transactions he is occasionally styled a gentleman.

Although in 1593 and 1594 Shakespeare published two narrative poems dedicated to the Earl of Southampton, *Venus and Adonis* and *The Rape of Lucrece,* and may well have written most or all of his sonnets in the middle nineties, Shakespeare's literary activity seems to have been almost entirely devoted to the theater. (It may be significant that the two narrative poems were written in years when the plague closed the theaters for several months.) In 1594 he was a charter member of a theatrical company called the Chamberlain's Men (which in 1603 changed its name to the King's Men); until he retired to Stratford (about 1611, apparently), he was with this remarkably stable company. From 1599 the company acted primarily at the Globe Theatre, in which Shakespeare held a one-tenth interest. Other Elizabethan dramatists are known to have acted, but no other is known also to have been entitled to a share in the profits of the playhouse.

Shakespeare's first eight published plays did not have his name on them, but this is not remarkable; the most popular play of the sixteenth century, Thomas Kyd's *The Spanish Tragedy,* went through many editions without naming Kyd, and Kyd's authorship is known only because a book on the profession of acting happens to quote (and attribute to Kyd) some lines on the interest of Roman emperors in the drama. What is remarkable is that after 1598 Shakespeare's name commonly appears on printed plays—some of which are not his. Another indication of his popularity comes from Francis Meres, author of *Palladis Tamia: Wit's Treasury* (1598): in this anthology of snippets accompanied by an essay on literature, many playwrights are mentioned, but Shakespeare's name occurs more often than any other, and Shakespeare is the only playwright whose plays are listed.

From his acting, playwriting, and share in a theater, Shakespeare seems to have made considerable money. He put it to work, making substantial investments in Stratford real estate. When he made his will (less than a month before he died), he sought to leave his property intact to his descendants. Of small bequests to relatives and to friends (including three actors, Richard Burbage, John Heminges, and Henry Condell), that to his wife of the second-best bed has provoked the most comment; perhaps it was the bed the couple had slept in, the best being reserved for visitors. In any case, had Shakespeare not excepted it, the bed would have gone (with the rest of his household possessions) to his daughter and her husband. On 25 April 1616 he was buried within the chancel of the church at Stratford. An unattractive monument to his memory, placed on a wall near the grave, says he died on 23 April. Over the grave itself are the lines, perhaps by Shakespeare, that (more than his literary fame) have kept his bones undisturbed in the crowded burial ground where old bones were often dislodged to make way for new:

> Good friend, for Jesus' sake forbear
> To dig the dust enclosèd here.
> Blessed be the man that spares these stones
> And cursed be he that moves my bones.

Thirty-seven plays, as well as some nondramatic poems, are held to constitute the Shakespeare canon. The dates of composition of most of the works are highly uncertain, but there is often evidence of a *terminus a quo* (starting point) and/or a *terminus ad quem* (terminal point) that provides a framework for intelligent guessing. For example, *Richard II* cannot be earlier than 1595, the publication date of some material to which it is indebted; *The Merchant of Venice* cannot be later than 1598, the year Francis Meres mentioned it. Sometimes arguments for a date hang on an alleged topical allusion, such as the lines about the unseasonable weather in *A Midsummer Night's Dream,* II.i.81–117, but such an allusion (if indeed it is an allusion) can be variously interpreted, and in any case there is always the possibility that a topical allusion was inserted during a revision, years after the composition of a play. Dates are often attributed on the basis of style, and although conjectures about style usually rest on other conjectures, sooner or later one must rely on one's literary sense. There is no real proof, for example, that *Othello* is not as early as *Romeo and Juliet,* but one feels *Othello* is later, and because the first record of its performance is 1604, one is glad enough to set its composition at that date and not push it back into Shakespeare's early years. The following chronology, then, is as much indebted to informed guesswork and sensitivity as it is to fact. The dates, necessarily imprecise, indicate something like a scholarly consensus.

PLAYS

1608–09	*Pericles*
1609–10	*Cymbeline*
1610–11	*The Winter's Tale*
1611	*The Tempest*
1612–13	*Henry VIII*

POEMS

1592	*Venus and Adonis*
1593–94	*The Rape of Lucrece*
1593–1600	*Sonnets*
1600–01	*The Phoenix and the Turtle*

Shakespeare's Theater

In Shakespeare's infancy, Elizabethan actors performed wherever they could—in great halls, at court, in the courtyards of inns. The innyards must have made rather unsatisfactory theaters: on some days they were unavailable because carters bringing goods to London used them as depots; when available, they had to be rented from the innkeeper; perhaps most important, London inns were subject to the Common Council of London, which was not well disposed toward theatricals. In 1574 the Common Council required that plays and playing places in London be licensed. It asserted that

> sundry great disorders and inconveniences have been found to ensue to this city by the inordinate haunting of great multitudes of people, specially youth, to plays, interludes, and shows, namely occasion of frays and quarrels, evil practices of incontinency in great inns having chambers and secret places adjoining to their open stages and galleries,

and ordered that innkeepers who wished licenses to hold performances put up a bond and make contributions to the poor.

The requirement that plays and innyard theaters be licensed, along with the other drawbacks of playing at inns, probably drove James Burbage (a carpenter-turned-actor) to rent in 1576 a plot of land northeast of the city walls and to build here—on property outside the jurisdiction of the city—England's first permanent construction designed for plays. He called it simply the Theatre. About all that is known of its construction is that it was wood. It soon had imitators, the most famous being the Globe (1599), built across the Thames (again outside the city's jurisdiction), out of timbers of the Theatre, which had been dismantled when Burbage's lease ran out.

There are three important sources of information about the structure of Elizabethan playhouses—drawings, a contract, and stage directions in plays. Of drawings, only the so-called De Witt drawing (c. 1596) of the Swan—really a friend's copy of De Witt's drawing—is of much significance. It shows a building of three tiers, with a stage jutting from a wall into the yard or center of the building. The tiers are roofed, and part of the stage is covered by a roof that projects from the rear and is supported at its front on two posts, but the groundlings, who paid a penny to stand in front of the stage, were exposed to the sky. (Performances in such a playhouse were held only in the daytime; artificial illumination was not used.) At the rear of the stage are two doors; above the stage is a gallery. The second major source of information, the contract for the Fortune, specifies that although the Globe is to be the model, the Fortune is to be square, eighty feet outside and fifty-five inside. The stage is to be forty-three feet broad, and is to extend into the middle of the yard (i.e., it is twenty-seven and a half feet deep). For patrons willing to pay more than the general admission charged of the groundlings, there were to be three galleries provided with seats. From the third chief source, stage directions, one learns that entrance to the stage was by doors, presumably spaced widely apart at the rear ("Enter one citizen at one door, and another at the other"), and that in addition to the platform stage there was occasionally some sort of curtained booth or alcove allowing for "discovery" scenes, and some sort of playing space "aloft" or "above" to represent (for example) the top of a city's walls or a room above the street. Doubtless each theater had its own peculiarities, but perhaps we can talk about a "typical" Elizabethan theater if we realize that no theater need exactly have fit the description, just as no father is the typical father with 3.7 children. This hypothetical theater is wooden, round or polygonal (in *Henry V* Shakespeare calls it a "wooden *O*"), capable of holding some eight hundred spectators standing in the yard around the projecting elevated stage and some fifteen hundred additional spectators seated in the three roofed galleries. The stage, protected by a "shadow" or "heavens" or roof, is entered by two doors; behind the doors is the "tiring house" (attiring house, i.e., dressing room), and above the doors is some sort of gallery that may sometimes hold spectators but that can be used (for example) as the bedroom from which Romeo—according to a stage direction in one text—"goeth down." Some evidence suggests that a throne can be lowered onto the platform stage, perhaps from the "shadow"; certainly characters can descend from the stage through a trap or traps into the cellar or "hell." Sometimes this space beneath the platform accommodates a sound-effects man or musician (in *Antony and Cleopatra* "music of the hautboys is under the stage") or an actor (in *Hamlet* the "Ghost cries under the stage"). Most characters simply walk on and off, but because there is no curtain in front of the platform, corpses will have to be carried off (Hamlet must lug Polonius' guts into the neighbor room), or will have to fall at the rear, where the curtain on the alcove or booth can be drawn to conceal them.

Such may have been the so-called "public theater." Another kind of theater, called the "private theater" because its much greater admission charge limited its audience to the wealthy or the prodigal, must be briefly mentioned. The private theater was basically a large room, entirely roofed and therefore artificially illuminated, with a stage at one end. In 1576 one such theater was established in Blackfriars, a Dominican priory in London that had been suppressed in 1538 and confiscated by the Crown and thus was not under the city's jurisdiction. All the actors in the Blackfriars theater were boys about eight to thirteen years old (in the public theaters similar boys played female parts; a boy Lady Macbeth played to a man Macbeth). This private theater had a precarious existence, and ceased operations in 1584. In 1596 James Burbage, who had already made theatrical history by building the Theatre, began to construct a second Blackfriars theater. He died in 1597, and for several years this second Blackfriars theater was used by a troupe of boys, but in 1608 two of Burbage's sons and five other actors (including Shakespeare) became joint operators of the theater, using it in the winter when the open-air Globe was unsuitable. Perhaps such a smaller theater, roofed, artificially illuminated, and with a tradition of a courtly audience, exerted an influence on Shakespeare's late plays.

Performances in the private theaters may well have had intermissions during which music was played, but in the public theaters the action was probably uninterrupted, flowing from scene to scene almost without a break. Actors would enter, speak, exit, and others would immediately enter and establish (if necessary) the new locale by a few properties and by words and gestures. Here are some samples of Shakespeare's scene painting:

> This is Illyria, lady.

> Well, this is the Forest of Arden.

> This castle hath a pleasant seat; the air
> Nimbly and sweetly recommends itself
> Unto our gentle senses.

On the other hand, it is a mistake to conceive of the Elizabethan stage as bare. Although Shakespeare's Chorus in *Henry V* calls the stage an "unworthy scaffold" and urges the spectators to "eke out our performance with your mind," there was considerable spectacle. The last act of *Macbeth,* for example, has five stage directions calling for "drum and colors," and another sort of appeal to the eye is indicated by the stage direction "Enter Macduff, with Macbeth's head." Some scenery and properties may have been substantial; doubtless a throne was used, and in one play of the period we encounter this direction: "Hector takes up a great piece of rock and casts at Ajax, who tears up a young tree by the roots and assails Hector." The matter is of some importance, and will be glanced at again in the next section.

The Texts of Shakespeare

Though eighteen of his plays were published during his lifetime, Shakespeare seems never to have supervised their publication. There is nothing unusual here; when a playwright sold a play to a theatrical company he surrendered his ownership of it. Normally a company would not publish the play, because to publish it meant to allow competitors to acquire the piece. Some plays, however, did get published: apparently treacherous actors sometimes pieced together a play for a publisher, sometimes a company in need of money sold a play, and sometimes a company allowed a play to be published that no longer drew audiences. That Shakespeare did not concern himself with publication, then, is scarcely remarkable; of his contemporaries only Ben Jonson carefully supervised the publication of his own plays. In 1623, seven years after Shakespeare's death, John Heminges and Henry Condell (two senior members of Shakespeare's company, who had performed with him for about twenty years) collected his plays—published and unpublished—into a large volume, commonly called the First Folio. (A folio is a volume consisting of sheets that have been folded once, each sheet thus making two leaves, or four pages. The eighteen plays published during Shakespeare's lifetime had been issued one play per volume in small books called quartos. Each sheet in a quarto has been folded twice, making four leaves, or eight pages.) The First Folio contains thirty-six plays; a thirty-seventh, *Pericles,* though not in the Folio is regarded as canonical. Heminges and Condell suggest in an address "To the great variety of readers" that the republished plays are presented in better form than in the quartos: "Before you were abused with diverse stolen and surreptitious copies, maimed and deformed by the frauds and stealths of injurious impostors that exposed them; even those, are now offered to your view cured and perfect of their limbs, and all the rest absolute in their numbers, as he [i.e., Shakespeare] conceived them."

Whoever was assigned to prepare the texts for publication in the First Folio seems to have taken his job seriously and yet not to have performed it with uniform care. The sources of the texts seem to have been, in general, good unpublished copies or the best published copies. The first play in the collection, *The Tempest,* is divided into acts and scenes, has unusually full stage directions and descriptions of spectacle, and concludes with a list of the characters, but the editor was not able (or willing) to present all of the succeeding texts so fully dressed. Later texts occasionally show signs of carelessness: in one scene of *Much Ado About Nothing* the names of actors, instead of characters, appear as speech prefixes, as they had in the quarto, which the Folio reprints; proofreading throughout the Folio is spotty and apparently was done without reference to the printer's copy; the pagination of *Hamlet* jumps from 156 to 257.

A modern editor of Shakespeare must first select his copy; no problem if the play exists only in the Folio, but a considerable problem if the relationship between a quarto and the Folio—or an early quarto and a later one—is unclear. When an editor has chosen what seems to him to be the most authoritative text or texts for his copy, he has not done with making decisions. First of all, he must reckon with Elizabethan spelling. If he is not producing a facsimile, he probably modernizes it, but ought he to preserve the old form of words that apparently were pronounced quite unlike their modern forms—"lanthorn," "alablaster"? If he preserves these forms, is he really preserving Shakespeare's forms or perhaps those of a compositor in the printing house? What is one to do when one finds "lanthorn" and "lantern" in adjacent lines? (The editors of this series in general, but not invariably, assume that words should be spelled in their modern form.) Elizabethan punctuation, too, presents problems. For example in the First Folio, the only text for the play, Macbeth rejects his wife's idea that he can wash the blood from his hand:

> no: this my Hand will rather
> The multitudinous Seas incarnardine,
> Making the Greene one, Red.

Obviously an editor will remove the superfluous capitals, and he will probably alter the spelling to "incarnadine," but will he leave the comma before "red," letting Macbeth speak of the sea as "the green one," or will he (like most modern editors) remove the comma and thus have Macbeth say that his hand will make the ocean *uniformly* red?

An editor will sometimes have to change more than spelling or punctuation. Macbeth says to his wife:

> I dare do all that may become a man,
> Who dares no more, is none.

For two centuries editors have agreed that the second line is unsatisfactory, and have emended "no" to "do": "Who dares do more is none." But when in the same play Ross says that fearful persons

> floate vpon a wilde and violent Sea
> Each way, and moue,

need "move" be emended to "none," as it often is, on the hunch that the compositor misread the manuscript? The editors of the Signet Classic Shakespeare have restrained themselves from making abundant emendations. In their minds they hear Dr. Johnson on the dangers of emending: "I have adopted the Roman sentiment, that it is more honorable to save a citizen than to kill an enemy." Some departures (in addition to spelling, punctuation, and lineation) from the copy text have of course been made, but the original readings are listed in a note following the play, so that the reader can evaluate them for himself.

The editors of the Signet Classic Shakespeare, following tradition, have added line numbers and in many cases act and scene divisions as well as indications of locale at the beginning of scenes. The Folio divided most of the plays into acts and some into scenes. Early eighteenth-century editors increased the divisions. These divisions, which provide a convenient way of referring to passages in the plays, have been retained, but when not in the text chosen as the basis for the Signet Classic text they are enclosed in square brackets [ ] to indicate that they are editorial additions. Similarly, although no play of Shakespeare's published during his lifetime was equipped with indications of locale at the heads of scene divisions, locales have here been added in square brackets for the convenience of the reader, who lacks the information afforded to spectators by costumes, properties, and gestures. The spectator can tell at a glance he is in the throne room, but without an editorial indication the reader may be puzzled for a while. It should be mentioned, incidentally, that there are a few authentic stage directions —perhaps Shakespeare's, perhaps a prompter's—that suggest locales: for example, "Enter Brutus in his orchard," and "They go up into the Senate house." It is hoped that the bracketed additions provide the reader with the sort of help provided in these two authentic directions, but it is equally hoped that the reader will remember that the stage was not loaded with scenery.

No editor during the course of his work can fail to recollect some words Heminges and Condell prefixed to the Folio:

It had been a thing, we confess, worthy to have been wished, that the author himself had lived to have set forth and overseen his own writings. But since it hath been ordained otherwise, and he by death departed from that right, we pray you do not envy his friends the

Introduction

I

Readers who come to *Henry IV* [*Part One*] from *Richard II* (and they are well advised who do so) find themselves in a changed world. The new king's second word is "shaken"—"So shaken as we are, so wan with care" (I.i.1). His realm's peace, "frighted," pants to catch her breath. The English earth, invoked in vain by Richard in the earlier play for aid against Henry's invading power (III.ii.4ff), like a perverted mother has been sucking "her own children's blood." Englishmen have met Englishmen "in the . . . furious close of civil butchery." The "edge" of war's knife has cut his master.

Though the new king assigns these troubles to the past, we are speedily assured they will not stay there. Present news is equally bloody. In the West, a thousand of Mortimer's men have been "butchered," and afterward mutilated. In the North, ten thousand Scottish corpses were seen by Sir Walter Blunt "balked in their own blood." Throughout the play we shall hear continually of this sort of thing: of "guns and drums and wounds" (I.iii.55) and "many a good tall fellow" destroyed (I.iii.61); of "bloody noses and cracked crowns" (II.iii.93); wearing "a garment all of blood" (III.ii.135); noblemen offered up "hot and bleeding" to "the fire-eyed maid of smoky war" (IV.i.113–14); ragamuffins tossed dead into a pit —"Tut, tut, good enough to toss; food for powder. . . ." (IV.ii. 66–67)—or consigned, maimed, to the town's end,

"to beg during life" (V.iii.38). Richard returned from
wars in Ireland in the earlier play, and the present king,
then Henry Hereford, known as Bolingbroke, invaded
England; but we never heard of doings like these. This
is indeed a changed world: the world of outrage that is
anticipated in the next-to-last scene of *Richard II* by the
brutal murder of the King and, earlier, in the deposition
scene (IV.i.121–49), by the warning of the Bishop of
Carlisle:

> What subject can give sentence on his king?
> And who sits here that is not Richard's subject? . . .
> My Lord of Hereford here, whom you call king,
> Is a foul traitor to proud Hereford's king;
> And if you crown him, let me prophesy
> The blood of English shall manure the ground,
> And future ages groan for this foul act;
> Peace shall go sleep with Turks and infidels,
> And, in this seat of peace, tumultuous wars
> Shall kin with kin, and kind with kind, confound;
> Disorder, horror, fear, and mutiny
> Shall here inhabit, and this land be called
> The field of Golgotha and dead men's skulls.
> O, if you raise this house against this house,
> It will the woefullest division prove
> That ever fell upon this cursèd earth!
> Prevent it, resist it, let it not be so,
> Lest child, child's children, cry against you woe.

The violence predicted by Carlisle takes over immediately in *1 Henry IV,* as we have seen. But the bishop's
enunciation of what is sometimes called "the Tudor myth"
—the thesis that an ever-watchful Providence brings retri-
bution on peoples who displace their lawful sovereigns,
and, specifically, that England's sufferings between the
murder of Richard in 1399 and the accession of the first
Tudor monarch in 1485 were a divinely appointed punishment for the' assault on Richard—the enunciation of
this doctrine better suits Shakespeare's earlier treatment
of these disorders in the Henry VI plays and *Richard III*
than the Henry IV plays. The world that produces Henry

is changed in this respect, too. The old scheme of celestial superintendence hangs loosely over it, to be glanced at in moments of introspection and anxiety; but to all dramatic intents and purposes, Henry's world, like Henry himself, is secular. One reason may be that Shakespeare saw in secularism the necessary condition of a usurper's success. A more compelling reason, doubtless, is that his attention had increasingly shifted from the interpretive moral and theological scheme with which his sources provided him toward the complexities and crosscurrents of human beings as they act and react on one another: in Yeats's words, toward "the fury and the mire of human veins."

The best anticipation of the mood of our play, from this point of view, is Richard's own warning, addressed to the man whose betrayal of him enabled Henry to seize the throne:

> Northumberland, thou ladder wherewithal
> The mounting Bolingbroke ascends my throne,
> The time shall not be many hours of age
> More than it is, ere foul sin, gathering head,
> Shall break into corruption. Thou shalt think,
> Though he divide the realm and give thee half,
> It is too little, helping him to all;
> He shall think that thou which knowest the way
> To plant unrightful kings, wilt know again,
> Being ne'er so little urged another way,
> To pluck him headlong from the usurped throne.
> The love of wicked men converts to fear,
> That fear to hate, and hate turns one or both
> To worthy danger and deservèd death.   (V.i.55–68)

These lines pay tribute to the overall theological scheme ("foul sin, gathering head"), but this fact should not blind us to the principles of *realpolitik* which they put forward as the mode of action that will govern in the hearts of Henry and his associates.

The irony of the new king's position, we soon learn, springs from these principles. As a successful usurper with the blood of a predecessor on his conscience, he is himself a principle of the disorder on which, as Shakespeare's Macbeth will learn at length, no lasting order can be built. Lawlessness springs up about him as if like Jason he had sown the dragon's teeth. It comes not only in the form of the Percys' rebellion and the behavior of his son, but in the knavery of Falstaff and the murky atmosphere of the inn at Rochester (to some extent an image of England), where all order is in decay and no man trusts another. All these are reflections cast by Henry in the mirror of the body politic. If there are highwaymen on the public road and other highwaymen at Glendower's plotting to snatch the Crown, these circumstances cannot be separated from the circumstance that one who has acted like a highwayman is king.

Thus the Tudor theme of the harsh wages of usurpation by no means vanishes from the play. Minimizing it as doctrine, Shakespeare makes it part of the poetic and dramatic texture, while he qualifies and complicates it by presenting to us in Henry a capable and even admirable king—one who, though never granted the security and peace he longs for, maintains his crown by a combination of strength, sagacity, severity, and lenience, and passes it on to an eventually deserving son. The ambivalence of his position is brought out by continual questioning of his title. The rebels question it on many occasions verbally (I.iii.10ff, 143ff; IV.iii.52ff; V.i.30ff) and, subsequently, by force of arms. The King himself seems to cast a doubt on it when he dresses others "in his coats" to confuse the enemy at Shrewsbury, as if royalty were a costume or blazon to be laid on at will. When Falstaff "acts" the King in the tavern, this doubt assumes a compelling visual shape, as does a further doubt whether "that father ruffian," as Hal calls Falstaff when he himself assumes the King's part, is more a ruffian in some respects than the deposer and murderer of Richard. Meantime, in the language of the play, this subject is teased at incessantly: we hear of the "Grace" that Hal will or will not have when he is king; of the "*true*[1] prince" knowable by instinct; of the "heir *apparent*"[1]—

---

[1] The italics are, of course, the editor's.

with a lurking pun in the second term; of false or cracked coins (bearing the King's image) to be passed current; of "nobles" appreciated to "royals"; and of many forms of "counterfeiting." Perhaps the ambiguities surrounding Henry's claim are expressed most succinctly in two remarks made by the Scottish Douglas during the battle. Douglas is engaged in killing all who wear the King's coats as fast as he can find them. "I fear thou art another counterfeit," he says as he sees Henry approach in the same garb. "And yet, in faith, thou bearest thee like a king." The first sentence suggests the emptiness of Henry's title in that he is not the rightful king; the second suggests the justness of his title in that he is a man who knows how to rule. We notice, however, that the King's life is saved neither by the stratagem of the coats nor by kingly "bearing," but by the chivalry of his son.

II

The *First Part of Henry IV* was published in 1598; it was probably written and acted in 1596–97. There are some topical allusions in the play to these years, notably the Second Carrier's reference to the high cost of oats that killed Robin Ostler (II.i.12). Topical in a more important sense, during the whole of the 1590's, was the play's general subject matter. Though contemporary concern about succession to the throne need not (though it may) have influenced Shakespeare's choice of materials for his English histories, it inevitably gave them an extra dimension. Elizabeth was now in her sixties, and there was no assured heir, only a multiplicity of candidates, including her sometimes favorite, the Earl of Essex. Many recalled anxiously the chaos in times past when the center of power in the monarchical system had ceased to be sharply defined and clearly visible. This had occurred to an extent after Henry VIII's death, and earlier after Henry V's, and still earlier after the murder of Richard II.

If Shakespeare was at all influenced by these anxieties, his rendering of them is on the whole buoyant and optimistic in his second English tetralogy and especially so in *1 Henry IV*. True, the England seen in this play and its immediate successor is far from reassuring. It has even been described as

> . . . an England, on the one side, of bawdy house and thieves'-kitchen, of waylaid merchants, badgered and bewildered Justices, and a peasantry wretched, betrayed, and recruited for the wars; an England, on the other side, of the chivalrous wolf pack of Hotspur and Douglas, and of state-sponsored treachery in the person of Prince John—the whole presided over by a sick King, hagridden by conscience, dreaming of a Crusade to the Holy Land as M. Remorse [i.e., Falstaff] thinks of slimming and repentance.[2]

But this is only half the picture. Beside it, for the first Henry IV play, we must place the warmth, wit, and high spirits of the tavern scenes, the impetuous charm of Hotspur, the amusing domesticities of Kate and Glendower's daughter, the touching loyalty of Francis, the affections that (along with sponging) bind Falstaff to Hal, and Hal's own magnanimity and self-command. For both the first and second plays, we must weigh heavily into the account the character of the story told. This, the greatest of monarchical success stories in English popular history, traces the evolution of an engaging scapegrace into one of the most admired of English kings. Chicanery and appetite in the first play, apathy and corruption in the second, form an effective theatrical background against which the oncoming sunbright majesty of the future Henry V may shine more brightly—as we are assured precisely that it will do on our first meeting with him (I.ii).

When Shakespeare turned to this subject in 1596–97, he found in his historical sources, mainly Holinshed's *Chronicles,* two dominant motifs. One was the moral and theological interpretation of the troubles attending Henry IV's reign in consequence of his usurpation. This

2 Danby, J. F., *Shakespeare's Doctrine of Nature: A Study of King Lear.* London: Faber and Faber, 1949, pp. 97–98.

we have already discussed. The other was the legend of the madcap youth of Henry's son and heir—a legend already exploited in an anonymous play of which we have today only a debased and possibly abbreviated text: *The Famous Victories of Henry the Fifth*. The *Famous Victories* contributes to *1 Henry IV* the germ of the robbery incident (though the Prince's involvement in a thieving episode is found in the chronicles as well); the germ of the tavern high jinks and parodying of authority; the germ of the expectation of Hal's reign as a golden age of rascals; and the germ of the reconciliation scene between the Prince and his father. The extent to which these hints are fleshed out and transfigured by Shakespeare's imagination may be seen in the character of Mistress Quickly. Her entire original in the *Famous Victories* is a sentence spoken by the Prince, favoring a rendezvous at "the old tavern in Eastcheap" because "there is a pretty wench that can talk well."

From the *Famous Victories* come also the names Gad's Hill (for the arranger of the robbery), Ned (our Ned Poins), and Jockey Oldcastle. The last was Shakespeare's name for Falstaff when the play was first performed, as references throughout the early seventeenth century show; Hal's addressing him as "my old lad of the castle" in the play as we have it (I.ii.43–44) is a survival from this. By the time the play was printed, the name had been altered to Falstaff for reasons that can now only be guessed at. Possibly there had been a protest by Oldcastle's descendants, one of whom was Lord Chamberlain during part of 1596–97. How the historical Oldcastle (d.1417), a man of character who was made High Sheriff of Herefordshire and eventually Lord Cobham, came to be metamorphosed into the roisterer of the *Famous Victories* is also an unsolved mystery, though no more mysterious than the dramatic imagination that exalted this dull stage roisterer, lacking eloquence, wit, mendacity, thirst, and fat, into the Falstaff we know.

On Holinshed and minor sources like Samuel Daniel's epic *The First Four Books of the Civil Wars between the Two Houses of Lancaster and York* [1595], Shakespeare based his treatment of the Percy rebellion, recasting the materials to give them an inner coherence. The Hotspur of history, for example, was twenty-three years older than Hal and two years older than the King himself, who at the date of the battle of Shrewsbury was only thirty-seven, his eldest son being then sixteen, and Prince John thirteen. Shakespeare followed the lead of Daniel and made Hotspur a youth, in order to establish dramatic rivalry between him and Hal. He then aged Henry rapidly so that by the time of the battle the King can speak of crushing his "old limbs in ungentle steel" and be the more appropriately rescued (this episode is also derived from Daniel) by his vigorous heir. For the same dramatic purpose, he assigned to Hal the triumph over Hotspur—though the inspiration for this may have come from misreading an ambiguous sentence in Holinshed. The reconciliation of Prince and King, touched on in the chronicles and dramatized briefly in the *Famous Victories* as occurring in Henry's latter years, he moved forward to a position before Shrewsbury, in order to enhance the human drama of father and son and further sharpen our anticipation of Hal's meeting with Hotspur. Hotspur's blunt uncourtly humor, the conception of Glendower as scholar and poet fired by a Celtic imagination, the entertaining clash of temperament and mood that this makes possible at Glendower's house, not only between Welshman and Englishman, but between romantic lovers and seasoned man and wife—all this again is Shakespeare's invention. His transformation of Holinshed, like his transformation of the *Famous Victories,* may best be indicated by a specific example. All of Hotspur's deliciously impetuous speech about the popinjay lord who came to Holmedon to demand his prisoners, not to mention the wonderfully ebullient scene in which it occurs, has behind it in Holinshed only seventeen words: "the King demanded of the Earl and his son such Scottish prisoners as were taken at Homeldon. . . ."

Hal's triumphant journey from tippling in taverns to glory on the field of battle derives from one other "source," more influential than any yet mentioned here.

This is the *psychomachia* of the morality plays—that is, the struggle of virtues and vices for possession of a man's soul, a theme acted again and again in the plays of the early sixteenth century, which the drama of Marlowe and Shakespeare superseded. In these plays, youthful virtue is beset by temptations and misleaders but customarily sees the true light at last and is saved. In the same general manner, Prince Hal "has to choose, Morality-fashion, between Sloth or Vanity, to which he is drawn by his bad companions, and Chivalry, to which he is drawn by his father and brothers. And he chooses Chivalry."[3]

III

The play that Shakespeare built from these miscellaneous materials is simple in its large outlines. It brings before us three contrasting environments at once, each with a commanding personality. The court is Henry's domain; the tavern is Falstaff's; the feudal countryside is Hotspur's. What essentially takes place during the first three acts is the progress of Hal, the one unattached player, from Falstaff's environment to Henry's. Hal then returns in the last scene of Act III to mobilize the tavern world for war, after which Falstaff's environment dissolves. We then have two environments, both military and political in nature, one of them dominated by Hotspur, the other (beginning with Act IV) increasingly by Hal. Falstaff, now in his turn the unattached man, makes appropriate comments on each.

Within this simple framework, Shakespeare accomplishes an articulation of complementary images, cross-references, and ironic contrasts that is without parallel in the history of English stage comedy. The highway robbery comments on the Percys' plot and also on the King's usurpation, as we saw a few moments ago. Gadshill, boasting of the quality of his confederates (II.i), antici-

---

[3] Tillyard, E. M. W. *Shakespeare's History Plays.* London: Chatto and Windus, 1944, p. 265.

pates Hotspur's misplaced confidence in the fidelity of his fellow rebels (II.iii). Falstaff bawling for his horse (II.ii) has satirical affinities with Hotspur chattering to the same purpose (II.iii). Hal describes Hotspur talking to his wife (II.iv) as if he had been an eavesdropper in the scene preceding, and points our attention to a tavern monomania in Francis which is perhaps reminiscent of Hotspur's monomania for "palisadoes, frontiers, parapets." Hotspur describes a presumed but perhaps wholly imaginary fight between Glendower and Mortimer in epic terms (I.iii); Falstaff does the same for a definitely imaginary contest with eleven men in buckram (II.iv). Falstaff keeps telling us he is about to reform; Hal actually does so. Hal's interview with his father (III.ii) is broadened and deepened for us in advance by the burlesque of it (II.iv) and by the failure of Hotspur to achieve a similar self-discipline (III.i). Glendower and Hotspur mirror each other in egoism, contrast vividly in the pedantic refinements of the one, the countrified heartiness of the other. Falstaff's remarks on honor, as everyone knows, complement those we have heard earlier from Hotspur; the comic account of Falstaff's conscripted derelicts corrects and supplements the description of Hal's army by a general who loves parades (IV.i.97ff) and the anticipation of destroying it by a general who loves carnage (IV.i.113ff); Falstaff's cynical "They'll fill a pit as well as better" hangs over the ensuing battle, enveloping especially those who are to fill a pit simply because the King has dressed them in his coats; etc. This list of cross-references could be extended almost indefinitely.

Only through such qualifying optics as these does Shakespeare allow us to view the simple Morality "choice" described by Professor Tillyard. Hotspur is one term in that choice—at first glance, a wholly negative term. He misjudges Henry, seeing only the King's duplicity. He misjudges Hal, seeing only the truant, overlooking Hal's sagacity and versatility. Magnanimity is also beyond his reach. His manners are rude, not courtly. His reaction to Glendower is both impolitic and provincial. Yet the play shows us there is much to be said on behalf of this misguided and hotheaded young man. In many respects, he is set apart from, and above, the company he keeps. In being free of scheming policy, he is differentiated from his uncle Worcester and the King. In fighting (for a time) the nation's battles, he has in the past surpassed Hal. He can be counted on when needed and is thereby distinguished from Glendower, Mortimer, and his father. His valor in battle is total. In this he is unlike Douglas, who makes a fine display of fearlessness but in the pinch flees. And he is naively frank-hearted. Hotspur, Worcester knows, would be moved to meet what seems the King's generous offer of amnesty with equal generosity, and the battle would probably not be fought.

Falstaff, the other term of the choice, is similarly complex. First of all, he is endowed by Shakespeare with a comic imagination that enables him (as Antony will later be enabled by the imagination of Cleopatra) to show his back above the element he lives in. His shattering of official clichés and stained-glass attitudes throughout the play is a measure of his penetration as well as, sometimes, his irresponsibility: "Why, Hal, 'tis my vocation, Hal. 'Tis no sin for a man to labor in his vocation" (I.ii.108–09); "A plague of sighing and grief, it blows a man up like a bladder" (II.iv.332–33); "Thou knowest in the state of innocency Adam fell, and what should poor Jack Falstaff do in the days of villainy? Thou seest I have more flesh than another man, and therefore more frailty" (III.iii.169–73); "Rebellion lay in his way, and he found it" (V.i.28). These show the same gift of comic insight that enables him to multiply images of himself as a shotten herring or a poulterer's hare, to raise the stock role of *miles gloriosus,* or braggart soldier, into the most rapturous flight of mendacity the comic stage has ever seen (II.iv), and to fling into the tense silence before the robbery one of those searching questions about the nature of man and his societies that a wide-eyed child will sometimes propound: "Zounds, will they not rob *us?*" (II.ii.64). (In *2 Henry IV,* appealing to "law of nature" to account for the way of a pike with a dace, he will make this Hobbist question a proposition).

Falstaff is also set apart by his genuine affections, his joy in his friends: "Gallants, lads, boys, hearts of gold, all the titles of good fellowship come to you!" (II.iv.278–80). He is even set apart by a certain kind of honesty. He will lie to others inexhaustibly, but that life is sweeter to him than honor, sack than killing, money in the pocket more gratifying than a fine squad of soldiers, he never seeks to hide from himself. Yet it would be folly to ignore that his honesty makes him no less a rascal, his affection no less a parasite, his perspicacity about some matters no less willful-blind about the rest. Falstaff is much more than —but he also is—a glutton, drunkard, liar, coward, and thief.

Hotspur and Falstaff are extremes, and we see the gulf that separates them when Hotspur goes down fighting while Falstaff plays dead to save his skin. But extremes (so runs the familiar saying) meet, and we see them meet when Falstaff, having taken Hotspur's body on his back, assures Hal he is "not a double man." The phrase reminds us that he and Hotspur are in some respects outsized versions of the same thing. Both are chivalric figures, Falstaff being, however backslidden, a knight; both exemplify ways in which chivalry may go to seed. "A hare-brained Hotspur, governed by a spleen," as his uncle Worcester describes him, can sacrifice to spleen a true knight's fealty and stain the honor he so prizes by making it the ground his egoism walks on. As for Falstaff, that "huge bombard of sack," that "roast Manningtree ox with the pudding in his belly": in his knight's bosom, "there's no room for faith, truth, nor honesty; . . . it is all filled up with guts and midriff."

Falstaff and Hotspur help us see that Hal's course is a mean between extremes. King Henry helps us see that Hal's mean is not a path of least resistance but a creative will that points toward a new kind of world. A master of appearances, as his description of his behavior in King Richard's time informs us (III.ii), Henry is at the same time their victim. If he seriously imagines that he would ever actually go on that Crusade whose "dear expedience" occupies his council at the opening of the play (I.i), he

is obviously self-deceived; if he does not intend to go,
it is a calculated charade. The sketches of Hotspur and
his son which he draws for us in the same scene are un-
mistakably sincere; but we soon discover they are wrong
—mere stereotypes of martial prowess and libertinism.
Henry does not really understand either his son or Hotspur. When he holds up Hotspur for a model in the reconciliation scene (III.ii), when he exhibits his delusion
that what he was to King Richard, Hotspur is now to
Hal, when he speaks of Hal's "barren pleasures" to us
who have just seen the tavern bulge with an energy and
feeling never to be matched at Henry's court, we understand how far he has become prisoner of a royalism that
is less imaginative than his son's. And when the battle
comes, we understand more clearly against this background the meaning of the contrasts there: the King "has
many marching in his coats"; the Prince offers to decide
the issue by taking the danger on himself alone; the King,
thinking in political terms, sends his enemies to execution and within these terms is perfectly right to do so;
the Prince thinks in larger terms and spares Douglas,
not for political reasons (though doubtless he is aware
of these), but because, as in his praise of Hotspur, he
can cherish "high deeds/Even in the bosom of our adversaries." Even Falstaff at his most ignominious, wound-
ing Hotspur's corpse and claiming credit for having killed
him, the Prince can bring himself to excuse; he will gild
his lie "with the happiest terms I have."

Thus by the play's end, Hal casts an inclusive shadow.
He has met the claims of Hotspur's world, of Falstaff's,
and of Henry's, without narrowing himself to any one.
He has practiced mercy as well as justice, politics as well
as friendship, shown himself capable of mockery as well
as reverence, detachment as well as commitment, and
brought into a practicable balance court, field, and tavern.
He is on the way to becoming the luminous figure toward
whom, in *Henry V*, Welshman, Irishman, Scot, and Englishman will alike be drawn. In this figure, combining
valor, courtliness, hard sense, and humor in an ideal
image of the potentialities of the English character, Shake-

speare seems to have discerned grounds for that optimism about the future of his country which permeates his historical vision in the plays from *Richard II* to *Henry V*. We ourselves may find in it, if not so local and particular an image, glimpses of an ideal form that remains relevant to us—such a form as Socrates and Glaucon, in the ninth book of the *Republic,* allude to in their discussion of the perfect city. Glaucon, the doubter, says: "But the city whose foundation we have been describing has its being only in words; there is no spot on earth where it exists." And Socrates replies: "No; but it is laid up in heaven as a pattern for him who wills to see, and seeing, to found that city in himself. Whether it exists anywhere, or ever will exist, is no matter."

MAYNARD MACK
Yale University

The History of Henry IV
[PART ONE]

[*Dramatis Personae*

King Henry the Fourth
Henry, Prince of Wales ᴴᴬᴸ }
Prince John of Lancaster } the King's sons
Earl of Westmoreland
Sir Walter Blunt
Thomas Percy, Earl of Worcester
Henry Percy, Earl of Northumberland
Henry Percy ("Hotspur"), his son
Edmund Mortimer, Earl of March
Richard Scroop, Archbishop of York
Archibald, Earl of Douglas
Owen Glendower
Sir Richard Vernon
Sir John Falstaff
Sir Michael, a friend of the Archbishop of York
Poins
Gadshill
Peto
Bardolph
Francis, a waiter
Lady Percy, Hotspur's wife and Mortimer's sister
Lady Mortimer, Glendower's daughter and Mortimer's wife
Mistress Quickly, hostess of the tavern
Sheriff, Vintner, Chamberlain, two Carriers, Ostler, Messengers, Travelers, Attendants

Scene: England and Wales]

The History of Henry IV

[PART ONE]

[ACT I

Scene I. *London. The palace.*]

Enter the King, Lord John of Lancaster, Earl of Westmoreland, [Sir Walter Blunt,] with others.

King. So shaken as we are, so wan with care,
Find we a time for frighted peace to pant°[1]
And breathe short-winded accents of new broils
To be commenced in stronds° afar remote.
No more the thirsty entrance of this soil   5
Shall daub her lips with her own children's blood,
No more shall trenching° war channel her fields,
Nor bruise her flow'rets with the armèd hoofs
Of hostile paces. Those opposèd eyes
Which, like the meteors° of a troubled heaven,   10
All of one nature, of one substance bred,°
Did lately meet in the intestine° shock
And furious close° of civil butchery,
Shall now in mutual well-beseeming° ranks
March all one way and be no more opposed   15
Against acquaintance, kindred, and allies.

---

[1] The degree sign (°) indicates a footnote, which is keyed to the text by line number. Text references are printed in **boldface** type; the annotation follows in roman type.
I.i.2 **pant** catch (her) breath   4 **stronds** shores   7 **trenching** (1) cutting (2) encroaching   10 **meteors** atmospheric disturbances   11 **All ... bred** i.e., because believed to originate from vapors   12 **intestine** internal   13 **close** grappling   14 **mutual well-beseeming** interdependent well-ordered

39

The edge of war, like an ill-sheathèd knife,
No more shall cut his master. Therefore, friends,
As far as to the sepulcher of Christ°—
20   Whose soldier now, under whose blessèd cross
We are impressèd and engaged° to fight—
Forthwith a power° of English shall we levy,
Whose arms were molded in their mother's womb
To chase these pagans in those holy fields
25   Over whose acres walked those blessèd feet
Which fourteen hundred years ago were nailed
For our advantage on the bitter cross.
But this our purpose now is twelvemonth old,
And bootless° 'tis to tell you we will go.
30   Therefor we meet not now.° Then let me hear
Of you, my gentle cousin° Westmoreland,
What yesternight our council did decree
In forwarding this dear expedience.°

Westmoreland. My liege, this haste was hot in question°
35   And many limits of the charge° set down
But yesternight; when all athwart° there came
A post° from Wales, loaden with heavy news,
Whose worst was that the noble Mortimer,
Leading the men of Herefordshire to fight
40   Against the irregular and wild° Glendower,
Was by the rude hands of that Welshman taken,
A thousand of his people butcherèd;
Upon whose dead corpse there was such misuse,
Such beastly shameless transformation
45   By those Welshwomen done, as may not be
Without much shame retold or spoken of.°

19 **As . . . Christ** i.e., to Jerusalem   21 **impressèd and engaged** conscripted and pledged (i.e., by Henry's vow after the murder of
Richard: cf. *Richard II*, V.vi.45–50)   22 **power** army   29 **bootless**
useless   30 **Therefor . . . now** that is not the reason we now meet
31 **gentle cousin** noble kinsman   33 **dear expedience** urgent enterprise   34 **hot in question** undergoing hot discussion   35 **limits of
the charge** apportionings of tasks and costs   36 **athwart** crosswise,
i.e., interfering   37 **post** messenger   40 **irregular and wild** i.e., as
border-raider and guerrilla   43–46 **such . . . spoken of** (the phras-
ing in Holinshed, Shakespeare's source, suggests that the dead English were castrated)

King. It seems then that the tidings of this broil
  Brake off our business for the Holy Land.

Westmoreland. This, matched with other, did, my
    gracious lord;
  For more uneven° and unwelcome news   50
  Came from the north, and thus it did import:
  On Holy-rood Day° the gallant Hotspur there,
  Young Harry Percy, and brave Archibald,
  That ever-valiant and approvèd Scot,
  At Holmedon° met, where they did spend   55
  A sad and bloody hour;
  As by discharge of their artillery
  And shape of likelihood° the news was told;
  For he that brought them,° in the very heat
  And pride of their contention° did take horse,   60
  Uncertain of the issue° any way.

King. Here is a dear, a true industrious° friend,
  Sir Walter Blunt, new lighted from his horse,
  Stained with the variation of each soil
  Betwixt that Holmedon and this seat° of ours,   65
  And he hath brought us smooth and welcome news.
  The Earl of Douglas is discomfited;
  Ten thousand bold Scots, two and twenty knights,
  Balked° in their own blood did Sir Walter see
  On Holmedon's plains. Of prisoners, Hotspur took   70
  Mordake, Earl of Fife and eldest son
  To beaten Douglas, and the Earl of Athol,
  Of Murray, Angus, and Menteith.
  And is not this an honorable spoil?
  A gallant prize? Ha, cousin, is it not?   75

Westmoreland. In faith it is. A conquest for a prince
    to boast of.

---

50 **uneven** cf. "smooth," line 66   52 **Holy-rood Day** September 14
55 **Holmedon** Humbleton in Northumberland   58 **shape of likelihood** probability   59 **them** i.e., the news   59–60 **heat . . . conten-
tion** peak of battle   61 **issue** outcome   62 **true industrious** loyally
zealous   65 **seat** dwelling, i.e., the palace   69 **Balked** (1) heaped
(2) thwarted

King. Yea, there thou mak'st me sad, and mak'st me
    sin
    In envy that my Lord Northumberland
    Should be the father to so blest a son:
80   A son who is the theme of honor's tongue,
    Amongst a grove the very straightest plant;
    Who is sweet fortune's minion° and her pride;
    Whilst I, by looking on the praise of him,
    See riot and dishonor stain the brow
85   Of my young Harry. O that it could be proved
    That some night-tripping fairy° had exchanged
    In cradle clothes our children where they lay,
    And called mine Percy, his Plantagenet!°
    Then would I have his Harry, and he mine.
90   But let him from my thoughts. What think you, coz,°
    Of this young Percy's pride? The prisoners
    Which he in this adventure hath surprised°
    To his own use he keeps, and sends me word
    I shall have none but Mordake, Earl of Fife.

Westmoreland. This is his uncle's teaching, this is
95   Worcester,
    Malevolent to you in all aspects,°
    Which makes him prune° himself and bristle up
    The crest of youth against your dignity.

King. But I have sent for him to answer this;
100   And for this cause awhile we must neglect
    Our holy purpose to Jerusalem.
    Cousin, on Wednesday next our council we
    Will hold at Windsor, so inform the lords:
    But come yourself with speed to us again,
105   For more is to be said and to be done
    Than out of anger can be utterèd.°

Westmoreland. I will, my liege.   *Exeunt.*

---

82. **minion** darling 86 **fairy** (fairies were thought sometimes to
steal a beautiful infant, leaving an ugly "changeling" in its place
88 **Plantagenet** family name of Henry IV 90 **coz** kinsman (short
for "cousin") 92 **surprised** taken 96 **Malevolent . . . aspects** (an
astrological expression comparing Worcester to a planet whose influence obstructs Henry's designs) 97 **prune** preen his feathers for
action (like a hawk) 106 **utterèd** transacted in public

[Scene II. *London. The Prince's lodging.*]

Enter Prince of Wales and Sir John Falstaff.

Falstaff. Now, Hal, what time of day is it, lad?

Prince. Thou art so fat-witted with drinking of old
sack,° and unbuttoning thee after supper, and sleep-
ing upon benches after noon, that thou hast forgotten to demand that truly which thou wouldest   5
truly know. What a devil hast thou to do with the
time of the day? Unless hours were cups of sack,
and minutes capons, and clocks the tongues of
bawds, and dials° the signs of leaping houses,° and
the blessed sun himself a fair hot wench in flame-   10
colored taffeta, I see no reason why thou shouldst
be so superfluous to° demand the time of the day.

Falstaff. Indeed you come near me° now, Hal; for we
that take purses go by° the moon and the seven
stars,° and not by Phoebus,° he, that wand'ring   15
knight so fair.° And I prithee, sweet wag, when thou
art a king, as, God save thy Grace°—Majesty I
should say, for grace thou wilt have none—

Prince. What, none?

I.ii.3 **sack** Spanish white wine   9 **dials** sundials   9 **leaping houses**
brothels   12 **so superfluous to** so irrelevant as to   13 **near me** i.e.,
close to understanding me (as if Hal were shooting at a mark)
14 **go by** (1) walk under (2) tell time by (3) regulate our lives by
14–15 **seven stars** constellation Pleiades   15 **Phoebus** the sun   15–
16 **he . . . fair** (Falstaff possibly quotes here, or sings, a line of a lost
ballad; the sun was readily thought of as an eternal wanderer or
"knight-errant")   17 **Grace** (Falstaff puns on "your Grace"—a title
which Hal as king will exchange for "your Majesty"—and spiritual
grace and, in lines 20–21, on grace before eating)

20   *Falstaff*. No, by my troth; not so much as will serve to
be prologue to an egg and butter.

Prince. Well, how then? Come, roundly, roundly.°

Falstaff. Marry,° then, sweet wag, when thou art king,
let not us that are squires of the night's body be
25   called thieves of the day's beauty.° Let us be
Diana's° foresters, gentlemen of the shade, minions°
of the moon; and let men say we be men of good
government,° being governed, as the sea is, by our
noble and chaste mistress the moon, under whose
30   countenance we steal.

Prince. Thou sayest well, and it holds well° too; for
the fortune of us that are the moon's men doth ebb
and flow like the sea, being governed as the sea is
by the moon. As, for proof now: a purse of gold
35   most resolutely snatched on Monday night and most
dissolutely spent on Tuesday morning; got with
swearing "Lay by," and spent with crying "Bring
in";° now in as low an ebb as the foot of the ladder,°
and by and by in as high a flow as the ridge of the
40   gallows.

Falstaff. By the Lord, thou say'st true, lad—and is not
my hostess of the tavern a most sweet wench?

22 **roundly** i.e., get to the point (but possibly with a glance at Falstaff's girth)   23 **Marry** (a mild oath, from "By the Virgin Mary")
24–25 **squires . . . beauty** (Falstaff's puns on "night/knight"—knights
were often attended by body-squires—and probably on "body/
beauty/booty." The "day's beauty" in one of its senses here is the
sun and balances "the night's body," which in one sense is the moon)
26 **Diana** goddess of the moon and the hunt (by identifying the hunt
with hunting for "booty"—and "beauty"—Falstaff presents himself
and his crew as Diana's companion foresters, her titled "Gentlemen
of the Shade," her "minions," who "steal"—i.e., [1] move silently
[2] take purses under her "countenance"—i.e., under [1] her face
[2] her protection)   26 **minions** servants and favorites   27–28 **of
good government** (1) well-behaved (2) ruled by a good ruler   31 **it
holds well** it's a good comparison   37–38 **Lay by . . . Bring in** (the
highwayman's commands: the first to his victims, the second to the
waiter in the tavern where he spends his gains)   38 **ladder** (leading
up to the gallows)

Prince. As the honey of Hybla,° my old lad of the castle°—and is not a buff jerkin° a most sweet robe of durance?

Falstaff. How now, how now, mad wag? What, in thy quips and thy quiddities?° What a plague have I to do with a buff jerkin?

Prince. Why, what a pox° have I to do with my hostess of the tavern?

Falstaff. Well, thou hast called her to a reckoning° many a time and oft.

Prince. Did I ever call for thee to pay thy part?

Falstaff. No; I'll give thee thy due, thou hast paid all there.

Prince. Yea, and elsewhere, so far as my coin would stretch; and where it would not, I have used my credit.

Falstaff. Yea, and so used it that, were it not here apparent that thou art heir apparent—But I prithee, sweet wag, shall there be gallows standing in England when thou art king? And resolution thus fubbed° as it is with the rusty curb of old father Antic° the law? Do not thou, when thou art king, hang a thief.

Prince. No; thou shalt.

Falstaff. Shall I? O rare! By the Lord, I'll be a brave° judge.

---

43 **Hybla** Sicilian source of fine honey　43–44 **old lad of the castle** rowdy (with pun on "Oldcastle," Falstaff's original name, and probably on "The Castle," a well-known London brothel)　44 **buff jerkin** tan (leather) jacket (a "robe of durance" because both durable and suggesting imprisonment [durance] because worn by the sheriff's officers)　46–47 **What . . . quiddities** "So you're in a witty mood, are you?"　49 **pox** (the Prince turns Falstaff's "plague" into a disease more characteristic of tavern hostesses)　51 **called her to a reckoning** (1) called her to a showdown (2) asked her for the bill 62 **resolution thus fubbed** courage (i.e., in the highwayman) thus cheated of its reward　63 **old father Antic** i.e., "that old screwball" 66 **brave** (1) excellent (2) handsomely decked out

Prince. Thou judgest false already. I mean, thou shalt
have the hanging of the thieves and so become a rare
70 hangman.

Falstaff. Well, Hal, well; and in some sort it jumps
with my humor° as well as waiting in the court, I
can tell you.

Prince. For obtaining of suits?°

75 *Falstaff.* Yea, for obtaining of suits, whereof the hangman hath no lean wardrobe. 'Sblood,° I am as
melancholy as a gib-cat° or a lugged° bear.

Prince. Or an old lion, or a lover's lute.

Falstaff. Yea, or the drone° of a Lincolnshire bagpipe.

80 *Prince.* What sayest thou to a hare,° or the melancholy
of Moorditch?°

Falstaff. Thou hast the most unsavory similes, and art
indeed the most comparative,° rascalliest, sweet
young prince. But, Hal, I prithee trouble me no
85 more with vanity.° I would to God thou and I knew
where a commodity° of good names were to be
bought. An old lord of the council rated° me the
other day in the street about you, sir, but I marked
him not; and yet he talked very wisely, but I re-
90 garded him not; and yet he talked wisely, and in the
street too.

71–72 **jumps with my humor** agrees with my frame of mind   74 **suits**
petitions for court favor (but Falstaff takes it in the sense of the
victim's garments, which were forfeit to the executioner)   76 **'Sblood**
by God's (i.e., Christ's) blood   77 **gib-cat** tomcat   77 **lugged** i.e.,
tied to a stake and baited by dogs, as entertainment   79 **drone**
single note of a bagpipe's bass pipe   80 **hare** (proverbially melancholy)   81 **Moorditch** foul London drainage ditch   83 **comparative**
full of (insulting) comparisons   85 **vanity** i.e., worldly considerations
(Falstaff here takes up one of his favorite humorous roles, assuming
for the next several lines the sanctimonious attitudes and vocabulary
of Elizabethan Puritanism)   86 **commodity** supply   87 **rated** scolded

Prince. Thou didst well, for wisdom cries out in the streets, and no man regards it.°

Falstaff. O, thou hast damnable iteration,° and art indeed able to corrupt a saint. Thou hast done much 95 harm upon me, Hal—God forgive thee for it! Before I knew thee, Hal, I knew nothing; and now am I, if a man should speak truly, little better than one of the wicked.° I must give over this life, and I will give it over! By the Lord, and° I do not, I 100 am a villain! I'll be damned for never a king's son in Christendom.

Prince. Where shall we take a purse tomorrow, Jack?

Falstaff. Zounds,° where thou wilt, lad! I'll make one. An° I do not, call me villain and baffle° me. 105

Prince. I see a good amendment of life in thee—from praying to purse-taking.

Falstaff. Why, Hal, 'tis my vocation,° Hal. 'Tis no sin for a man to labor in his vocation.

Enter Poins.

Poins! Now shall we know if Gadshill have set a 110 match.° O, if men were to be saved by merit,° what hole in hell were hot enough for him? This is the most omnipotent villain that ever cried "Stand!" to a true° man.

92–93 **Thou . . . it** (Hal quotes Proverbs 1:20–24: "Wisdom crieth without, and putteth forth her voice in the streets . . . saying . . . 'I have stretched out my hand, and no man regarded' ") 94 **damnable iteration** i.e., a sinful way of repeating and (mis)applying holy texts 99 **the wicked** (Puritan idiom for those who were not Puritans; cf. "saint" in 95, which glances at the Puritans' way of referring collectively to themselves) 100 **and** if 104 **Zounds** by God's (i.e., Christ's) wounds 105 **An** if 105 **baffle** hang upside down (a punishment allotted perjured knights) 108 **vocation** calling (with reference to the Puritan stress on a man's being "called" by God to his work) 110–11 **set a match** arranged a robbery 111 **merit** i.e., good works (in Puritan doctrine wholly insufficient for salvation) 114 **true** honest

115 *Prince.* Good morrow, Ned.

Poins. Good morrow, sweet Hal. What says Monsieur
   Remorse? What says Sir John Sack and Sugar?°
   Jack, how agrees the devil and thee about thy soul,
   that thou soldest him on Good Friday last for a cup
120   of Madeira and a cold capon's leg?

Prince. Sir John stands to his word, the devil shall
   have his bargain; for he was never yet a breaker of
   proverbs. He will give the devil his due.

Poins. Then art thou damned for keeping thy word
125   with the devil.

Prince. Else he had been damned for cozening° the
   devil.

Poins. But, my lads, my lads, tomorrow morning, by
   four o'clock early, at Gad's Hill!° There are pil-
130   grims going to Canterbury with rich offerings,° and
   traders riding to London with fat purses. I have
   vizards° for you all; you have horses for yourselves.
   Gadshill lies tonight in Rochester. I have bespoke
   supper tomorrow night in Eastcheap.° We may do
135   it as secure as sleep. If you will go, I will stuff your
   purses full of crowns; if you will not, tarry at home
   and be hanged!

Falstaff. Hear ye, Yedward:° if I tarry at home and
   go not, I'll hang you for going.

140 *Poins.* You will, chops?°

Falstaff. Hal, wilt thou make one?

Prince. Who, I rob? I a thief? Not I, by my faith.

Falstaff. There's neither honesty, manhood, nor good

---

117 **Sack and Sugar** (sack sweetened with sugar was particularly
the drink of the elderly, but there may be a pun, in this context, on
sackcloth, symbol of penance)   126 **cozening** cheating   129 **Gad's
Hill** (a place notorious for holdups on the road from Rochester to
London)   130 **offerings** i.e., for the shrine of St. Thomas à Becket
132 **vizards** masks   134 **Eastcheap** London street and district   138
Yedward (dialect form of Edward)   140 **chops** "fat-face"

fellowship in thee, nor thou cam'st not of the blood
royal° if thou darest not stand for° ten shillings.   *145*

Prince. Well then, once in my days I'll be a madcap.

Falstaff. Why, that's well said.

Prince. Well, come what will, I'll tarry at home.

Falstaff. By the Lord, I'll be a traitor then, when thou
art king.   *150*

Prince. I care not.

Poins. Sir John, I prithee, leave the Prince and me
alone. I will lay him down such reasons for this
adventure that he shall go.

Falstaff. Well, God give thee the spirit of persuasion *155*
and him the ears of profiting, that what thou speak-
est may move° and what he hears may be believed,
that the true prince may (for recreation sake) prove
a false thief; for the poor abuses of the time want
countenance.° Farewell; you shall find me in East-   *160*
cheap.

Prince. Farewell, the° latter spring! Farewell, All-
hallown summer!°   [*Exit Falstaff.*]

Poins. Now, my good sweet honey lord, ride with us
tomorrow. I have a jest to execute that I cannot   *165*
manage alone. Falstaff, Bardolph, Peto, and Gadshill
shall rob those men that we have already waylaid;°
yourself and I will not be there; and when they have
the booty, if you and I do not rob them, cut this
head off from my shoulders.   *170*

Prince. How shall we part with them in setting forth?

---

145 **royal** (pun on "royal," a ten-shilling coin)   145 **stand for** (1)
pass for (as a coin) (2) contest for (in a robbery)   155–57 **God . . .
move** (mimicry again of the Puritans, who claimed to act only when
the spirit moved in them)   159–60 **want countenance** lack protection (royal and aristocratic)   162 **the** (sometimes used in the sixteenth century for "thou" and "you")   162–63 **All-hallown summer**
(Poins compares Falstaff's youthfulness in old age to the belated
summer that occurs around All Hallows day)   167 **waylaid** set our
trap for

Poins. Why, we will set forth before or after them and appoint them a place of meeting, wherein it is at our pleasure to fail; and then will they adventure upon
175 the exploit themselves, which they shall have no sooner achieved, but we'll set upon them.

Prince. Yea, but 'tis like that they will know us by our horses, by our habits,° and by every other appointment,° to be ourselves.

180 *Poins.* Tut! Our horses they shall not see—I'll tie them in the wood; our vizards we will change after we leave them; and, sirrah,° I have cases of buckram for the nonce,° to immask our noted outward garments.

185 *Prince.* Yea, but I doubt° they will be too hard for us.

Poins. Well, for two of them, I know them to be as true-bred cowards as ever turned back; and for the third, if he fight longer than he sees reason, I'll forswear arms. The virtue of this jest will be the
190 incomprehensible° lies that this same fat rogue will tell us when we meet at supper: how thirty, at least, he fought with; what wards,° what blows, what extremities he endured; and in the reproof° of this lives the jest.

195 *Prince.* Well, I'll go with thee. Provide us all things necessary and meet me tomorrow night° in Eastcheap. There I'll sup. Farewell.

Poins. Farewell, my lord.   *Exit.*

Prince. I know you all, and will awhile uphold
200 The unyoked humor° of your idleness.

---

178 **habits** dress   178–79 **appointment** piece of equipment   182
sirrah (term of address showing great familiarity)   182–183 **cases
... nonce** outer coverings of coarse linen for the purpose   185 **doubt**
fear   190 **incomprehensible** unlimited   192 **wards** strategies of defense (in swordsmanship)   193 **reproof** disproof   196 **tomorrow
night** (they will meet for the robbery tomorrow morning, but Hal
is thinking ahead to the jest on Falstaff that night)   200 **unyoked
humor** undisciplined inclinations

Yet herein will I imitate the sun,° — *parelleled with king*
Who doth permit the base contagious° clouds
To smother up his beauty from the world,
That, when he please again to be himself,
Being wanted,° he may be more wond'red at   *205*
By breaking through the foul and ugly mists
Of vapors that did seem to strangle him.
If all the year were playing holidays,
To sport would be as tedious as to work;
But when they seldom come, they wished-for come,   *210*
And nothing pleaseth but rare accidents.°
So when this loose behavior I throw off
And pay the debt I never promisèd, — *to be the king*
By how much better than my word I am,
By so much shall I falsify men's hopes;°   *215*
And, like bright metal on a sullen° ground,
My reformation, glitt'ring o'er my fault,
Shall show more goodly and attract more eyes
Than that which hath no foil° to set it off.
I'll so offend to make offense a skill,   *220*
Redeeming time° when men think least I will.   *Exit.*

201 **sun** (royalty's traditional symbol)   202 **contagious** (clouds were
thought to breed pestilence)   205 **wanted** lacked, missed   211 **rare
accidents** unexpected or uncommon events   215 **hopes** expectations
216 **sullen** dull   219 **foil** contrasting background   221 **Redeeming
time** making amends (Hal alludes to Ephesians 5:7ff, which bears in
a general way on much that has been said in this scene: "Be not ye
therefore partakers with them, for ye were sometimes darkness, but
now are ye light in the Lord: walk as children of light. . . . See then
that ye walk circumspectly, not as fools, but as wise. Redeeming the
time, because the days are evil).

[Scene III. *Windsor. The council chamber.*]

*Enter the King, Northumberland, Worcester,
Hotspur, Sir Walter Blunt, with others.*

King. My blood hath been too cold and temperate,
    Unapt to stir at these indignities,
    And you have found me,° for accordingly
    You tread upon my patience; but be sure
5   I will from henceforth rather be myself,°
    Mighty and to be feared, than my condition,°
    Which hath been smooth as oil, soft as young down,
    And therefore lost that title of respect
    Which the proud soul ne'er pays but to the proud.

Worcester. Our house, my sovereign liege, little de-
10   serves
    The scourge of greatness to be used on it—
    And that same greatness too which our own hands
    Have holp° to make so portly.°

Northumberland.   My lord—

King. Worcester, get thee gone, for I do see
15   Danger and disobedience in thine eye.
    O, sir, your presence is too bold and peremptory,
    And majesty might never yet endure
    The moody frontier° of a servant brow.
    You have good leave to leave us: when we need
20   Your use and counsel, we shall send for you.
                   Exit Worcester.
    You were about to speak.

I.iii.3 **found me** found me out   5 **myself** i.e., what I am as king
6 **my condition** i.e., what I am by nature   13 **holp** helped   13 **portly**
stately   18 **frontier** rampart (as if Worcester were an enemy fortress)

Northumberland.   Yea, my good lord.
  Thóse prisoners in your Highness' name demanded
  Which Harry Percy here at Holmedon took,
  Were, as he says, not with such strength denied
  As is deliverèd to your Majesty.   25
  Either envy,° therefore, or misprision°
  Is guilty of this fault, and not my son.

Hotspur. My liege, I did deny no prisoners.
  But I remember, when the fight was done,
  When I was dry with rage and extreme toil,   30
  Breathless and faint, leaning upon my sword,
  Came there a certain lord, neat and trimly dressed,
  Fresh as a bridegroom, and his chin new reaped°
  Showed like a stubble land at harvest home.
  He was perfumèd like a milliner,   35
  And 'twixt his finger and his thumb he held
  A pouncet box,° which ever and anon
  He gave his nose, and took't away again;
  Who° therewith angry, when it next came there,
  Took it in snuff;° and still he smiled and talked;   40
  And as the soldiers bore dead bodies by,
  He called them untaught knaves, unmannerly,
  To bring a slovenly unhandsome corse°
  Betwixt the wind and his nobility.
  With many holiday and lady° terms   45
  He questioned° me, amongst the rest demanded
  My prisoners in your Majesty's behalf.
  I then, all smarting with my wounds being cold,
  To be so pest'red with a popingay,°
  Out of my grief° and my impatience   50
  Answered neglectingly, I know not what—
  He should, or he should not; for he made me mad
  To see him shine so brisk, and smėll so sweet,

---

26 **envy** malice   26 **misprision** misapprehension   33 **reaped** i.e.,
with the closely clipped beard of a man of fashion   37 **pouncet box**
perfume box   39 **Who** i.e., his nose   40 **Took it in snuff** (proverbial,
meaning "took offense," but here with pun on "snuffing" the perfume)   43 **corse** corpse   45 **holiday and lady** fastidious and effemi-
nate   46 **questioned** talked to   49 **popingay** parrot (here, one who
is gaudy in dress and chatters emptily)   50 **grief** pain

And talk so like a waiting gentlewoman
Of guns and drums and wounds—God save the
55   mark!°—
And telling me the sovereignest° thing on earth
Was parmacity° for an inward bruise,
And that it was great pity, so it was,
This villainous saltpeter should be digged
60   Out of the bowels of the harmless earth,
Which many a good tall° fellow had destroyed
So cowardly, and but for these vile guns,
He would himself have been a soldier.
This bald unjointed chat of his, my lord,
65   I answered indirectly,° as I said,
And I beseech you, let not his report
Come current° for an accusation
Betwixt my love and your high Majesty.

Blunt. The circumstance considerèd, good my lord,
70   Whate'er Lord Harry Percy then had said
To such a person, and in such a place,
At such a time, with all the rest retold,
May reasonably die, and never rise
To do him wrong,° or any way impeach
75   What then he said, so° he unsay it now.

King. Why, yet he doth deny his prisoners,
But with proviso and exception,
That we at our own charge shall ransom straight
His brother-in-law, the foolish Mortimer;
80   Who, on my soul, hath willfully betrayed
The lives of those that he did lead to fight
Against that great magician, damned Glendower—
Whose daughter, as we hear, that Earl of March
Hath lately married. Shall our coffers, then,
85   Be emptied to redeem a traitor home?

---

55 **God save the mark** (a ritual phrase originally used to invoke a blessing, but here expressing scorn)   56 **sovereignest** best   57 **parmacity** spermaceti (medicinal substance found in sperm whales)   61 **tall** stalwart   65 **indirectly** absently   67 **Come current** (1) be accepted (i.e., as of true coin) (2) intrude   74 **To do him wrong** i.e., to be held against him   75 **so** provided

Shall we buy treason, and indent° with fears°
When they have lost and forfeited themselves?
No, on the barren mountains let him starve!
For I shall never hold that man my friend
Whose tongue shall ask me for one penny cost   *90*
To ransom home revolted Mortimer.

Hotspur. Revolted Mortimer?
He never did fall off, my sovereign liege,
But by the chance of war. To prove that true
Needs no more but one tongue for all those wounds,   *95*
Those mouthèd wounds,° which valiantly he took
When on the gentle Severn's sedgy bank,
In single opposition hand to hand,
He did confound° the best part of an hour
In changing hardiment° with great Glendower.   *100*
Three times they breathed,° and three times did they
    drink,
Upon agreement, of swift Severn's flood;
Who° then affrighted with their bloody looks
Ran fearfully among the trembling reeds
And hid his crisp° head in the hollow bank,   *105*
Bloodstainèd with these valiant combatants.
Never did bare and rotten policy°
Color° her working with such deadly wounds;
Nor never could the noble Mortimer
Receive so many, and all willingly.   *110*
Then let not him be slanderèd with revolt.°

King. Thou dost belie° him, Percy, thou dost belie him!
He never did encounter with Glendower.
I tell thee, he durst as well have met the devil alone
As Owen Glendower for an enemy.   *115*

---

86 **indent** bargain   86 **fears** (1) cowards (2) traitors, i.e., those wh
by "fear" have yielded to the enemy and so become traitors "to be
feared"   96 **mouthèd wounds** i.e., wounds that speak for him
(based on the likeness of a bloody flesh wound to a mouth)   99 **con-
found** spend   100 **changing hardiment** battling   101 **breathed**
paused for breath   103 **Who** i.e., the river   105 **crisp** (used punningly to mean both "curled" [of a man's head] and "rippling" [of a
river]; "head" also refers punningly to a river's force)   107 **policy**
cunning   108 **Color** (1) disguise (2) redden (i.e., with blood)   111
revolt treason   112 **belie** misrepresent

Art thou not ashamed? But, sirrah,° henceforth
Let me not hear you speak of Mortimer.
Send me your prisoners with the speediest means,
Or you shall hear in such a kind from me
120   As will displease you. My Lord Northumberland,
We license your departure with your son.
Send us your prisoners, or you will hear of it.

                  Exit King, [with Blunt, and train].

Hotspur. And if° the devil come and roar for them,
I will not send them. I will after straight
125   And tell him so, for I will ease my heart,
Albeit I make a hazard of° my head.

Northumberland. What, drunk with choler?° Stay, and
    pause awhile.
Here comes your uncle.

               Enter Worcester.

Hotspur.   Speak of Mortimer?
Zounds, I will speak of him, and let my soul
130   Want mercy if I do not join with him!
Yea, on his part I'll empty all these veins,
And shed my dear blood drop by drop in the dust,
But I will lift the downtrod Mortimer
As high in the air as this unthankful king,
135   As this ingrate and cank'red° Bolingbroke.°

Northumberland. Brother, the King hath made your
    nephew mad.

Worcester. Who struck this heat up after I was gone?

Hotspur. He will forsooth have all my prisoners;
And when I urged the ransom once again
140   Of my wife's brother, then his cheek looked pale,
And on my face he turned an eye of death,
Trembling even at the name of Mortimer.

Worcester. I cannot blame him. Was not he pro-
    claimed

116 **sirrah** (term of address to an inferior, here insulting)   123 **And**
if if   126 **make a hazard of** risk   127 **choler** anger   135 **cank'red**
infected   135 **Bolingbroke** i.e., the king

By Richard that dead is, the next of blood?°

Northumberland. He was, I heard the proclamation: *145*
And then it was when the unhappy king
(Whose wrongs in us° God pardon!) did set forth
Upon his Irish expedition;
From whence he intercepted° did return
To be deposed, and shortly murderèd.   *150*

Worcester. And for whose death we in the world's wide
      mouth
Live scandalized and foully spoken of.

Hotspur. But soft, I pray you, did King Richard then
Proclaim my brother Edmund Mortimer
Heir to the crown?

Northumberland.   He did, myself did hear it.   *155*

Hotspur. Nay, then I cannot blame his cousin king,
That wished him on the barren mountains starve.
But shall it be that you, that set the crown
Upon the head of this forgetful man,
And for his sake wear the detested blot   *160*
Of murderous subornation°—shall it be
That you a world of curses undergo,
Being the agents or base second means,
The cords, the ladder, or the hangman rather?
O, pardon me that I descend so low   *165*
To show the line° and the predicament°
Wherein you range under this subtle king!
Shall it for shame be spoken in these days,
Or fill up chronicles in time to come,
That men of your nobility and power   *170*
Did gage° them both in an unjust behalf
(As both of you, God pardon it, have done)
To put down Richard, that sweet lovely rose,

144 **next of blood** i.e., heir to the throne   147 **in us** at our hands
149 **intercepted** interrupted   161 **murderous subornation** confederacy in murder   166 **line** degree, station (but also "hangman's rope"
[cf. line 164] and "tether" [cf. line 167])   166 **predicament** category
(but also "perilous position")   171 **gage** pledge

And plant this thorn, this canker° Bolingbroke?
175   And shall it in more shame be further spoken
That you are fooled, discarded, and shook off
By him for whom these shames ye underwent?
No, yet time serves wherein you may redeem
Your banished honors and restore yourselves
180   Into the good thoughts of the world again;
Revenge the jeering and disdained contempt
Of this proud king, who studies day and night
To answer all the debt he owes to you
Even with the bloody payment of your deaths.
Therefore I say—

185 *Worcester.*   Peace, cousin, say no more;
And now I will unclasp a secret book,
And to your quick-conceiving° discontents
I'll read you matter deep and dangerous,
As full of peril and adventurous spirit
190   As to o'erwalk a current roaring loud
On the unsteadfast footing of a spear.

Hotspur. If he fall in, good night, or sink, or swim!°
Send danger from the east unto the west,
So honor cross it from the north to south,
195   And let them grapple. O, the blood more stirs
To rouse a lion than to start a hare!

Northumberland. Imagination of some great exploit
Drives him beyond the bounds of patience.

Hotspur. By heaven, methinks it were an easy leap
200   To pluck bright honor from the pale-faced moon,
Or dive into the bottom of the deep,
Where fathom line could never touch the ground,
And pluck up drownèd honor by the locks,
So° he that doth redeem her thence might wear
205   Without corrival° all her dignities;
But out upon this half-faced fellowship!°

174 **canker** dog-rose (an inferior rose, but with suggestions of "can-
kerworm" and "ulcer")   187 **quick-conceiving** eagerly responsive
192 **good . . . swim** i.e., the man is doomed whether he sinks at once
or is swept away by the current   204 **So** provided   205 **corrival**
partner   206 **out . . . fellowship** down with this half-and-half sharing
(of honors)

Worcester. He apprehends a world of figures° here,
  But not the form of what he should attend.
  Good cousin, give me audience for a while.

Hotspur. I cry you mercy.°   210

Worcester. Those same noble Scots that are your
    prisoners—

Hotspur. I'll keep them all.
  By God, he shall not have a Scot of them!
  No, if a Scot° would save his soul, he shall not.
  I'll keep them, by this hand!

Worcester.   You start away   215
  And lend no ear unto my purposes.
  Those prisoners you shall keep.

Hotspur.   Nay, I will! That's flat!
  He said he would not ransom Mortimer,
  Forbade my tongue to speak of Mortimer,
  But I will find him when he lies asleep,   220
  And in his ear I'll hollo "Mortimer."
  Nay, I'll have a starling shall be taught to speak
  Nothing but "Mortimer," and give it him
  To keep his anger still in motion.

Worcester. Hear you, cousin, a word.   225

Hotspur. All studies° here I solemnly defy°
  Save how to gall and pinch this Bolingbroke;
  And that same sword-and-buckler° Prince of Wales,
  But that I think his father loves him not
  And would be glad he met with some mischance,   230
  I would have him poisonèd with a pot of ale.°

Worcester. Farewell, kinsman: I'll talk to you
  When you are better tempered to attend.

---

207 **figures** (1) figures of speech (2) airy fancies (as opposed
to substantial "form," line 208)   210 **cry you mercy** beg your
pardon   214 **Scot** (pun on "scot," meaning "small payment")
226 **studies** interests   226 **defy** reject   228 **sword-and-buckler** "low-
down" (sword and shield were arms of the lower classes)   231 **ale**
(a further glance at Hal's presumed low tastes, gentlemen's drink
being wine)

Northumberland. Why, what a wasp-stung and impa-
  tient fool
235 Art thou to break into this woman's mood,
  Tying thine ear to no tongue but thine own!

Hotspur. Why, look you, I am whipped and scourged
  with rods,
  Nettled, and stung with pismires,° when I hear
  Of this vile politician, Bolingbroke.
240 In Richard's time—what do you call the place?
  A plague upon it! It is in Gloucestershire;
  'Twas where the madcap duke his uncle kept,°
  His uncle York—where I first bowed my knee
  Unto this king of smiles, this Bolingbroke—
245 'Sblood!—when you and he came back from Ravens-
  purgh°—

Northumberland. At Berkeley Castle.

Hotspur. You say true.
  Why, what a candy deal° of courtesy
  This fawning greyhound then did proffer me!
250 "Look when his infant fortune came to age,"
  And "gentle Harry Percy," and "kind cousin"—
  O, the devil take such cozeners!°—God forgive me!
  Good uncle, tell your tale; I have done.

Worcester. Nay, if you have not, to it again.
  We will stay your leisure.

255 *Hotspur.*   I have done, i' faith.

Worcester. Then once more to your Scottish prisoners:
  Deliver them up without their ransom straight,
  And make the Douglas' son your only mean
  For powers in Scotland—which, for divers reasons
260 Which I shall send you written, be assured
  Will easily be granted. [*To Northumberland*] You,
  my lord,

238 **pismires** ants   242 **kept** dwelt   245 **Ravenspurgh** harbor in
Yorkshire (where Hotspur's father had gone to take sides with
Bolingbroke—who was returning from exile on the Continent—
against the absent King Richard II)   248 **candy deal** sugared bit
252 **cozeners** cheats (with pun on "cousin" of previous line)

Your son in Scotland being thus employed,
Shall secretly into the bosom creep
Of that same noble prelate well-beloved,
The Archbishop.   265

Hotspur. Of York, is it not?

Worcester. True; who bears hard°
His brother's death at Bristow,° the Lord Scroop.
I speak not this in estimation,°
As what I think might be, but what I know   270
Is ruminated, plotted, and set down,
And only stays but to behold the face
Of that occasion that shall bring it on.

Hotspur. I smell it.° Upon my life, it will do well.

Northumberland. Before the game is afoot thou still
let'st slip.°   275

Hotspur. Why, it cannot choose but be a noble plot.
And then the power of Scotland and of York
To join with Mortimer, ha?

Worcester.   And so they shall.

Hotspur. In faith, it is exceedingly well aimed.

Worcester. And 'tis no little reason bids us speed   280
To save our heads by raising of a head;°
For, bear ourselves as even as we can,
The King will always think him in our debt,
And think we think ourselves unsatisfied,
Till he hath found a time to pay us home.°   285
And see already how he doth begin
To make us strangers to his looks of love.

Hotspur. He does, he does! We'll be revenged on him.

Worcester. Cousin, farewell. No further go in this
Than I by letters shall direct your course.   290

267 **bears hard** (because his brother had been executed by Henry)
268 **Bristow** Bristol   269 **in estimation** as a guess   274 **smell it**
i.e., like a hound catching the scent   275 **let'st slip** let loose (the
dogs)   281 **head** army   285 **home** i.e., with a "home" thrust

When time is ripe, which will be suddenly,°
I'll steal to Glendower and Lord Mortimer,
Where you and Douglas, and our pow'rs at once,
As I will fashion it, shall happily meet,
295   To bear our fortunes in our own strong arms,
Which now we hold at much uncertainty.

Northumberland. Farewell, good brother. We shall
thrive, I trust.

Hotspur. Uncle, adieu. O, let the hours be short
Till fields and blows and groans applaud our sport!
Exeunt.

291 **suddenly** speedily

[ACT II

Scene I. *Rochester. An inn yard.*]

Enter a Carrier with a lantern in his hand.

First Carrier. Heigh-ho! An it be not four by the day,°
I'll be hanged. Charles' wain° is over the new chimney, and yet our horse not packed. What, ostler!

Ostler. [*Within*] Anon, anon.

First Carrier. I prithee, Tom, beat° Cut's saddle, put   *5*
a few flocks in the point;° poor jade is wrung in the
withers° out of all cess.°

Enter another Carrier.

Second Carrier. Peas and beans are as dank here as a
dog, and that is the next° way to give poor jades the
bots.° This house is turned upside down since Robin   *10*
Ostler died.

First Carrier. Poor fellow never joyed since the price
of oats rose; it was the death of him.

Second Carrier. I think this be the most villainous
house in all London road for fleas, I am stung like   *15*
a tench.°

II.i.1 **by the day** in the morning   2 **Charles' wain** the Great Bear
5 **beat** i.e., to soften it   6 **a few flocks in the point** a little padding
in the pommel   6–7 **wrung in the withers** rubbed raw at the shoulders   7 **out of all cess** to excess   9 **next** nearest   10 **bots** worms
16 **tench** fish with red spots (as if flea-bitten)

First Carrier. Like a tench? By the mass, there is ne'er a king christen could be better bit than I have been° since the first cock.°

20 *Second Carrier*. Why, they will allow us ne'er a jordan,° and then we leak in your chimney,° and your chamber-lye° breeds fleas like a loach.°

First Carrier. What, ostler! Come away and be hanged! Come away!

25 *Second Carrier*. I have a gammon° of bacon and two razes° of ginger, to be delivered as far as Charing Cross.

First Carrier. God's body! The turkeys in my pannier° are quite starved. What, ostler! A plague on thee,
30 hast thou never an eye in thy head? Canst not hear? And 'twere not as good deed as drink to break the pate on thee, I am a very villain. Come, and be hanged! Hast no faith in thee?

Enter Gadshill.

Gadshill. Good morrow, carriers, what's o'clock?

35 *First Carrier*. I think it be two o'clock.

Gadshill. I prithee lend me thy lantern to see my gelding in the stable.

First Carrier. Nay, by God, soft!° I know a trick worth two of that, i' faith.

40 *Gadshill*. I pray thee lend me thine.

Second Carrier. Ay, when? Canst tell?° Lend me thy lantern, quoth he? Marry, I'll see thee hanged first!

17–18 **there . . . been** i.e., not even a Christian king (though kings get the best of everything) could have surpassed my record in flea-bites   19 **the first cock** midnight   20–21 **jordan** chamberpot   21 **chimney** fireplace   22 **chamber-lye** urine   22 **loach** fish that breeds often   25 **gammon** haunch   26 **razes** roots   28 **pannier** basket   38 **soft** i.e., "listen to him!"   41 **Ay, when? Canst tell?** (standard retort to an inopportune request)

Gadshill. Sirrah carrier, what time do you mean to come to London?

Second Carrier. Time enough to go to bed with a candle,° I warrant thee. Come, neighbor Mugs, we'll call up the gentlemen, they will along with company, for they have great charge.°   *Exeunt [Carriers]*.   45

Gadshill. What, ho! Chamberlain!

Enter Chamberlain.

Chamberlain. "At hand,° quoth pickpurse."   50

Gadshill. That's even as fair as "at hand, quoth the chamberlain"; for thou variest no more from picking of purses than giving direction doth from laboring: thou layest the plot how.

Chamberlain. Good morrow, Master Gadshill. It holds   55
current° that I told you yesternight: there's a frank-
lin° in the Wild° of Kent hath brought three hundred marks° with him in gold, I heard him tell it to
one of his company last night at supper—a kind of
auditor,° one that hath abundance of charge too,   60
God knows what. They are up already and call for
eggs and butter, they will away presently.

Gadshill. Sirrah, if they meet not with Saint Nicholas'
clerks,° I'll give thee this neck.

Chamberlain. No, I'll none of it; I pray thee keep that   65
for the hangman; for I know thou worshippest Saint
Nicholas as truly as a man of falsehood may.

Gadshill. What talkest thou to me of the hangman? If
I hang, I'll make a fat pair of gallows; for if I hang,

45–46 **Time . . . candle** (evasively spoken, the carriers being suspicious of Gadshill)   48 **charge** luggage   50 **At hand** (a popular
tag meaning "Ready, sir!" but relevant here to the Chamberlain's
filching way of life, as Gadshill points out)   56 **current** true   56–
57 **franklin** rich farmer   57 **Wild** weald, open country   57–58 **three
hundred marks** £200 (Elizabethan value)   60 **auditor** revenue officer   63–64 **Saint Nicholas' clerks** highwaymen (St. Nicholas was
reckoned the patron of all travelers, including traveling thieves)

70 old Sir John hangs with me, and thou knowest he is
no starveling. Tut! There are other Troyans° that
thou dream'st not of, the which for sport sake are
content to do the profession some grace; that would
(if matters should be looked into) for their own
75 credit sake make all whole. I am joined with no foot-
landrakers,° no long-staff sixpenny strikers,° none
of these mad mustachio purple-hued maltworms;°
but with nobility and tranquillity,° burgomasters and
great oneyers,° such as can hold in,° such as will
80 strike sooner than speak,° and speak sooner than
drink, and drink sooner than pray—and yet, zounds,
I lie, for they pray continually to their saint, the commonwealth, or rather, not pray to her, but prey on
her, for they ride up and down on her and make her
85 their boots.°

Chamberlain. What, the commonwealth their boots?
Will she hold out water in foul way?°

Gadshill. She will, she will! Justice hath liquored° her.
We steal as in a castle, cocksure. We have the re-
90 ceipt of fernseed,° we walk invisible.

Chamberlain. Nay, by my faith, I think you are more
beholding to the night than to fernseed for your
walking invisible.

Gadshill. Give me thy hand. Thou shalt have a share
95 in our purchase,° as I am a true man.

Chamberlain. Nay, rather let me have it, as you are a
false thief.

---

71 **Troyans** good fellows   75–76 **foot-landrakers** footloose vaga-
bonds   76 **long-staff sixpenny strikers** men who would pull you
from your horse with long staves even to steal sixpence   77 **mustachio purple-hued maltworms** big-mustached purple-faced drunk-
ards   78 **tranquillity** (Gadshill's witty coinage, on the analogy of
"nobility": people who don't have to scrounge their living)   79 **oneyers** ones (?)   79 **hold in** keep confidence   80 **speak** i.e., say "hands
up"   85 **boots** (with pun on "boots/booty")   87 **in foul way** on
muddy roads   88 **liquored** (1) greased (as with boots) (2) made her
drunk   89–90 **receipt of fernseed** recipe of fernseed (popularly
supposed to render one invisible)   95 **purchase** (euphemism for
loot)

Gadshill. Go to; "homo" is a common name to all
     men.° Bid the ostler bring my gelding out of the
     stable. Farewell, you muddy knave.   [*Exeunt.*]   100

[Scene II. *The highway, near Gad's Hill.*]

Enter Prince, Poins, and Peto, etc.

Poins. Come, shelter, shelter! I have removed Falstaff's
     horse, and he frets° like a gummed velvet.

Prince. Stand close.   [*They step aside.*]

Enter Falstaff.

Falstaff. Poins! Poins, and be hanged! Poins!

Prince. [*Comes forward*] Peace, ye fat-kidneyed rascal!   5
     What a brawling dost thou keep!

Falstaff. Where's Poins, Hal?

Prince. He is walked up to the top of the hill; I'll go
     seek him.   [*Steps aside.*]

Falstaff. I am accursed to rob in that thief's company.   10
     The rascal hath removed my horse and tied him I
     know not where. If I travel but four foot by the
     squire° further afoot, I shall break my wind. Well,
     I doubt not but to die a fair death for all this, if I
     scape hanging for killing that rogue. I have forsworn   15
     his company hourly any time this two and twenty
     years, and yet I am bewitched with the rogue's com-
     pany. If the rascal have not given me medicines to
     make me love him, I'll be hanged. It could not be
     else: I have drunk medicines. Poins! Hal! A plague   20

98–99 **homo . . . men** the Latin for man, *homo* is a term that covers
all men, true (i.e., honest) or false   II.ii.2 **frets** chafes (with pun
on the fretting or fraying of velvet as the gum used to stiffen it
wore away)   13 **squire** rule

upon you both! Bardolph! Peto! I'll starve° ere I'll
rob a foot further. And 'twere not as good a deed
as drink to turn true man and to leave these rogues,
I am the veriest varlet that ever chewed with a tooth.
25   Eight yards of uneven ground is threescore and ten
miles afoot with me, and the stony-hearted villains
know it well enough. A plague upon it when thieves
cannot be true one to another! (*They whistle.*)
Whew! A plague upon you all! Give me my horse,
30   you rogues! Give me my horse and be hanged!

Prince. [*Comes forward*] Peace, ye fat-guts! Lie down,
lay thine ear close to the ground, and list if thou
canst hear the tread of travelers.

Falstaff. Have you any levers to lift me up again, being
35   down? 'Sblood, I'll not bear mine own flesh so far
afoot again for all the coin in thy father's exchequer.
What a plague mean ye to colt° me thus?

Prince. Thou liest, thou art not colted, thou art uncolted.°

40   *Falstaff.* I prithee, good Prince Hal, help me to my
horse, good king's son.

Prince. Out, ye rogue! Shall I be your ostler?

Falstaff. Hang thyself in thine own heir-apparent garters!° If I be ta'en, I'll peach° for this. And I have
45   not ballads made on you all, and sung to filthy tunes,
let a cup of sack be my poison. When a jest is so
forward—and afoot too—I hate it.

Enter Gadshill [and Bardolph].

Gadshill. Stand!

Falstaff. So I do, against my will.

---

21 **starve** die   37 **colt** trick   38–39 **uncolted** i.e., unhorsed   43–
44 **heir-apparent garters** (Falstaff adapts a proverbial phrase to fit
a crown prince)   44 **peach** inform on you

Poins. O, 'tis our setter;° I know his voice. [*Comes*   50
forward] Bardolph, what news?

Bardolph. Case ye, case ye! On with your vizards!
There's money of the King's coming down the hill;
'tis going to the King's exchequer.

Falstaff. You lie, ye rogue! 'Tis going to the King's   55
tavern.

Gadshill. There's enough to make us all—

Falstaff. To be hanged.

Prince. Sirs, you four shall front them in the narrow
lane; Ned Poins and I will walk lower: if they scape   60
from your encounter, then they light on us.

Peto. How many be there of them?

Gadshill. Some eight or ten.

Falstaff. Zounds, will they not rob us?

Prince. What, a coward, Sir John Paunch?   65

Falstaff. Indeed, I am not John of Gaunt° your grandfather, but yet no coward, Hal.

Prince. Well, we leave that to the proof.°

Poins. Sirrah Jack, thy horse stands behind the hedge.
When thou need'st him, there thou shalt find him.   70
Farewell and stand fast.

Falstaff. Now cannot I strike him, if I should be
hanged.

Prince. [*Aside to Poins*] Ned, where are our disguises?

Poins. [*Aside to Prince*] Here, hard by. Stand close.   75
                         [*Exeunt Prince and Poins.*]

---

50 **setter** one who makes arrangements for a robbery   66 **John of
Gaunt** Hal's grandfather (but in reply to "Sir John Paunch" Falstaff
puns on "gaunt/thin" which Hal evidently is [cf. II.iv.244–48])
68 **proof** test

Falstaff. Now, my masters, happy man be his dole,° say I. Every man to his business.

Enter the Travelers.

Traveler. Come, neighbor. The boy shall lead our horses down the hill; we'll walk afoot awhile and
80 ease our legs.

Thieves. Stand!

Traveler. Jesus bless us!

Falstaff. Strike! Down with them! Cut the villains' throats! Ah, whoreson caterpillars!° Bacon-fed
85 knaves! They hate us youth. Down with them! Fleece them!

Traveler. O, we are undone, both we and ours forever!

Falstaff. Hang ye, gorbellied° knaves, are ye undone? No, ye fat chuffs;° I would your store° were here!
90 On, bacons, on! What, ye knaves, young men must live. You are grandjurors,° are ye? We'll jure ye, faith!   *Here they rob them and bind them. Exeunt.*

Enter the Prince and Poins [disguised].

Prince. The thieves have bound the true men. Now could thou and I rob the thieves and go merrily to
95 London, it would be argument° for a week, laughter for a month, and a good jest forever.

Poins. Stand close! I hear them coming.
                              [They stand aside.]

Enter the thieves again.

Falstaff. Come, my masters, let us share, and then to horse before day. And the Prince and Poins be not
100 two arrant° cowards, there's no equity stirring.°

---

76 **happy man be his dole** may happiness be our lot   84 **whoreson caterpillars** miserable parasites   88 **gorbellied** great-bellied   89 **chuffs** misers   89 **store** total wealth   91 **grandjurors** i.e., men of substance (as required for service on a grand jury)   95 **be argument** make conversation   100 **arrant** thorough   100 **no equity stirring** i.e., no justice left alive

There's no more valor in that Poins than in a wild
duck.

Prince. Your money!	*As they are sharing, the Prince and Poins set upon them. They all run away, and Falstaff, after a blow or two, runs away too, leaving the booty behind them.*
Poins. Villains!	

Prince. Got with much ease. Now merrily to horse. The   *105*
thieves are all scattered, and possessed with fear so
strongly that they dare not meet each other: each
takes his fellow for an officer. Away, good Ned. Falstaff sweats to death and lards the lean earth as he
walks along. Were't not for laughing, I should pity   *110*
him.°

Poins. How the fat rogue roared!   *Exeunt.*

[Scene III. *Northumberland. Warkworth Castle.*]

Enter Hotspur solus,° reading a letter.

Hotspur. "But, for mine own part, my lord, I could be
well contented to be there, in respect of the love I
bear your house."° He could be contented—why is
he not then? In respect of the love he bears our
house! He shows in this he loves his own barn better   *5*
than he loves our house. Let me see some more. "The
purpose you undertake is dangerous"—why, that's
certain! 'Tis dangerous to take a cold, to sleep, to
drink; but I tell you, my lord fool, out of this nettle,
danger, we pluck this flower, safety. "The purpose   *10*
you undertake is dangerous, the friends you have

105–11 **Got . . . him** (printed as verse by Pope and many later
editors, with line breaks after "horse/fear/other/officer/death/
along/him") II.iii.s.d. **solus** alone (Latin)   3 **house** family

named uncertain, the time itself unsorted,° and your
whole plot too light for the counterpoise of so great
an opposition." Say you so, say you so? I say unto
15 you again, you are a shallow, cowardly hind,° and
you lie. What a lack-brain is this! By the Lord, our
plot is a good plot as ever was laid; our friends true
and constant: a good plot, good friends, and full of
expectation; an excellent plot, very good friends.
20 What a frosty-spirited rogue is this! Why, my Lord
of York° commends the plot and the general course
of the action. Zounds, and I were now by this rascal,
I could brain him with his lady's fan. Is there not my
father, my uncle, and myself; Lord Edmund Mor-
25 timer, my Lord of York, and Owen Glendower? Is
there not, besides, the Douglas? Have I not all their
letters to meet me in arms by the ninth of the next
month, and are they not some of them set forward
already? What a pagan° rascal is this, an infidel! Ha!
30 you shall see now, in very sincerity of fear and cold
heart will he to the King and lay open all our proceedings. O, I could divide myself and go to buffets°
for moving such a dish of skim milk with so honorable an action! Hang him, let him tell the King! We
35 are prepared. I will set forward tonight.

Enter his Lady.

How now, Kate? I must leave you within these two
hours.

Lady. O my good lord, why are you thus alone?
For what offense have I this fortnight been
40 A banished woman from my Harry's bed?
Tell me, sweet lord, what is't that takes from thee
Thy stomach,° pleasure, and thy golden sleep?
Why dost thou bend thine eyes upon the earth,
And start so often when thou sit'st alone?

---

12 **unsorted** unsuitable   15 **hind** menial   20–21 **my Lord of York**
the Archbishop of York (cf. I.iii.264 ff)   29 **pagan** faithless   32 **divide . . . buffets** split myself into two, and set the halves fighting
42 **stomach** appetite

Why hast thou lost the fresh blood in thy cheeks   45
And given my treasures and my rights of thee
To thick-eyed musing and cursed° melancholy?
In thy faint slumbers I by thee have watched,°
And heard thee murmur tales of iron wars,
Speak terms of manage to thy bounding steed,   50
Cry "Courage! To the field!" And thou hast talked
Of sallies and retires, of trenches, tents,
Of palisadoes,° frontiers,° parapets,
Of basilisks,° of cannon, culverin,°
Of prisoners' ransom, and of soldiers slain,   55
And all the currents° of a heady° fight.
Thy spirit within thee hath been so at war,
And thus hath so bestirred thee in thy sleep,
That beads of sweat have stood upon thy brow
Like bubbles in a late-disturbèd stream,   60
And in thy face strange motions have appeared,
Such as we see when men restrain their breath
On some great sudden hest.° O, what portents are
        these?
Some heavy business hath my lord in hand,
And I must know it, else he loves me not.   65

Hotspur. What, ho!

        [*Enter a Servant.*]

                Is Gilliams with the packet gone?

Servant. He is, my lord, an hour ago.

Hotspur. Hath Butler brought those horses from the
        sheriff?

Servant. One horse, my lord, he brought even now.

Hotspur. What horse? A roan, a crop-ear, is it not?   70

Servant. It is, my lord.

---

47 **cursed** peevish   48 **watched** lain awake   53 **palisadoes** defenses
made of stakes   53 **frontiers** fortifications   54 **basilisks, culverin**
(sizes and types of cannon)   56 **currents** occurrences   56 **heady**
violent   63 **hest** (1) command? (2) resolution?

Hotspur. That roan shall be my throne. Well, I will
back him straight. O Esperance!° Bid Butler lead
him forth into the park.°

[*Exit Servant.*]

75 *Lady.* But hear you, my lord.

Hotspur. What say'st thou, my lady?

Lady. What is it carries you away?°

Hotspur. Why, my horse, my love—my horse!

Lady. Out, you mad-headed ape! A weasel hath not
80 such a deal of spleen° as you are tossed with. In
faith, I'll know your business, Harry, that I will! I
fear my brother Mortimer doth stir about his title
and hath sent for you to line° his enterprise; but if
you go°—

85 *Hotspur.* So far afoot, I shall be weary, love.

Lady. Come, come, you paraquito,° answer me directly
unto this question that I ask. In faith, I'll break thy
little finger, Harry, and if thou wilt not tell me all
things true.°

90 *Hotspur.* Away, away, you trifler! Love? I love thee not;
I care not for thee, Kate. This is no world
To play with mammets° and to tilt° with lips.
We must have bloody noses and cracked crowns,°
And pass them current too. Gods me,° my horse!
What say'st thou, Kate? What wouldst thou have
95   with me?

---

73 **Esperance** hope (part of the Percy motto)   72–74 **That . . . park**
(Pope and many later editors print as verse; with line breaks after
"throne/Esperance/park"   77 **away** (1) i.e., from home (2) from
your usual self   80 **spleen** caprice   83 **line** strengthen   79–84 **Out
. . . go** (printed by Pope and many later editors as verse, but with a
variety of lineations)   86 **paraquito** parrot   86–89 **Come . . . true**
(printed by Pope and many later editors as verse, with line breaks
after "me/ask/Harry/true"   92 **mammets** dolls   92 **tilt** duel   93
crowns (1) heads (2) coins—which when "cracked" were hard to
"pass current" (possibly there is an allusion to the "crown" of
kingship, which, though not genuine when usurped, may be passed
current by force)   94 **Gods me** God save me

Lady. Do you not love me? Do you not indeed?
   Well, do not then; for since you love me not,
   I will not love myself. Do you not love me?
   Nay, tell me if you speak in jest or no.

Hotspur. Come, wilt thou see me ride?   100
   And when I am a-horseback, I will swear
   I love thee infinitely. But hark you, Kate:
   I must not have you henceforth question me
   Whither I go, nor reason whereabout.
   Whither I must, I must, and—to conclude,   105
   This evening must I leave you, gentle Kate.
   I know you wise—but yet no farther wise
   Than Harry Percy's wife; constant you are—
   But yet a woman; and for secrecy,
   No lady closer—for I well believe   110
   Thou wilt not utter what thou dost not know,
   And so far will I trust thee, gentle Kate—

Lady. How? So far?

Hotspur. Not an inch further. But hark you, Kate:
   Whither I go, thither shall you go too;   115
   Today will I set forth, tomorrow you.
   Will this content you, Kate?

Lady.   It must of force.° *Exeunt.*

[Scene IV. *Eastcheap. The tavern.°*]

Enter Prince and Poins.

Prince. Ned, prithee come out of that fat° room and
   lend me thy hand to laugh a little.

Poins. Where hast been, Hal?

117 **of force** of necessity   II.iv.s.d. **tavern** (the tavern is said to be
in Eastcheap, but it is never explicitly named; references to a boar
in *Henry IV* [*Part Two*] suggest it is the Boar's Head)   1 **fat** hot

Prince. With three or four loggerheads° amongst three
or fourscore hogsheads. I have sounded the very
bass-string of humility. Sirrah, I am sworn brother
to a leash° of drawers° and can call them all by their
christen names, as Tom, Dick, and Francis. They
take it already upon their salvation° that, though I
be but Prince of Wales, yet I am the king of courtesy,
and tell me flatly I am no proud Jack° like Falstaff,
but a Corinthian,° a lad of mettle, a good boy (by
the Lord, so they call me!), and when I am King of
England I shall command all the good lads in Eastcheap. They call drinking deep, dyeing scarlet;° and
when you breathe in your watering,° they cry "hem!"
and bid you play it off.° To conclude, I am so good
a proficient in one quarter of an hour that I can drink
with any tinker in his own language during my life.
I tell thee, Ned, thou hast lost much honor that thou
wert not with me in this action. But, sweet Ned—
to sweeten which name of Ned, I give thee this
pennyworth of sugar,° clapped even now into my
hand by an under-skinker,° one that never spake
other English in his life than "Eight shillings and
sixpence," and "You are welcome," with this shrill
addition, "Anon,° anon, sir! Score° a pint of bas-
tard° in the Half-moon,"° or so—but, Ned, to drive
away the time till Falstaff come, I prithee do thou
stand in some by-room while I question my puny
drawer to what end he gave me the sugar; and do
thou never leave calling "Francis!" that his tale to
me may be nothing but "Anon!" Step aside, and I'll
show thee a precedent.°

---

4 **loggerheads** blockheads 7 **leash** trio 7 **drawers** tapsters 9 **take
. . . salvation** pledge their salvation 11 **Jack** fellow 12 **Corinthian** gay blade 15 **dyeing scarlet** i.e., from the complexion it
gives a man 16 **breathe in your watering** pause for breath while
drinking 17 **play it off** down it 23 **sugar** i.e., for sweetening wine
(cf. I.ii.117) 24 **under-skinker** under-tapster 27 **Anon** i.e., (I'm
coming) at once 27 **Score** charge 27–28 **bastard** Spanish wine
28 **Half-moon** one of the inn's rooms 34 **precedent** example

Poins. Francis!   35

Prince. Thou art perfect.

Poins. Francis!   [*Poins steps aside.*]

           Enter [*Francis, a*] *Drawer.*

Francis. Anon, anon, sir. Look down into the Pom-
    garnet,° Ralph.

Prince. Come hither, Francis.   40

Francis. My lord?

Prince. How long hast thou to serve,° Francis?

Francis. Forsooth, five years, and as much as to—

Poins. [*Within*] Francis!

Francis. Anon, anon, sir.   45

Prince. Five year! By'r Lady,° a long lease for the clink-
    ing of pewter. But, Francis, darest thou be so valiant
    as to play the coward with thy indenture° and show
    it a fair pair of heels and run from it?

Francis. O Lord, sir, I'll be sworn upon all the books   50
    in England I could find in my heart—

Poins. [*Within*] Francis!

Francis. Anon, sir.

Prince. How old art thou, Francis?

Francis. Let me see: about Michaelmas° next I shall   55
    be—

Poins. [*Within*] Francis!

Francis. Anon, sir. Pray stay a little, my lord.

Prince. Nay, but hark you, Francis. For the sugar thou
    gavest me—'twas a pennyworth, was't not?   60

38-39 **Pomgarnet** Pomegranate (another of the inn's rooms)   42
serve i.e., as an apprentice (apprenticeship ran for seven years)
46 **By'r Lady** by Our Lady (mild oath)   48 **indenture** contract
55 **Michaelmas** September 29

Francis. O Lord! I would it had been two!

Prince. I will give thee for it a thousand pound. Ask
me when thou wilt, and thou shalt have it.

Poins. [Within] Francis!

65 *Francis.* Anon, anon.

Prince. Anon, Francis?° No, Francis; but tomorrow,
Francis; or, Francis, a Thursday; or indeed, Francis,
when thou wilt. But, Francis—

Francis. My lord?

70 *Prince.* Wilt thou rob this leathern-jerkin, crystal-
button, not-pated, agate-ring, puke-stocking, caddis-
garter, smooth-tongue, Spanish-pouch?°

Francis. O Lord, sir, who do you mean?

Prince. Why then, your brown bastard is your only
75 drink; for look you, Francis, your white canvas doublet will sully. In Barbary, sir, it cannot come to so
much.°

Francis. What, sir?

Poins. [Within] Francis!

80 *Prince.* Away, you rogue! Dost thou not hear them call?

> *Here they both call him. The Drawer stands
> amazed, not knowing which way to go.*

> *Enter Vintner.°*

Vintner. What, stand'st thou still, and hear'st such a
calling? Look to the guests within. *[Exit Francis.]*

---

66 **Anon, Francis?** (Hal pretends to take Francis' "anon"—at once—
to Poins as meaning he wants the thousand pounds at once)   70–
72 **this . . . Spanish-pouch** i.e., the innkeeper, whose middle-class
appearance Hal details: leather jacket with crystal buttons, short
hair, agate ring, wool stockings, plain worsted (not fancy) garters,
ingratiating (and probably unctuous) speech, money pouch of Spanish leather   74–77 **Why . . . much** (semi-nonsense; but the implica-
tion seems clear that Francis must stick to his trade)   80 s.d.
Vintner the innkeeper

My lord, old Sir John, with half a dozen more, are
at the door. Shall I let them in?

Prince. Let them alone awhile, and then open the door.   *85*
[*Exit Vintner.*] Poins!

Poins. [*Within*] Anon, anon, sir.

Enter Poins.

Prince. Sirrah, Falstaff and the rest of the thieves are at
the door. Shall we be merry?

Poins. As merry as crickets, my lad. But hark ye; what   *90*
cunning match have you made with this jest of the
drawer? Come, what's the issue?°

Prince. I am now of all humors that have showed themselves humors since the old days of goodman Adam
to the pupil age of this present twelve o'clock at   *95*
midnight.°

[*Enter Francis.*]

What's o'clock, Francis?

Francis. Anon, anon, sir.   [*Exit.*]

Prince. That ever this fellow should have fewer words
than a parrot, and yet the son of a woman! His in-   *100*
dustry is upstairs and downstairs, his eloquence
the parcel of a reckoning.° I am not yet of Percy's mind,
the Hotspur of the North: he that kills me some six
or seven dozen of Scots at a breakfast, washes his
hands, and says to his wife, "Fie upon this quiet   *105*
life! I want work." "O my sweet Harry," says she,
"how many hast thou killed today?" "Give my roan
horse a drench,"° says he, and answers "Some fourteen," an hour after, "a trifle, a trifle." I prithee call
in Falstaff. I'll play Percy, and that damned brawn°   *110*

92 **issue** outcome, point (of the jest)   93–96 **I . . . midnight** I am
ready for every kind of gaiety that men have invented since the
beginning of the world   100–02 **His industry . . . reckoning** his
whole activity is running up and down stairs, his whole conversation
the totaling of bills   108 **drench** dose of medicine   110 **brawn** fat
boar

shall play Dame Mortimer his wife. "Rivo!"° says
the drunkard. Call in Ribs, call in Tallow.

Enter Falstaff, [Gadshill, Bardolph, and Peto;

Francis follows with wine].

Poins. Welcome, Jack. Where hast thou been?

Falstaff. A plague of° all cowards, I say, and a ven-
115   geance too! Marry and amen! Give me a cup of sack,
boy. Ere I lead this life long, I'll sew netherstocks,°
and mend them and foot them too. A plague of all
cowards! Give me a cup of sack, rogue. Is there no
virtue extant?   *He drinketh.*

120 *Prince.* Didst thou never see Titan° kiss a dish of butter
(pitiful-hearted Titan!) that melted at the sweet tale
of the sun's? If thou didst, then behold that compound.

Falstaff. You rogue, here's lime° in this sack too! There
125   is nothing but roguery to be found in villainous man.
Yet a coward is worse than a cup of sack with lime
in it—a villainous coward! Go thy ways, old Jack,
die when thou wilt; if manhood, good manhood, be
not forgot upon the face of the earth, then am I a
130   shotten herring.° There lives not three good men un-
hanged in England; and one of them is fat, and grows
old. God help the while! A bad world, I say. I would
I were a weaver; I could sing psalms° or anything. A
plague of all cowards, I say still!

135 *Prince.* How now, woolsack? What mutter you?

Falstaff. A king's son! If I do not beat thee out of thy

---

111 **Rivo** (drinking cry of uncertain meaning)   114 **of** on   116
netherstocks stockings   120 **Titan** the sun (of which Hal is possibly reminded by Falstaff's broad face, and his melting effect on
the sack)   124 **lime** (added to make poor wine seem dry and clear)
130 **shotten herring** herring that has cast its roe (and is therefore
long and lean)   132–33 **God . . . psalms** (Falstaff reassumes his
role of comic Puritan: English weavers were often psalm-singing
Protestants who had fled from the Roman Catholic continent)

kingdom with a dagger of lath° and drive all thy
subjects afore thee like a flock of wild geese, I'll never
wear hair on my face more. You Prince of Wales?

Prince. Why, you whoreson round man, what's the   140
matter?

Falstaff. Are not you a coward? Answer me to that—
and Poins there?

Poins. Zounds, ye fat paunch, and ye call me coward,
by the Lord, I'll stab thee.   145

Falstaff. I call thee coward? I'll see thee damned ere I
call thee coward, but I would give a thousand pound
I could run as fast as thou canst. You are straight
enough in the shoulders; you care not who sees your
back. Call you that backing of your friends? A plague   150
upon such backing, give me them that will face me.
Give me a cup of sack. I am a rogue if I drunk today.

Prince. O villain, thy lips are scarce wiped since thou
drunk'st last.

Falstaff. All is one for that. (*He drinketh.*) A plague   155
of all cowards, still say I.

Prince. What's the matter?

Falstaff. What's the matter? There be four of us here
have ta'en a thousand pound this day morning.

Prince. Where is it, Jack, where is it?   160

Falstaff. Where is it? Taken from us it is. A hundred
upon poor four of us!

Prince. What, a hundred, man?

Falstaff. I am a rogue if I were not at half-sword° with
a dozen of them two hours together. I have scaped   165
by miracle. I am eight times thrust through the dou-

---

137 **dagger of lath** wooden dagger (by this phrase Falstaff associates
himself with a character called "the Vice" in the old religious plays,
who drove the devil offstage by beating him with a wooden dagger)
164 **at half-sword** infighting at close quarters

blet,° four through the hose;° my buckler cut
through and through; my sword hacked like a hand-
saw—*ecce signum!*° I never dealt° better since I was
170 a man. All would not do. A plague of all cowards!
Let them speak. If they speak more or less than
truth, they are villains and the sons of darkness.°

Prince. Speak, sirs. How was it?

Gadshill. We four set upon some dozen—

175 *Falstaff.* Sixteen at least, my lord.

Gadshill. And bound them.

Peto. No, no, they were not bound.

Falstaff. You rogue, they were bound, every man of
them, or I am a Jew else—an Ebrew Jew.

180 *Gadshill.* As we were sharing, some six or seven fresh
men set upon us—

Falstaff. And unbound the rest, and then come in the
other.°

Prince. What, fought you with them all?

185 *Falstaff.* All? I know not what you call all, but if I
fought not with fifty of them, I am a bunch of radish!° If there were not two or three and fifty° upon
poor old Jack, then am I no two-legged creature.

Prince. Pray God you have not murd'red some of them.

190 *Falstaff.* Nay, that's past praying for. I have peppered
two of them. Two I am sure I have paid,° two rogues
in buckram suits. I tell thee what, Hal—if I tell thee
a lie, spit in my face, call me horse. Thou knowest

166–67 doublet Elizabethan upper garment   167 hose Elizabethan
breeches   169 ecce signum behold the evidence (Latin; spoken as he
shows his sword)   169 dealt i.e., dealt blows   172 sons of darkness
i.e., damned (but cf. also I.ii.24)   183 other others   186–87 bunch
of radish (again an object long and lean)   187 three and fifty (fifty-
three was the number of Spanish ships popularly reputed to have
opposed Sir Richard Grenville at the battle of the Azores in 1591;
Falstaff thus humorously claims for his fight the status of a national
epic)   191 paid settled with

my old ward:° here I lay, and thus I bore my point.
Four rogues in buckram let drive at me.　　　195

Prince. What, four? Thou saidst but two even now.

Falstaff. Four, Hal. I told thee four.

Poins. Ay, ay, he said four.

Falstaff. These four came all afront and mainly° thrust
at me. I made me no more ado but took all their　200
seven points in my target, thus.

Prince. Seven? Why, there were but four even now.

Falstaff. In buckram?

Poins. Ay, four, in buckram suits.

Falstaff. Seven, by these hilts, or I am a villain else.　　205

Prince. [*Aside to Poins*] Prithee let him alone. We shall
have more anon.

Falstaff. Dost thou hear me, Hal?

Prince. Ay, and mark° thee too, Jack.

Falstaff. Do so, for it is worth the list'ning to. These　210
nine in buckram that I told thee of—

Prince. So, two more already.

Falstaff. Their points being broken—

Poins. Down fell their hose.°

Falstaff. Began to give me ground; but I followed me　215
close, came in, foot and hand, and with a thought°
seven of the eleven I paid.

Prince. O monstrous! Eleven buckram men grown out
of two!

Falstaff. But, as the devil would have it, three misbe-　220

194 **ward** fencing posture　199 **mainly** mightily　209 **mark** pay
close attention to　214 **Down fell their hose** (Poins wittily takes
"points" in the sense of laces holding the breeches to the doublet)
216 **with a thought** quick as a thought

gotten knaves in Kendal green came at my back and
let drive at me; for it was so dark, Hal, that thou
couldest not see thy hand.

Prince. These lies are like their father that begets them
225 —gross as a mountain, open, palpable. Why, thou
clay-brained guts, thou knotty-pated° fool, thou
whoreson obscene greasy tallow-catch°—

Falstaff. What, art thou mad? Art thou mad? Is not
the truth the truth?

230 *Prince.* Why, how couldst thou know these men in Kendal green when it was so dark thou couldst not see
thy hand? Come, tell us your reason. What sayest
thou to this?

Poins. Come, your reason, Jack, your reason.

235 *Falstaff.* What, upon compulsion? Zounds, and I were
at the strappado° or all the racks in the world, I
would not tell you on compulsion. Give you a reason on compulsion? If reasons° were as plentiful as
blackberries, I would give no man a reason upon
240 compulsion, I.

Prince. I'll be no longer guilty of this sin; this sanguine°
coward, this bed-presser, this horseback-breaker,
this huge hill of flesh—

Falstaff. 'Sblood, you starveling, you eel-skin, you dried
245 neat's-tongue,° you bull's pizzle,° you stockfish°—
O for breath to utter what is like thee!—you tailor's
yard, you sheath, you bowcase, you vile standing
tuck!°

Prince. Well, breathe awhile, and then to it again; and

---

226 **knotty-pated** blockheaded   227 **tallow-catch** (1) pan to catch
drippings under roasting meat? (2) tallow-keech, i.e., roll of fat for
making candles?   236 **strappado** instrument of torture   238 **reasons**
(pronounced like "raisins," and hence comparable to blackberries)
241 **sanguine** ruddy (and hence valorous-seeming)   245 **neat's-
tongue** ox-tongue   245 **pizzle** penis   245 **stockfish** dried codfish
247-48 **standing tuck** upright rapier

when thou hast tired thyself in base comparisons,   250
hear me speak but this.

Poins. Mark, Jack.

Prince. We two saw you four set on four, and bound
them and were masters of their wealth. Mark now
how a plain tale shall put you down. Then did we   255
two set on you four and, with a word,° outfaced you
from your prize, and have it; yea, and can show it
you here in the house. And, Falstaff, you carried your
guts away as nimbly, with as quick dexterity, and
roared for mercy, and still run and roared, as ever   260
I heard bullcalf. What a slave art thou to hack thy
sword as thou hast done, and then say it was in fight!
What trick, what device, what starting hole° canst
thou now find out to hide thee from this open and
apparent shame?   265

Poins. Come, let's hear, Jack. What trick hast thou
now?

Falstaff. By the Lord, I knew ye as well as he that made
ye. Why, hear you, my masters. Was it for me to
kill the heir apparent? Should I turn upon the true   270
prince? Why, thou knowest I am as valiant as Her-
cules, but beware instinct. The lion will not touch
the true prince.° Instinct is a great matter. I was now
a coward on instinct. I shall think the better of myself, and thee, during my life—I for a valiant lion,   275
and thou for a true prince. But, by the Lord, lads,
I am glad you have the money. Hostess, clap to the
doors. Watch tonight, pray tomorrow.° Gallants,
lads, boys, hearts of gold, all the titles of good fellowship come to you! What, shall we be merry? Shall   280
we have a play extempore?

---

256 **with a word** (1) in brief? (2) with a mere shout to scare you?
263 **starting hole** hiding place   272–73 **The lion . . . prince** (a traditional belief about lions)   278 **Watch . . . tomorrow** cf. Matthew
26:41 "Watch and pray, that ye enter not into temptation." (Falstaff
puns on "watch," which means "carouse" as well as "keep vigil")

Prince. Content—and the argument° shall be thy running away.

Falstaff. Ah, no more of that, Hal, and thou lovest me!

Enter Hostess.

285 *Hostess.* O Jesu, my lord the Prince!

Prince. How now, my lady the hostess? What say'st thou to me?

Hostess. Marry, my lord, there is a nobleman of the court at door would speak with you. He says he 290 comes from your father.

Prince. Give him as much as will make him a royal man,° and send him back again to my mother.

Falstaff. What manner of man is he?

Hostess. An old man.

295 *Falstaff.* What doth gravity° out of his bed at midnight? Shall I give him his answer?

Prince. Prithee do, Jack.

Falstaff. Faith, and I'll send him packing.   *Exit.*

Prince. Now, sirs. By'r Lady, you fought fair; so did 300 you, Peto; so did you, Bardolph. You are lions too, you ran away upon instinct, you will not touch the true prince; no—fie!

Bardolph. Faith, I ran when I saw others run.

Prince. Faith, tell me now in earnest, how came Fal-305 staff's sword so hacked?

Peto. Why, he hacked it with his dagger, and said he would swear truth out of England but he would make you believe it was done in fight, and persuaded us to do the like.

282 **argument** subject   291–92 **royal man** cf. "noble" in the previous speech, but with a pun on the "royal," a coin worth ten shillings, which was of greater value than the "noble," worth six shillings eight pence   295 **gravity** i.e., sober age

Bardolph. Yea, and to tickle our noses with speargrass   310
to make them bleed, and then to beslubber our garments with it and swear it was the blood of true men.
I did that° I did not this seven year before—I
blushed to hear his monstrous devices.

Prince. O villain! Thou stolest a cup of sack eighteen   315
years ago and wert taken with the manner,° and ever
since thou hast blushed extempore. Thou hadst fire°
and sword on thy side, and yet thou ran'st away.
What instinct hadst thou for it?

Bardolph. My lord, do you see these meteors?° Do you   320
behold these exhalations?°

Prince. I do.

Bardolph. What think you they portend?

Prince. Hot livers and cold purses.°

Bardolph. Choler,° my lord, if rightly taken.   325

Prince. No, if rightly taken, halter.

Enter Falstaff.

Here comes lean Jack; here comes bare-bone. How
now, my sweet creature of bombast?° How long is't
ago, Jack, since thou sawest thine own knee?

Falstaff. My own knee? When I was about thy years,   330
Hal, I was not an eagle's talent° in the waist; I could
have crept into any alderman's thumb-ring. A plague
of sighing and grief, it blows a man up like a bladder.
There's villainous news abroad. Here was Sir John
Bracy from your father: you must to the court in   335

313 **that** what   316 **taken with the manner** caught with the goods
317 **fire** i.e., the alcoholic hue of Bardolph's face   320, 321 **meteors,
exhalations** i.e., the pimples and other features of Bardolph's face,
spoken of as if they were meteorological portents   324 **Hot livers
and cold purses** (the two notable results of excessive drink)   325
Choler anger (Bardolph implies that he is choleric, and therefore no
coward; Hal proceeds to understand "choler" as "collar," which in
Bardolph's case will be—if "rightly taken"—the hangman's noose)
328 **bombast** cotton stuffing   331 **talent** talon

the morning. That same mad fellow of the north, Percy, and he of Wales that gave Amamon the bastinado, and made Lucifer cuckold, and swore the devil his true liegeman upon the cross of a Welsh
340 hook°—what a plague call you him?

Poins. Owen Glendower.

Falstaff. Owen, Owen—the same; and his son-in-law Mortimer, and old Northumberland, and that sprightly Scot of Scots, Douglas, that runs a-horse-
345 back up a hill perpendicular—

Prince. He that rides at high speed and with his pistol kills a sparrow flying.

Falstaff. You have hit it.

Prince. So did he never the sparrow.

350 *Falstaff.* Well, that rascal hath good metal° in him; he will not run.

Prince. Why, what a rascal art thou then, to praise him so for running!

Falstaff. A-horseback, ye cuckoo! But afoot he will not
355 budge a foot.

Prince. Yes, Jack, upon instinct.

Falstaff. I grant ye, upon instinct. Well, he is there too, and one Mordake, and a thousand bluecaps° more. Worcester is stol'n away tonight; thy father's beard
360 is turned white with the news; you may buy land now as cheap as stinking mack'rel.

Prince. Why then, it is like, if there come a hot June, and this civil buffeting hold, we shall buy maiden-heads as they buy hobnails, by the hundreds.°

337–40 he of Wales . . . hook (Falstaff alludes to Glendower's supposed magical powers: he has cudgeled a devil named Amamon, made horns grow on Lucifer, and forced the devil to swear allegiance to him on the cross of a weapon that has no cross)   350 good metal (with pun on "mettle," spirit, courage)   358 bluecaps Scots   362–64 If there . . . hundreds (the Prince applies the analogy of selling cheap what won't keep to the reactions of virgins as they see all the men going off to war)

Falstaff. By the mass, lad, thou sayest true; it is like we   365
shall have good trading that way. But tell me, Hal,
art not thou horrible afeard? Thou being heir apparent, could the world pick thee out three such enemies again as that fiend Douglas, that spirit Percy,
and that devil Glendower? Art thou not horribly   370
afraid? Doth not thy blood thrill° at it?

Prince. Not a whit, i' faith. I lack some of thy instinct.

Falstaff. Well, thou wilt be horribly chid tomorrow
when thou comest to thy father. If thou love me,
practice an answer.   375

Prince. Do thou stand for my father and examine me
upon the particulars of my life.

Falstaff. Shall I? Content. This chair shall be my state,°
this dagger my scepter, and this cushion my crown.

Prince. Thy state is taken for° a joined-stool, thy golden   380
scepter for a leaden dagger, and thy precious rich
crown for a pitiful bald crown.

Falstaff. Well, and the fire of grace be not quite out of
thee, now shalt thou be moved. Give me a cup of
sack to make my eyes look red, that it may be   385
thought I have wept; for I must speak in passion,
and I will do it in King Cambyses' vein.°

Prince. Well, here is my leg.

Falstaff. And here is my speech. Stand aside, nobility.°

Hostess. O Jesu, this is excellent sport, i' faith!   390

Falstaff. Weep not, sweet queen,° for trickling tears are
vain.

---

371 **thrill** shiver (with fear)   378 **state** chair of state   380 **taken for**
(either "seen to be merely," or, alternatively, this is a meditative
comment, possibly an aside, in the detached vein of I.ii.199 and
II.iv.481, with "thy" referring to the King)   387 **King Cambyses'**
vein i.e., the old ranting style of Preston's *King Cambyses* (1569)
389 **nobility** (addressed to his motley ragamuffins)   391 **queen** (addressed to the Hostess, who is evidently tearful with laughter; probably with a standard pun on *quean* = tart, prostitute)

Hostess. O, the Father, how he holds his countenance!°

Falstaff. For God's sake, lords, convey my tristful°
queen!
For tears do stop the floodgates of her eyes.

395 *Hostess.* O Jesu, he doth it as like one of these harlotry°
players as ever I see!

Falstaff. Peace, good pintpot. Peace, good tickle-brain.
Harry, I do not only marvel where thou spendest
thy time, but also how thou art accompanied. For
400 though the camomile,° the more it is trodden on, the
faster it grows, so° youth, the more it is wasted, the
sooner it wears. That thou art my son I have partly
thy mother's word, partly my own opinion, but
chiefly a villainous trick° of thine eye and a foolish
405 hanging of thy nether lip that doth warrant me. If
then thou be son to me, here lies the point: why,
being son to me, art thou so pointed at? Shall the
blessed sun of heaven prove a micher and eat blackberries?° A question not to be asked. Shall the son°
410 of England prove a thief and take purses? A question
to be asked. There is a thing, Harry, which thou
hast often heard of, and it is known to many in our
land by the name of pitch. This pitch (as ancient
writers do report) doth defile; so doth the company
415 thou keepest. For, Harry, now I do not speak to
thee in drink, but in tears; not in pleasure, but in
passion; not in words only, but in woes also: and
yet there is a virtuous man whom I have often noted
in thy company, but I know not his name.

---

392 **holds his countenance** keeps a straight face   393 **tristful** sad
395 **harlotry** rascally   400 **camomile** aromatic herb (Falstaff proceeds to satirize the highflown style of the court by using a manner
of speech called euphuism—from John Lyly's fictional narrative,
Euphues [1578] which introduced it—based on similes drawn from
natural history, intricate balance, antithesis, and repetition of sounds,
words, and ideas)   401 **so** (some editors emend to "yet," but the
imperfect logical correspondence of "though . . . so" may be part
of Falstaff's mockery)   404 **trick** mannerism (possibly a twitch)
408–09 **prove . . . blackberries** be a truant from duty and go black-
berrying   409 **son** (with pun on "sun," the royal symbol)

Prince. What manner of man, and it like your Majesty?　*420*

Falstaff. A goodly portly° man, i' faith, and a corpulent;° of a cheerful look, a pleasing eye, and a most
noble carriage; and, as I think, his age some fifty,
or, by'r Lady, inclining to threescore; and now I remember me, his name is Falstaff. If that man should　*425*
be lewdly given,° he deceiveth me; for, Harry, I see
virtue in his looks. If then the tree may be known by
the fruit,° as the fruit by the tree, then, peremptorily°
I speak it, there is virtue in that Falstaff. Him keep
with, the rest banish. And tell me now, thou naughty　*430*
varlet, tell me where hast thou been this month?

Prince. Dost thou speak like a king? Do thou stand for
me, and I'll play my father.

Falstaff. Depose me? If thou dost it half so gravely, so
majestically, both in word and matter, hang me up　*435*
by the heels for a rabbit-sucker° or a poulter's hare.

Prince. Well, here I am set.

Falstaff. And here I stand. Judge, my masters.

Prince. Now, Harry, whence come you?

Falstaff. My noble lord, from Eastcheap.　*440*

Prince. The complaints I hear of thee are grievous.

Falstaff. 'Sblood, my lord, they are false! Nay, I'll tickle
ye for a young prince,° i' faith.

Prince. Swearest thou, ungracious boy? Henceforth
ne'er look on me. Thou art violently carried away　*445*
from grace. There is a devil haunts thee in the likeness of an old fat man; a tun° of man is thy companion. Why dost thou converse with that trunk of

---

421 **portly** stately　421–22 **corpulent** well filled out　426 **lewdly
given** inclined to evil-doing　427–28 **If . . . fruit** cf. Matthew 12:33:
"The tree is known by his fruit"　428 **peremptorily** decisively　436
rabbit-sucker suckling rabbit　442–43 **I'll . . . prince** I'll act a prince
that will amuse you　447 **tun** hogshead

humors,° that bolting-hutch° of beastliness, that
450   swoll'n parcel of dropsies,° that huge bombard° of
sack, that stuffed cloakbag of guts, that roasted
Manningtree° ox with the pudding in his belly, that
reverend vice,° that gray iniquity,° that father
ruffian,° that vanity° in years? Wherein is he good,
455   but to taste sack and drink it? Wherein neat and
cleanly, but to carve a capon and eat it? Wherein
cunning, but in craft?° Wherein crafty, but in
villainy? Wherein villainous, but in all things?
Wherein worthy, but in nothing?

460 *Falstaff.* I would your Grace would take me with you.°
Whom means your Grace?

Prince. That villainous abominable misleader of youth,
Falstaff, that old white-bearded Satan.

Falstaff. My lord, the man I know.

465 *Prince.* I know thou dost.

Falstaff. But to say I know more harm in him than in
myself were to say more than I know. That he is old,
the more the pity, his white hairs do witness it; but
that he is, saving your reverence, a whoremaster,
470   that I utterly deny. If sack and sugar be a fault, God
help the wicked! If to be old and merry be a sin,
then many an old host that I know is damned. If to
be fat be to be hated, then Pharaoh's lean kine° are
to be loved. No, my good lord: banish Peto, banish
475   Bardolph, banish Poins; but for sweet Jack Falstaff,
kind Jack Falstaff, true Jack Falstaff, valiant Jack

448–49 **trunk of humors** receptacle of body fluids (with allusion
to the diseases that were thought to be the product of these fluids)
449 **bolting-hutch** sifting-bin (where impurities collect)   450 **dropsies** internal fluids   450 **bombard** leather wine vessel   452 **Manningtree** town in Essex (where at annual fairs plays were acted and,
evidently, great oxen were stuffed and barbecued)   453–54 **vice,
iniquity, ruffian, vanity** (names intended to associate Falstaff with
characters of the old morality plays, all of whom were corrupters
of virtue. But unlike Falstaff, who ought to know better, *they* were
young)   456–57 **Wherein cunning but in craft** i.e., wherein skillful
but in underhanded skills   460 **take me with you** let me follow your
meaning   473 **kine** cows (cf. Genesis 41:19–21)

Falstaff, and therefore more valiant being, as he is,
old Jack Falstaff, banish not him thy Harry's company, banish not him thy Harry's company, banish
plump Jack, and banish all the world!   *480*

Prince. I do, I will.   [*A knocking heard.*
          Exeunt Hostess, Francis, and Bardolph.]

          Enter Bardolph, running.

Bardolph. O, my lord, my lord! The sheriff with a most
monstrous watch° is at the door.

Falstaff. Out, ye rogue! Play out the play, I have much
to say in the behalf of that Falstaff.   *485*

          Enter the Hostess.

Hostess. O Jesu, my lord, my lord!

Prince. Heigh, heigh, the devil rides upon a fiddlestick!
What's the matter?

Hostess. The sheriff and all the watch are at the door.
They are come to search the house. Shall I let   *490*
them in?

Falstaff. Dost thou hear, Hal? Never call a true piece
of gold a counterfeit. Thou art essentially made without seeming so.°

Prince. And thou a natural coward without instinct.   *495*

Falstaff. I deny your major.° If you will deny the sheriff,
so; if not, let him enter. If I become not a cart° as
well as another man, a plague on my bringing up!
I hope I shall as soon be strangled with a halter as
another.   *500*

Prince. Go hide thee behind the arras.° The rest walk
up above. Now, my masters, for a true face and good
conscience.

---

483 **watch** group of constables   492–94 **Never . . . so** (a difficult
passage, perhaps meaning that Falstaff, as a true piece of gold
despite appearances, should not be turned over to the sheriff by a
royal friend who is also true gold despite appearances)   496 **major**
i.e., major premise, with pun on "mayor"   497 **cart** hangman's cart
501 **arras** wall-hanging

Falstaff. Both which I have had; but their date is out,
505   and therefore I'll hide me.   *Exit.*

Prince. Call in the sheriff.
                    [*Exeunt all but the Prince and Peto.*]

                    Enter Sheriff and the Carrier.

Now, master sheriff, what is your will with me?

Sheriff. First, pardon me, my lord. A hue and cry
    Hath followed certain men unto this house.

510 *Prince.* What men?

Sheriff. One of them is well known, my gracious lord—
    A gross fat man.

Carrier.   As fat as butter.

Prince. The man, I do assure you, is not here,
    For I myself at this time have employed him.°
515   And, sheriff, I will engage my word to thee
    That I will by tomorrow dinner time
    Send him to answer thee, or any man,
    For anything he shall be charged withal;
    And so let me entreat you leave the house.

520 *Sheriff.* I will, my lord. There are two gentlemen
    Have in this robbery lost three hundred marks.

Prince. It may be so. If he have robbed these men,
    He shall be answerable; and so farewell.

Sheriff. Good night, my noble lord.

525 *Prince.* I think it is good morrow, is it not?

Sheriff. Indeed, my lord, I think it be two o'clock.
                    Exit [*with Carrier*].

Prince. This oily rascal is known as well as Paul's. Go
    call him forth.

513-14 **The man . . . him** (Hal's reply is equivocal: Falstaff is not
"here," in the heir-apparent's presence, but "employed" behind the
arras)

Peto. Falstaff! Fast asleep behind the arras, and snort-
　　ing° like a horse.　　　　　　　　　　　　　　　　　*530*

Prince. Hark how hard he fetches breath. Search his
　　pockets.
　　　He searcheth his pocket and findeth certain papers.
　　What hast thou found?

Peto. Nothing but papers, my lord.

Prince. Let's see what they be. Read them.　　　　　*535*

[*Peto reads*] "Item, A capon　.　.　.　.　2s. 2d.
　　　　　　　Item, Sauce　.　.　.　.　.　　4d.
　　　　　　　Item, Sack two gallons　.　.　5s. 8d.
　　　　　　　Item, Anchovies and sack
　　　　　　　　　after supper　.　.　.　2s. 6d.　*540*
　　　　　　　Item, Bread　.　.　.　.　.　ob."°

Prince. O monstrous! But one halfpennyworth of bread
　　to this intolerable deal° of sack! What there is else,
　　keep close; we'll read it at more advantage. There
　　let him sleep till day. I'll to the court in the morn-　*545*
　　ing. We must all to the wars, and thy place shall be
　　honorable. I'll procure this fat rogue a charge of
　　foot,° and I know his death will be a march of twelve
　　score.° The money shall be paid back again with
　　advantage.° Be with me betimes° in the morning,　*550*
　　and so good morrow, Peto.

Peto. Good morrow, good my lord.　　　　　*Exeunt.*

529–30 **snorting** snoring　541 **ob.** obolus, halfpenny　543 **deal** lot
547–48 **charge of foot** company of infantry　548–49 **twelve score**
twelve score paces　550 **advantage** interest　550 **betimes** early

[ACT III

Scene I. *Wales. A room.*]

*Enter Hotspur, Worcester, Lord Mortimer, Owen
Glendower.*

Mortimer. These promises are fair, the parties sure,
And our induction° full of prosperous hope.

Hotspur. Lord Mortimer, and cousin Glendower, will
you sit down? And uncle Worcester. A plague upon
5 it! I have forgot the map.

Glendower. No, here it is. Sit, cousin Percy, sit, good
cousin Hotspur, for by that name as oft as Lancaster
doth speak of you, his cheek looks pale, and with
a rising sigh he wisheth you in heaven.

10 *Hotspur.* And you in hell, as oft as he hears Owen
Glendower spoke of.°

Glendower. I cannot blame him. At my nativity
The front of heaven was full of fiery shapes
Of burning cressets,° and at my birth
15 The frame and huge foundation of the earth
Shakèd like a coward.

III.i.2 **induction** beginning   3–11 **Lord . . . spoke of** (many editors
revise to read as verse, with line breaks after "down/it/is/Hotspur/
you/sigh/hell/of"; or, leaving Hotspur's lines as prose, revise Glendower's speech to read as verse with breaks after "Percy/name/you
sigh/heaven")   14 **cressets** beacons

96

Hotspur. Why, so it would have done at the same season
    if your mother's cat had but kittened, though your-
    self had never been born.

Glendower. I say the earth did shake when I was born.   *20*

Hotspur. And I say the earth was not of my mind,
    If you suppose as fearing you it shook.

Glendower. The heavens were all on fire, the earth did
    tremble.

Hotspur. O, then the earth shook to see the heavens on
    fire,
    And not in fear of your nativity.   *25*
    Diseasèd nature oftentimes breaks forth
    In strange eruptions; oft the teeming earth
    Is with a kind of colic pinched and vexed
    By the imprisoning of unruly wind
    Within her womb, which, for enlargement striving,   *30*
    Shakes the old beldame° earth and topples down
    Steeples and mossgrown towers. At your birth
    Our grandam earth, having this distemp'rature,°
    In passion° shook.

Glendower.   Cousin, of many men
    I do not bear these crossings. Give me leave   *35*
    To tell you once again that at my birth
    The front of heaven was full of fiery shapes,
    The goats ran from the mountains, and the herds
    Were strangely clamorous to the frighted fields.
    These signs have marked me extraordinary,   *40*
    And all the courses of my life do show
    I am not in the roll of common men.
    Where is he living, clipped in with° the sea
    That chides the banks of England, Scotland, Wales,
    Which calls me pupil or hath read to° me?   *45*
    And bring him out that is but woman's son
    Can trace° me in the tedious ways of art°
    And hold me pace in deep experiments.

31 **beldame** grandmother (cf. "grandam," line 33)   33 **distemp'rature** physical disorder   34 **passion** pain   43 **clipped in with** em-
braced by   45 **read to** tutored   47 **trace** follow   47 **art** magic

Hotspur. I think there's no man speaks better Welsh.°
50　　I'll to dinner.

Mortimer. Peace, cousin Percy; you will make him
　　mad.

Glendower. I can call spirits from the vasty deep.

Hotspur. Why, so can I, or so can any man;
　　But will they come when you do call for them?

55　*Glendower.* Why, I can teach you, cousin, to command
　　the devil.

Hotspur. And I can teach thee, coz, to shame the
　　devil—
　　By telling truth. Tell truth and shame the devil.
　　If thou have power to raise him, bring him hither,
60　　And I'll be sworn I have power to shame him hence.
　　O, while you live, tell truth and shame the devil!

Mortimer. Come, come, no more of this unprofitable
　　chat.

Glendower. Three times hath Henry Bolingbroke made
　　head
　　Against my power; thrice from the banks of Wye
65　　And sandy-bottomed Severn have I sent him
　　Booteless° home and weather-beaten back.

Hotspur. Home without boots, and in foul weather too?
　　How scapes he agues,° in the devil's name?

Glendower. Come, here is the map. Shall we divide our
　　right°
70　　According to our threefold order ta'en?

Mortimer. The Archdeacon hath divided it
　　Into three limits° very equally.
　　England, from Trent and Severn hitherto,
　　By south and east is to my part assigned;

49 **speaks better Welsh** (1) brags better (2) talks more unintelligibly
66 **Booteless** profitless (probably trisyllabic)　68 **agues** i.e., catching cold　69 **our right** i.e., the kingdom they hope to win　72 **limits**
regions

All <u>westward</u>, Wales beyond the Severn shore,   75
And all the fertile land within that bound,
To Owen <u>Glendower</u>; and, dear coz, to you
The remnant <u>northward lying off</u> from Trent.
And our indentures tripartite° are drawn,
Which being sealèd interchangeably°   80
(A business that this night may execute),
Tomorrow, cousin Percy, you and I
And my good Lord of Worcester will set forth
To meet your father and the Scottish power,
As is appointed us, at Shrewsbury.   85
My father Glendower is not ready yet,
Nor shall we need his help these fourteen days.
[*To Glendower*] Within that space you may have
    drawn together
Your tenants, friends, and neighboring gentlemen.

Glendower. A shorter time shall send me to you, lords;   90
And in my conduct shall your ladies come,
From whom you now must steal and take no leave,
For there will be a world of water shed
Upon the parting of your wives and you.

Hotspur. Methinks my moiety,° north from Burton
    here,   95
In quantity equals not one of yours.
See how this river comes me cranking° in
And cuts me from the best of all my land
A huge half-moon, a monstrous cantle° out.
I'll have the current in this place dammed up,   100
And here the smug° and silver Trent shall run
In a new channel fair and evenly.
It shall not wind with such a deep indent
To rob me of so rich a bottom° here.

Glendower. Not wind? It shall, it must! You see it doth.   105

Mortimer. Yea, but mark how he bears his course, and

---

79 **indentures tripartite** three-way agreements   80 **interchangeably**
i.e., by all three parties   95 **moiety** share   97 **cranking** winding
99 **cantle** piece   101 **smug** smooth   104 **bottom** valley

runs me up with like advantage° on the other side,
gelding the opposèd continent° as much as on the
other side it takes from you.°

Worcester. Yea, but a little charge° will trench° him
here
And on this north side win this cape of land;
And then he runs straight and even.

Hotspur. I'll have it so, a little charge will do it.

Glendower. I'll not have it alt'red.

115 *Hotspur.* Will not you?

Glendower. No, nor you shall not.

Hotspur. Who shall say me nay?

Glendower. Why, that will I.

Hotspur. Let me not understand you then; speak it in
120 Welsh.

Glendower. I can speak English, lord, as well as you;
For I was trained up in the English court,
Where, being but young, I framèd to the harp
Many an English ditty lovely well,
125 And gave the tongue a helpful ornament°—
A virtue that was never seen in you.

Hotspur. Marry, and I am glad of it with all my heart!
I had rather be a kitten and cry mew
Than one of these same meter ballad-mongers.°
130 I had rather hear a brazen canstick turned°
Or a dry wheel grate on the axletree,
And that would set my teeth nothing on edge,
Nothing so much as mincing° poetry.

---

107 **advantage** i.e., disadvantage   108 **gelding the opposèd continent**
cutting out of the opposite bank   106–09 **Yea . . . you** (revised by
most editors to four or five lines of verse, with little agreement about
lineation)   110 **charge** cost   110 **trench** make a new course for
125 **gave . . . ornament** (1) ornamented the words with music? (2)
benefited the English language by my poems?   129 **meter ballad-
mongers** singers of doggerel ballads   130 **canstick turned** i.e., can-
dlestick in process of being burnished (and therefore raucously
scraped)   133 **mincing** affected

'Tis like the forced gait of a shuffling nag.

Glendower. Come, you shall have Trent turned. *135*

Hotspur. I do not care. I'll give thrice so much land
To any well-deserving friend;
But in the way of bargain, mark ye me,
I'll cavil on the ninth part of a hair.
Are the indentures drawn? Shall we be gone? *140*

Glendower. The moon shines fair; you may away by
night.
I'll haste the writer, and withal
Break with° your wives of your departure hence.
I am afraid my daughter will run mad,
So much she doteth on her Mortimer. *Exit.* *145*

Mortimer. Fie, cousin Percy, how you cross my father!

Hotspur. I cannot choose. Sometime he angers me
With telling me of the moldwarp° and the ant,
Of the dreamer Merlin and his prophecies,
And of a dragon and a finless fish, *150*
A clip-winged griffin and a moulten raven,
A couching° lion and a ramping° cat,
And such a deal of skimble-skamble° stuff
As puts me from my faith. I tell you what—
He held me last night at least nine hours *155*
In reckoning up the several devils' names
That were his lackeys. I cried "hum," and "Well,
go to!"
But marked him not a word. O, he is as tedious
As a tired horse, a railing wife;
Worse than a smoky house. I had rather live *160*
With cheese and garlic in a windmill far
Than feed on cates° and have him talk to me
In any summer house in Christendom.

---

143 **Break with** inform 148 **moldwarp** mole, i.e., Henry 152
couching, ramping (Hotspur ridicules heraldic crouching and rearing
beasts; evidently Glendower talked of ancient prophecies which held
that the kingdom of the mole should be divided by the lion, dragon
and wolf, which were the crests of Percy, Glendower, and Mortimer)
153 **skimble-skamble** meaningless 162 **cates** delicacies

Mortimer. In faith, he is a worthy gentleman,
165   Exceedingly well read and profited
        In strange concealments,° valiant as a lion,
        And wondrous affable, and as bountiful
        As mines of India. Shall I tell you, cousin?
        He holds your temper in a high respect
170   And curbs himself even of his natural scope°
        When you come 'cross his humor.° Faith, he does.
        I warrant you that man is not alive
        Might so have tempted him as you have done
        Without the taste of danger and reproof.
175   But do not use it oft, let me entreat you.

Worcester. In faith, my lord, you are too willful-blame,°
        And since your coming hither have done enough
        To put him quite besides his patience.
        You must needs learn, lord, to amend this fault.
        Though sometimes it show greatness, courage,
180   blood°—
        And that's the dearest grace **it** renders you—
        Yet oftentimes it doth present° harsh rage,
        Defect of manners, want of government,°
        Pride, haughtiness, opinion,° and disdain;
185   The least of which haunting a nobleman
        Loseth men's hearts, and leaves behind a stain
        Upon the beauty of all parts besides,
        Beguiling them of commendation.

Hotspur. Well, I am schooled. Good manners be your
           speed!°
190   Here come our wives, and let us take our leave.

           Enter Glendower with the Ladies.

Mortimer. This is the deadly spite° that angers me—
        My wife can speak no English, I no Welsh.

165–66 **profited . . . concealments** expert in secret arts   170 **scope**
tendencies   171 **come 'cross his humor** clash with his temperament
176 **too willful-blame** blamable for too much willfulness   180 **blood**
spirit   182 **present** indicate   183 **government** self-control   184 **opinion** arrogance   189 **be your speed** bring you success   191 **spite** mis-
fortune

Glendower. My daughter weeps; she'll not part with
          you,
    She'll be a soldier too, she'll to the wars.

Mortimer. Good father, tell her that she and my aunt
          Percy   *195*
    Shall follow in your conduct speedily.
    Glendower speaks to her in Welsh, and she answers
                           him in the same.

Glendower. She is desperate here.
    A peevish self-willed harlotry,° one that no per-
    suasion can do good upon.
                       The Lady speaks in Welsh.

Mortimer. I understand thy looks. That pretty Welsh°   *200*
    Which thou pourest down from these swelling
      heavens°
    I am too perfect in; and, but for shame,
    In such a parley° should I answer thee.
                     The Lady again in Welsh.
    I understand thy kisses, and thou mine,
    And that's a feeling disputation.°   *205*
    But I will never be a truant, love,
    Till I have learnt thy language; for thy tongue
    Makes Welsh as sweet as ditties highly penned,°
    Sung by a fair queen in a summer's bow'r,
    With ravishing division,° to her lute.   *210*

Glendower. Nay, if you melt, then will she run mad.
               The Lady speaks again in Welsh.

Mortimer. O, I am ignorance itself in this!

Glendower. She bids you on the wanton° rushes lay
          you down
    And rest your gentle head upon her lap,
    And she will sing the song that pleaseth you   *21!*

---

198 **harlotry** ninny, fool   200 **That pretty Welsh** i.e., her tears
201 **heavens** i.e., her eyes   203 **parley** meeting (of tears)   205 **feeling disputation** dialogue by (1) touching (2) the feelings   208 **highly
penned** i.e., lofty   210 **division** musical variation   213 **wanton** lux-
urious

And on your eyelids crown the god of sleep,°
Charming your blood with pleasing heaviness,
Making such difference 'twixt wake and sleep
As is the difference betwixt day and night
220 The hour before the heavenly-harnessed team°
Begins his golden progress in the east.

Mortimer. With all my heart I'll sit and hear her sing.
By that time will our book,° I think, be drawn.

Glendower. Do so, and those musicians that shall play
to you
225 Hang in the air a thousand leagues from hence,
And straight they shall be here: sit, and attend.

Hotspur. Come, Kate, thou art perfect in lying down.
Come, quick, quick, that I may lay my head in thy
lap.

230 *Lady Percy.* Go, ye giddy goose.   *The music plays.*

Hotspur. Now I perceive the devil understands Welsh,
And 'tis no marvel he is so humorous,°
By'r Lady, he is a good musician.

Lady Percy. Then should you be nothing but musical,
235 For you are altogether governed by humors.
Lie still, ye thief, and hear the lady sing in Welsh.

Hotspur. I had rather hear Lady, my brach,° howl in
Irish.

Lady Percy. Wouldst thou have thy head broken?

240 *Hotspur.* No.

Lady Percy. Then be still.

Hotspur. Neither! 'Tis a woman's fault.

Lady Percy. Now God help thee!

Hotspur. To the Welsh lady's bed.

---

216 **crown the god of sleep** i.e., give sleep sovereignty   220 **the heavenly-harnessed team** the horses of the sun   223 **book** agreement
232 **humorous** capricious   237 **brach** bitch-hound

Lady Percy. What's that?

Hotspur. Peace! She sings.

                 Here the Lady sings a Welsh song.
  Come, Kate, I'll have your song too.

Lady Percy. Not mine, in good sooth.°

Hotspur. Not yours, in good sooth? Heart, you swear
  like a comfit-maker's° wife. "Not you, in good   250
  sooth!" and "as true as I live!" and "as God shall
  mend me!" and "as sure as day!"
  And givest such sarcenet surety° for thy oaths
  As if thou never walk'st further than Finsbury.°
  Swear me, Kate, like a lady as thou art,   255
  A good mouth-filling oath, and leave "in sooth"
  And such protest of pepper gingerbread°
  To velvet guards° and Sunday citizens.
  Come, sing.

Lady Percy. I will not sing.   260

Hotspur. 'Tis the next way to turn tailor° or be redbreast-teacher.° And the indentures be drawn, I'll
  away within these two hours; and so come in when
  ye will.   *Exit.*

Glendower. Come, come, Lord Mortimer. You are as
  slow   265
  As hot Lord Percy is on fire to go.
  By this our book is drawn; we'll but seal,
  And then to horse immediately.

Mortimer.   With all my heart.
                                 Exeunt.

---

248 **sooth** truth   250 **comfit-maker's** confectioner's   253 **sarcenet surety** flimsy security ("sarcenet"—a thin silk)   254 **Finsbury** favorite resort near London (frequented by the middle-class groups whom Hotspur satirizes)   257 **pepper gingerbread** i.e., insubstantial, crumbling in the mouth   258 **velvet guards** i.e., shopkeepers, who favored velvet trimmings for Sunday wear   261 **tailor** (like weavers, tailors were famed for singing at their work)   261–62 **redbreast-teacher** singing master to songbirds

[Scene II. *London. The palace.*]

Enter the King, Prince of Wales, and others.

King. Lords, give us leave: the Prince of Wales and I
 Must have some private conference; but be near at
  hand,
 For we shall presently have need of you.
           Exeunt Lords.
 I know not whether God will have it so

5 For some displeasing service I have done,
 That, in his secret doom,° out of my blood°
 He'll breed revengement and a scourge for me;
 But thou dost in thy passages° of life
 Make me believe that thou art only marked

10 For the hot vengeance and the rod of heaven
 To punish my mistreadings.° Tell me else,
 Could such inordinate° and low desires,
 Such poor, such bare, such lewd, such mean at-
  tempts,
 Such barren pleasures, rude society,

15 As thou art matched withal° and grafted to,
 Accompany the greatness of thy blood
 And hold their level with thy princely heart?

Prince. So please your Majesty, I would I could
 Quit° all offenses with as clear excuse

20 As well° as I am doubtless I can purge
 Myself of many I am charged withal.
 Yet such extenuation let me beg

III.ii.6 **doom** judgment 6 **blood** i.e., heirs 8 **passages** courses
9–11 **thou . . . mistreadings** i.e., (1) heaven is punishing me through
you (2) heaven will punish you to punish me 12 **inordinate** i.e.,
out of order (for one of your rank) 15 **withal** with 19 **Quit** clear
myself of 20 **As well** and as well

As, in reproof of many tales devised,
Which oft the ear of greatness needs must hear
By smiling pickthanks and base newsmongers, 　25
I may, for some things true wherein my youth
Hath faulty wand'red and irregular,
Find pardon on my true submission.°

King. God pardon thee! Yet let me wonder, Harry,
  At thy affections,° which do hold a wing 　30
  Quite from the flight of all thy ancestors.
  Thy place in council thou hast rudely lost,
  Which by thy younger brother is supplied,
  And art almost an alien to the hearts
  Of all the court and princes of my blood. 　35
  The hope and expectation of thy time°
  Is ruined, and the soul of every man
  Prophetically do forethink thy fall.
  Had I so lavish of my presence been,
  So common-hackneyed in the eyes of men, 　40
  So stale and cheap to vulgar company,
  Opinion,° that did help me to the crown,
  Had still kept loyal to possession°
  And left me in reputeless banishment,
  A fellow of no mark nor likelihood. 　45
  By being seldom seen, I could not stir
  But, like a comet, I was wond'red at;
  That men would tell their children, "This is he!"
  Others would say, "Where? Which is Bolingbroke?"
  And then I stole all courtesy from heaven,° 　50
  And dressed myself in such humility
  That I did pluck allegiance from men's hearts,
  Loud shouts and salutations from their mouths
  Even in the presence of the crownèd King.

22–28 **Yet ... submission** yet let me beg such extenuation that when
I have confuted many manufactured charges ("which the ear of
greatness is bound to hear from informers and tattletales") I may
be pardoned for some true faults of which my youth has been
guilty　30 **affections** tastes　36 **time** reign　42 **Opinion** public opinion　43 **possession** i.e., Richard II　50 **I ... heaven** I took a godlike
graciousness on myself

55   Thus did I keep my person fresh and new,
    My presence, like a robe pontifical,
    Ne'er seen but wond'red at; and so my state,
    Seldom but sumptuous, showed like a feast
    And won by rareness such solemnity.

60   The skipping King, he ambled up and down
    With shallow jesters and rash bavin° wits,
    Soon kindled and soon burnt; carded° his state;
    Mingled his royalty with cap'ring fools;
    Had his great name profanèd with their scorns

65   And gave his countenance, against his name,°
    To laugh at gibing boys and stand the push°
    Of every beardless vain comparative;°
    Grew a companion to the common streets,
    Enfeoffed himself to popularity;°

70   That, being daily swallowed by men's eyes,
    They surfeited with honey and began
    To loathe the taste of sweetness, whereof a little
    More than a little is by much too much.
    So, when he had occasion to be seen,

75   He was but as the cuckoo is in June,
    Heard, not regarded—seen, but with such eyes
    As, sick and blunted with community,°
    Afford no extraordinary gaze,
    Such as is bent on sunlike majesty

80   When it shines seldom in admiring eyes;
    But rather drowsed and hung their eyelids down,
    Slept in his face, and rend'red such aspect
    As cloudy° men use to their adversaries,
    Being with his presence glutted, gorged, and full.

85   And in that very line, Harry, standest thou;
    For thou hast lost thy princely privilege
    With vile participation.° Not an eye
    But is aweary of thy common sight,

---

61 **bavin** brushwood (which flares and burns out)   62 **carded** debased   65 **his name** i.e., (1) his kingly title (2) his kingly authority
66 **stand the push** put up with the impudence   67 **comparative** deviser of insulting comparisons   69 **Enfeoffed . . . popularity** bound himself to low company   77 **with community** by familiarity (with the king)   83 **cloudy** sullen (but also with reference to "clouds" obscuring the royal "sun")   87 **participation** companionship

Save mine, which hath desired to see thee more;
Which now doth that I would not have it do—　　90
Make blind itself with foolish tenderness.°

Prince. I shall hereafter, my thrice-gracious lord,
Be more myself.

King.　　　　　For all the world,
As thou art to this hour was Richard then
When I from France set foot at Ravenspurgh;　　95
And even as I was then is Percy now.
Now, by my scepter, and my soul to boot,
He hath more worthy interest° to the state — Hotspur
Than thou the shadow of succession;
For of no right, nor color° like to right,　　100
He doth fill fields with harness° in the realm,
Turns head against the lion's armèd jaws,
And, being no more in debt to years than thou,
Leads ancient lords and reverend bishops on
To bloody battles and to bruising arms.　　105
What never-dying honor hath he got
Against renownèd Douglas! whose high deeds,
Whose hot incursions and great name in arms
Holds from all soldiers chief majority°
And military title capital°　　110
Through all the kingdoms that acknowledge Christ.
Thrice hath this Hotspur, Mars in swathling clothes,
This infant warrior, in his enterprises
Discomfited great Douglas; ta'en him once,
Enlargèd him, and made a friend of him,　　115
To fill the mouth of deep defiance up°
And shake the peace and safety of our throne.
And what say you to this? Percy, Northumberland,
The Archbishop's grace of York, Douglas, Mortimer
Capitulate° against us and are up.°　　120
But wherefore do I tell these news to thee?

---

91 tenderness i.e., tears　**98 worthy interest** claim based on worth (as
compared with a "shadow" claim by inheritance)　**100 color** pretense　**101 harness** armor　**109 majority** preeminence　**110 capital**
topmost　**116 To fill . . . up** to deepen the noise of defiance　**120
Capitulate** (1) make a "head" or armed force? (2) draw up "heads"
of an argument?　**120 up** in arms

Why, Harry, do I tell thee of my foes,
Which art my nearest and dearest° enemy?
Thou that art like enough, through vassal fear,
125 Base inclination, and the start of spleen,
To fight against me under Percy's pay,
To dog his heels and curtsy at his frowns,
To show how much thou art degenerate.

Prince. Do not think so, you shall not find it so.
130 And God forgive them that so much have swayed
Your Majesty's good thoughts away from me.
I will redeem all this on Percy's head
And, in the closing of some glorious day,
Be bold to tell you that I am your son,
135 When I will wear a garment all of blood,
And stain my favors° in a bloody mask,
Which, washed away, shall scour my shame with it.
And that shall be the day, whene'er it lights,
That this same child of honor and renown,
140 This gallant Hotspur, this all-praisèd knight,
And your unthought-of Harry chance to meet.
For every honor sitting on his helm,
Would they were multitudes, and on my head
My shames redoubled! For the time will come
145 That I shall make this northern youth exchange
His glorious deeds for my indignities.
Percy is but my factor,° good my lord,
To engross° up glorious deeds on my behalf;
And I will call him to so strict account
150 That he shall render every glory up,
Yea, even the slightest worship of his time,°
Or I will tear the reckoning from his heart.
This in the name of God I promise here;
The which if he be pleased I shall perform,
155 I do beeseech your Majesty may salve
The long-grown wounds of my intemperance.
If not, the end of life cancels all bands,°

---

123 **dearest** (1) most loved (2) costliest 136 **favors** features
147 **factor** agent 148 **engross** hoard 151 **worship of his time**
honor he has gained in his lifetime 157 **bands** bonds, promises

And I will die a hundred thousand deaths
Ere break the smallest parcel° of this vow.

King. A hundred thousand rebels die in this!   160
    Thou shalt have charge and sovereign trust herein.

               Enter Blunt.

How now, good Blunt? Thy looks are full of speed.

Blunt. So hath the business° that I come to speak of.
    Lord Mortimer of Scotland hath sent word
    That Douglas and the English rebels met   165
    The eleventh of this month at Shrewsbury.
    A mighty and a fearful head they are,
    If promises be kept on every hand,
    As ever off'red foul play in a state.

King. The Earl of Westmoreland set forth today;   170
    With him my son, Lord John of Lancaster:
    For this advertisement is five days old.
    On Wednesday next, Harry, you shall set forward;
    On Thursday we ourselves will march. Our meeting
    Is Bridgenorth; and, Harry, you shall march   175
    Through Gloucestershire; by which account,
    Our business valuèd,° some twelve days hence
    Our general forces at Bridgenorth shall meet.
    Our hands are full of business. Let's away:
    Advantage feeds him° fat while men delay. *Exeunt.*   180

        [Scene III. *Eastcheap. The tavern.*]

        Enter Falstaff and Bardolph.

Falstaff. Bardolph, am I not fall'n away vilely since this
    last action? Do I not bate?° Do I not dwindle? Why,

---

159 **parcel** item   163 **So hath the business** i.e., the business too has
speed (must be dealt with speedily)   177 **Our business valuèd** having sized up what we have to do   180 **him** itself   III.iii.2 **bate** lose
weight

my skin hangs about me like an old lady's loose
gown! I am withered like an old apple-john.° Well,
5   I'll repent, and that suddenly, while I am in some
liking.° I shall be out of heart° shortly, and then I
shall have no strength to repent. And I have not forgotten what the inside of a church is made of, I am
a peppercorn,° a brewer's horse.° The inside of a
10   church! Company, villainous company, hath been
the spoil of me.

Bardolph. Sir John, you are so fretful you cannot live
long.

Falstaff. Why, there is it! Come, sing me a bawdy song,
15   make me merry. I was as virtuously given as a gentleman need to be, virtuous enough: swore little, diced
not above seven times a week, went to a bawdy house
not above once in a quarter of an hour, paid money
that I borrowed three or four times,° lived well, and
20   in good compass;° and now I live out of all order,
out of all compass.

Bardolph. Why, you are so fat, Sir John, that you must
needs be out of all compass—out of all reasonable
compass, Sir John.

25   *Falstaff.* Do thou amend thy face, and I'll amend my
life. Thou art our admiral,° thou bearest the lantern
in the poop—but 'tis in the nose of thee: thou art
the Knight of the Burning Lamp.

Bardolph. Why, Sir John, my face does you no harm.

30   *Falstaff.* No, I'll be sworn. I make as good use of it as
many a man doth of a death's-head° or a memento
mori.° I never see thy face·but I think upon hellfire

4 **old apple-john** apple with shriveled skin   5–6 **am in some liking**
(1) am in the mood (2) still have some flesh left   6 **out of heart** (1)
out of the mood (2) out of shape   9 **peppercorn, brewer's horse**
(Falstaff this time picks objects *not* long and thin, but dry, withered,
decrepit)   16–19 **diced . . . times** (probably spoken with significant
pauses after "diced not," "once," "borrowed")   20 **compass** order
(but Bardolph takes it in the sense of "size")   26 **admiral** flagship
(recognizable by its lantern)   31 **death's-head** ring with a skull
31–32 **memento mori** reminder of death

and Dives° that lived in purple; for there he is in his
robes, burning, burning. If thou wert any way given
to virtue, I would swear by thy face; my oath should   *35*
be "By this fire, that's God's angel."° But thou art
altogether given over, and wert indeed, but for the
light in thy face, the son of utter darkness. When
thou ran'st up Gad's Hill in the night to catch my
horse, if I did not think thou hadst been an ignis   *40*
fatuus° or a ball of wildfire,° there's no purchase in
money. O, thou art a perpetual triumph,° an everlasting bonfire-light! Thou hast saved me a thousand
marks in links° and torches, walking with thee in the
night betwixt tavern and tavern; but the sack that   *45*
thou hast drunk me would have bought me lights as
good cheap° at the dearest chandler's° in Europe.
I have maintained that salamander° of yours with
fire any time this two and thirty years. God reward
me for it!   *50*

Bardolph. 'Sblood, I would my face were in your belly!°

Falstaff. God-a-mercy! So should I be sure to be heart-
burned.

Enter Hostess.

How now, Dame Partlet° the hen? Have you enquired yet who picked my pocket?   *55*

Hostess. Why, Sir John, what do you think, Sir John?
Do you think I keep thieves in my house? I have
searched, I have enquired, so has my husband, man
by man, boy by boy, servant by servant. The tithe°
of a hair was never lost in my house before.   *60*

---

33 **Dives** uncharitable rich man who burns in hell (Luke 16:19–31)
36 **angel** (alluding to the Scriptural accounts of angels manifesting
themselves as fire, or possibly to the seraphs, highest order of angels,
who were fire)   40–41 **ignis fatuus** will-o'-the-wisp   41 **ball of wildfire** firework   42 **triumph** i.e., of the Roman kind, with torches
44 **links** flares   47 **good cheap** cheaply   47 **chandler's** candle mak-
er's   48 **salamander** lizard supposed to live in fire   51 **I . . . belly**
(proverbial retort, to which Falstaff's reply gives new life)   54 **Dame
Partlet** (traditional name for a hen, and well suited to the clucking
Hostess)   59 **tithe** tenth part

Falstaff. Ye lie, hostess. Bardolph was shaved and lost many a hair, and I'll be sworn my pocket was picked. Go to, you are a woman, go!

Hostess. Who, I? No;° I defy thee! God's light, I was
65   never called so in mine own house before!

Falstaff. Go to, I know you well enough.

Hostess. No, Sir John; you do not know me, Sir John. I know you, Sir John. You owe me money, Sir John, and now you pick a quarrel to beguile me of it. I
70   bought you a dozen of shirts to your back.

Falstaff. Dowlas,° filthy dowlas! I have given them away to bakers' wives; they have made bolters° of them.

Hostess. Now, as I am a true woman, holland° of eight
75   shillings an ell.° You owe money here besides, Sir John, for your diet and by-drinkings,° and money lent you, four and twenty pound.

Falstaff. He had his part of it; let him pay.

Hostess. He? Alas, he is poor; he hath nothing.

80   *Falstaff.* How? Poor? Look upon his face. What call you rich?° Let them coin his nose, let them coin his cheeks. I'll not pay a denier.° What, will you make a younker° of me? Shall I not take mine ease in mine inn but I shall have my pocket picked? I have lost a
85   seal ring of my grandfather's worth forty mark.

Hostess. O Jesu, I have heard the Prince tell him, I know not how oft, that that ring was copper!

Falstaff. How? The Prince is a Jack,° a sneak-up.°

---

64 **No** (the Hostess suspects that any word or phrase of Falstaff's may contain hidden innuendoes about her moral character; she sometimes retorts with comments containing amusing innuendoes about herself that she is too ignorant to understand)   71 **Dowlas** coarse linen   72 **bolters** sieves   74 **holland** fine linen   75 **ell** one and a quarter yards   76 **by-drinkings** drinks between meals   81 **rich** (referring to its red gold-and-copper hues)   82 **denier** tenth of a penny   83 **younker** greenhorn   88 **Jack** rascal   88 **sneak-up** sneak

'Sblood, and he were here, I would cudgel him like
a dog if he would say so.   *90*

*Enter the Prince [and Poins], marching, and
Falstaff meets them, playing upon his truncheon°
                 like a fife.*

How now, lad? Is the wind in that door,° i' faith?
Must we all march?

Bardolph. Yea, two and two,° Newgate fashion.

Hostess. My lord, I pray you hear me.

Prince. What say'st thou, Mistress Quickly? How doth   *95*
thy husband? I love him well, he is an honest man.

Hostess. Good my lord, hear me.

Falstaff. Prithee let her alone and list to me.

Prince. What say'st thou, Jack?

Falstaff. The other night I fell asleep here behind the   *100*
arras and had my pocket picked. This house is turned
bawdy house; they pick pockets.

Prince. What didst thou lose, Jack?

Falstaff. Wilt thou believe me, Hal, three or four bonds
of forty pound apiece and a seal ring of my grand-   *105*
father's.

Prince. A trifle, some eightpenny matter.

Hostess. So I told him, my lord, and I said I heard your
Grace say so; and, my lord, he speaks most vilely of
you, like a foulmouthed man as he is, and said he   *110*
would cudgel you.

Prince. What! He did not?

Hostess. There's neither faith, truth, nor womanhood
in me else.

90s.d. **truncheon** cudgel   91 **Is . . . door** i.e., is that how things are
going   93 **two and two** i.e., bound in pairs like prisoners on the way
to (Newgate) prison

115 *Falstaff*. There's no more faith in thee than in a stewed
prune,° nor no more truth in thee than in a drawn°
fox; and for womanhood, Maid Marian may be the
deputy's wife of the ward to thee.° Go, you thing, go!

Hostess. Say, what thing, what thing?

120 *Falstaff*. What thing? Why, a thing to thank God on.

Hostess. I am no thing to thank God on, I would thou
shouldst know it! I am an honest man's wife, and,
setting thy knighthood aside, thou art a knave to
call me so.

125 *Falstaff*. Setting thy womanhood aside, thou art a beast
to say otherwise.

Hostess. Say, what beast, thou knave, thou?

Falstaff. What beast? Why, an otter.

Prince. An otter, Sir John? Why an otter?

130 *Falstaff*. Why, she's neither fish nor flesh; a man knows
not where to have her.

Hostess. Thou art an unjust man in saying so. Thou
or any man knows where to have me, thou knave,
thou!

135 *Prince*. Thou say'st true, hostess, and he slanders thee
most grossly.

Hostess. So he doth you, my lord, and said this other
day you ought° him a thousand pound.

Prince. Sirrah, do I owe you a thousand pound?

140 *Falstaff*. A thousand pound, Hal? A million! Thy love
is worth a million, thou owest me thy love.

115–16 **stewed prune** (evidently chosen by Falstaff because stewed
prunes were associated with bawdy houses)   116 **drawn** drawn from
his lair and trying every trick to get back to it   117–18 **Maid Marian
... thee** a disreputable female in country May games is chaste as the
wife of the ward's most respectable citizen in comparison with you
138 **ought** owed

Hostess. Nay, my lord, he called you Jack and said he would cudgel you.

Falstaff. Did I, Bardolph?

Bardolph. Indeed, Sir John, you said so.   *145*

Falstaff. Yea, if he said my ring was copper.

Prince. I say 'tis copper. Darest thou be as good as thy word now?

Falstaff. Why, Hal, thou knowest, as thou art but man, I dare; but as thou art Prince, I fear thee as I fear   *150* the roaring of the lion's whelp.

Prince. And why not as the lion?

Falstaff. The King himself is to be feared as the lion. Dost thou think I'll fear thee as I fear thy father? Nay, and I do, I pray God my girdle break.   *155*

Prince. O, if it should, how would thy guts fall about thy knees! But, sirrah, there's no room for faith, truth, nor honesty in this bosom of thine. It is all filled up with guts and midriff. Charge an honest woman with picking thy pocket? Why, thou whore-   *160* son, impudent, embossed° rascal,° if there were anything in thy pocket but tavern reckonings, mem-orandums of bawdy houses, and one poor penny-worth of sugar candy to make thee long-winded— if thy pocket were enriched with any other injuries°   *165* but these, I am a villain. And yet you will stand to it; you will not pocket up wrong. Art thou not ashamed?

Falstaff. Dost thou hear, Hal? Thou knowest in the state of innocency Adam fell, and what should poor   *170* Jack Falstaff do in the days of villainy? Thou seest I have more flesh than another man, and therefore more frailty. You confess then, you picked my pocket?

---

161 **embossed** (1) swollen (2) foaming at the mouth (of a deer)
161 **rascal** (1) rogue (2) lean young deer   165 **injuries** i.e., things whose loss you call injuries

175 *Prince.* It appears so by the story.

    Falstaff. Hostess, I forgive thee, go make ready break-
    fast, love thy husband, look to thy servants, cherish
    thy guests. Thou shalt find me tractable to any hon-
    est reason. Thou seest I am pacified still. Nay, prithee
180   be gone.   *Exit Hostess.*
    Now, Hal, to the news at court. For the robbery, lad
    —how is that answered?

    Prince. O my sweet beef, I must still be good angel to
    thee. The money is paid back again.

185 *Falstaff.* O, I do not like that paying back! 'Tis a double
    labor.

    Prince. I am good friends with my father, and may do
    anything.

    Falstaff. Rob me the exchequer the first thing thou
190   doest, and do it with unwashed hands° too.

    Bardolph. Do, my lord.

    Prince. I have procured thee, Jack, a charge of foot.

    Falstaff. I would it had been of horse. Where shall I
    find one that can steal well? O for a fine thief° of the
195   age of two and twenty or thereabouts! I am heinously
    unprovided. Well, God be thanked for these rebels,
    they offend none but the virtuous: I laud them, I
    praise them.

    Prince. Bardolph!

200 *Bardolph.* My lord?

    Prince. Go bear this letter to Lord John of Lancaster,
    To my brother John; this to my Lord of Westmore-
    land.   *[Exit Bardolph.]*
    Go, Peto, to horse, to horse; for thou and I
    Have thirty miles to ride yet ere dinner time.
                           [Exit Peto.]

---

190 **with unwashed hands** with no delay   194 **thief** i.e., to steal a
horse

Jack, meet me tomorrow in the Temple Hall   205
At two o'clock in the afternoon.
There shalt thou know thy charge, and there receive
Money and order for their furniture.°
The land is burning, Percy stands on high,
And either we or they must lower lie.   [*Exit.*]   210

Falstaff. Rare words! Brave world! Hostess, my breakfast, come.
O, I could wish this tavern were my drum!°   [*Exit.*]

---

208 **furniture** equipment   212 **drum** recruiting center

[ACT IV

Scene I. *The rebel camp, near Shrewsbury.*]

[*Enter Hotspur, Worcester, and Douglas.*]

Hotspur. Well said, my noble Scot. If speaking truth
　　In this fine age were not thought flattery,
　　Such attribution° should the Douglas have
　　As not a soldier of this season's stamp
5　　Should go so general current° through the world.
　　By God, I cannot flatter, I do defy°
　　The tongues of soothers!° But a braver place
　　In my heart's love hath no man than yourself.
　　Nay, task me° to my word; approve me, lord.

10　*Douglas.* Thou art the king of honor.
　　No man so potent breathes upon the ground
　　But I will beard° him.

Enter one with letters.

Hotspur.　　　　　　Do so, and 'tis well.—
　　What letters hast thou there?—I can but thank you.

Messenger. These letters come from your father.

IV.i.3 **attribution** recognition　5 **go so general current** be as widely
accepted (the image is of a coin of recent mintage: "this season's
stamp")　6 **defy** despise　7 **soothers** flatterers　9 **task me** try me,
test me　12 **beard** oppose

120

Hotspur. Letters from him? Why comes he not himself?   15

Messenger. He cannot come, my lord, he is grievous
sick.

Hotspur. Zounds! How has he the leisure to be sick
In such a justling° time? Who leads his power?
Under whose government° come they along?

Messenger. His letters bears° his mind, not I, my lord.   20

Worcester. I prithee tell me, doth he keep his bed?

Messenger. He did, my lord, four days ere I set forth,
And at the time of my departure thence
He was much feared° by his physicians.

Worcester. I would the state of time had first been
whole   25
Ere he by sickness had been visited.
His health was never better worth than now.

Hotspur. Sick now? Droop now? This sickness doth
infect
The very lifeblood of our enterprise.
'Tis catching hither, even to our camp.   30
He writes me here that inward sickness—
And that his friends by deputation°
Could not so soon be drawn; nor did he think it meet
To lay so dangerous and dear a trust
On any soul removed but on his own.   35
Yet doth he give us bold advertisement,
That with our small conjunction° we should on,
To see how fortune is disposed to us;
For, as he writes, there is no quailing now,
Because the King is certainly possessed°   40
Of all our purposes. What say you to it?

Worcester. Your father's sickness is a maim to us.

18 **justling** jostling, unquiet   19 **government** command   20 **bears**
(a singular verb with plural subject is not uncommon in Elizabethan
English)   24 **feared** feared for   32 **deputation** a deputy   37 **con-
junction** combination of forces   40 **possessed** informed

Hotspur. A perilous gash, a very limb lopped off.
       And yet, in faith, it is not! His present want
45   Seems more than we shall find it. Were it good
       To set° the exact wealth of all our states
       All at one cast? To set so rich a main°
       On the nice° hazard of one doubtful hour?
       It were not good; for therein should we read
50   The very bottom and the soul° of hope,
       The very list,° the very utmost bound
       Of all our fortunes.

Douglas.   Faith, and so we should.
       Where now remains a sweet reversion,°
       We may boldly spend upon the hope of what is to
          come in.
55   A comfort of retirement° lives in this.

Hotspur. A rendezvous, a home to fly unto,
       If that the devil and mischance look big°
       Upon the maidenhead of our affairs.

Worcester. But yet I would your father had been here.
60   The quality and hair° of our attempt
       Brooks° no division. It will be thought
       By some that know not why he is away,
       That wisdom, loyalty, and mere dislike
       Of our proceedings kept the Earl from hence.
65   And think how such an apprehension
       May turn the tide of fearful° faction
       And breed a kind of question in our cause.
       For well you know we of the off'ring side°
       Must keep aloof from strict arbitrament,°
70   And stop all sight-holes, every loop° from whence
       The eye of reason may pry in upon us.
       This absence of your father's draws° a curtain

---

46 **set** risk   47 **main** (1) stake (in gambling) (2) army   48 **nice** precarious   50 **soul** (1) essence (2) sole (cf. "bottom")   51 **list** limit
53 **reversion** inheritance still to be received   55 **A comfort of retirement** a security to fall back on   57 **big** menacingly   60 **hair** nature
61 **Brooks** allows of   66 **fearful** timid   68 **we of the off'ring side** we who take the offensive   69 **arbitrament** evaluation   70 **loop** loophole   72 **draws** draws aside

That shows the ignorant a kind of fear
Before not dreamt of.

Hotspur.   You strain too far.
I rather of his absence make this use: *75*
It lends a luster and more great opinion,°
A larger dare to our great enterprise,
Than if the Earl were here; for men must think,
If we, without his help, can make a head°
To push against a kingdom, with his help   *80*
We shall o'erturn it topsy-turvy down.
Yet all goes well; yet all our joints are whole.

Douglas. As heart can think. There is not such a word
Spoke of in Scotland as this term of fear.

Enter Sir Richard Vernon.

Hotspur. My cousin Vernon, welcome, by my soul.   *85*

Vernon. Pray God my news be worth a welcome, lord.
The Earl of Westmoreland, seven thousand strong,
Is marching hitherwards; with him Prince John.

Hotspur. No harm. What more?

Vernon.   And further, I have learned
The King himself in person is set forth,   *90*
Or hitherwards intended speedily,
With strong and mighty preparation.

Hotspur. He shall be welcome too. Where is his son,
The nimble-footed madcap Prince of Wales,
And his comrades, that daffed° the world aside   *95*
And bid it pass?

Vernon.   All furnished, all in arms;
All plumed like estridges° that with the wind
Bated° like eagles having lately bathed;
Glittering in golden coats like images;
As full of spirit as the month of May
And gorgeous as the sun at midsummer;   *100*

76 **opinion** prestige   79 **a head** (1) an army (2) headway   95 **daffed**
thrust   97 **estridges** ostriches (ostrich plumes are the emblem of the
Prince of Wales)   98 **Bated** shook their wings

Wanton° as youthful goats, wild as young bulls.
I saw young Harry with his beaver° on,
His cushes° on his thighs, gallantly armed,
105 Rise from the ground like feathered Mercury,
And vaulted with such ease into his seat
As if an angel dropped down from the clouds
To turn and wind° a fiery Pegasus
And witch the world with noble horsemanship.

Hotspur. No more, no more! Worse than the sun in
110   March,
This praise doth nourish agues.° Let them come.
They come like sacrifices in their trim,
And to the fire-eyed maid° of smoky war
All hot and bleeding will we offer them.
115 The mailèd Mars shall on his altars sit
Up to the ears in blood. I am on fire
To hear this rich reprisal° is so nigh,
And yet not ours. Come, let me taste my horse,
Who is to bear me like a thunderbolt
120 Against the bosom of the Prince of Wales.
Harry to Harry shall, hot horse to horse,
Meet, and ne'er part till one drop down a corse.
O that Glendower were come!

Vernon.   There is more news.
I learned in Worcester, as I rode along,
125 He cannot draw his power this fourteen days.

Douglas. That's the worst tidings that I hear of yet.

Worcester. Ay, by my faith, that bears a frosty sound.

Hotspur. What may the King's whole battle° reach
    unto?

Vernon. To thirty thousand.

Hotspur.   Forty let it be.
130   My father and Glendower being both away,

102 **Wanton** exuberant   103 **beaver** helmet   104 **cushes** thigh armor   108 **wind** wheel about   111 **agues** chills and fever (the spring
sun was believed to set them going)   113 **maid** Bellona, goddess of
war   117 **reprisal** prize   128 **battle** army

The powers of us may serve so great a day.
Come, let us take a muster speedily.
Doomsday is near. Die all, die merrily.

Douglas. Talk not of dying. I am out of fear
Of death or death's hand for this one half year.   135
                                        Exeunt.

[Scene II. *A road near Coventry.*]

Enter Falstaff [and] Bardolph.

Falstaff. Bardolph, get thee before to Coventry; fill me
a bottle of sack. Our soldiers shall march through.
We'll to Sutton Co'fil' tonight.

Bardolph. Will you give me money, captain?

Falstaff. Lay out,° lay out.   5

Bardolph. This bottle makes an angel.°

Falstaff. And if it do, take it for thy labor; and if it
make twenty, take them all; I'll answer the coinage.
Bid my lieutenant Peto meet me at town's end.

Bardolph. I will, captain. Farewell.   *Exit.*   10

Falstaff. If I be not ashamed of my soldiers, I am a
soused gurnet.° I have misused the King's press°
damnably. I have got, in exchange of a hundred and
fifty soldiers, three hundred and odd pounds. I press
me none but good householders, yeomen's sons;° in-   15

IV.ii.5 **Lay out** i.e., pay out of your own pocket   6 **angel** coin worth,
at various times, six shillings eight pence to ten shillings (Bardolph
means that Falstaff now owes him an angel, but Falstaff jokingly
takes "make" in the literal sense—as if the bottle were minting
angels; he tells Bardolph to take them all and he will guarantee they
are not counterfeit)   12 **soused gurnet** pickled fish   12 **press** power
of conscription   15 **good householders, yeomen's sons** i.e., men of
some means who could pay to be let off

quire me out contracted bachelors, such as had been
asked twice on the banes°—such a commodity of
warm° slaves as had as lief hear the devil as a drum,
such as fear the report of a caliver° worse than a
struck fowl or a hurt wild duck. I pressed me none
but such toasts-and-butter, with hearts in their bellies no bigger than pins' heads, and they have bought
out their services; and now my whole charge consists
of ancients,° corporals, lieutenants, gentlemen of
companies°—slaves as ragged as Lazarus° in the
painted cloth,° where the glutton's dogs licked his
sores; and such as indeed were never soldiers, but
discarded unjust° serving-men, younger sons to
younger brothers, revolted° tapsters, and ostlers
trade-fall'n;° the cankers° of a calm world and a long
peace; ten times more dishonorable ragged than an
old fazed ancient;° and such have I to fill up the
rooms of them as have bought out their services that
you would think that I had a hundred and fifty tattered prodigals lately come from swine-keeping, from
eating draff° and husks. A mad fellow met me on the
way, and told me I had unloaded all the gibbets and
pressed the dead bodies. No eye hath seen such scare-
crows. I'll not march through Coventry with them,
that's flat. Nay, and the villains march wide betwixt
the legs, as if they had gyves° on, for indeed I had
the most of them out of prison. There's not a shirt
and a half in all my company, and the half-shirt is
two napkins tacked together and thrown over the
shoulders like a herald's coat without sleeves; and
the shirt, to say the truth, stol'n from my host at
Saint Albans, or the red-nose innkeeper of Daventry.

17 **asked twice on the banes** i.e., on the verge of marriage (banns
[banes] were announcements of intent to marry, published usually
three times at weekly intervals) 18 **warm** comfortable 19 **caliver**
musket 24 **ancients** ensigns 24–25 **gentlemen of companies** lesser
officers 25 **Lazarus** the beggar in the Dives parable (Luke 16:19–31)
26 **painted cloth** painted wall-hanging 28 **unjust** dishonest 29 **revolted** runaway 30 **trade-fall'n** unemployed 30 **cankers** parasites
32 **fazed ancient** tattered flag 36 **draff** pig-swill (the prodigal son,
in Luke 15:15–16, was so hungry he longed for draff) 41 **gyves** fet-
ters

But that's all one; they'll find linen enough on every
hedge.°

Enter the Prince [and the] Lord of Westmoreland.

Prince. How now, blown° Jack?° How now, quilt?   50

Falstaff. What, Hal? How now, mad wag? What a devil
dost thou in Warwickshire? My good Lord of Westmoreland, I cry you mercy. I thought your honor
had already been at Shrewsbury.

Westmoreland. Faith, Sir John, 'tis more than time that   55
I were there, and you too, but my powers are there
already. The King, I can tell you, looks for us all, we
must away all night.

Falstaff. Tut, never fear me: I am as vigilant as a cat
to steal cream.   60

Prince. I think, to steal cream indeed, for thy theft hath
already made thee butter. But tell me, Jack, whose
fellows are these that come after?

Falstaff. Mine, Hal, mine.

Prince. I did never see such pitiful rascals.   65

Falstaff. Tut, tut, good enough to toss;° food for powder, food for powder, they'll fill a pit as well as better.
Tush, man, mortal men, mortal men.

Westmoreland. Ay, but, Sir John, methinks they are exceeding poor and bare, too beggarly.

Falstaff. Faith, for their poverty, I know not where
they had that, and for their bareness, I am sure they
never learned that of me.

Prince. No, I'll be sworn, unless you call three fingers°
in the ribs bare. But, sirrah, make haste. Percy is   75
already in the field.   *Exit.*

---

49 **hedge** i.e., where linen was put out to dry   50 **blown** (1) swelled
(2) short of wind   50 **Jack** (1) Falstaff's name (2) soldier's quilted
jacket   66 **toss** i.e., on the end of a pike   74 **three fingers** i.e., of fat

Falstaff. What, is the King encamped?

Westmoreland. He is, Sir John. I fear we shall stay too
long.

80 *Falstaff.* Well, to the latter end of a fray and the beginning of a feast fits a dull fighter and a keen guest.

Exeunt.°

[Scene III. *The rebel camp, near Shrewsbury.*]

Enter Hotspur, Worcester, Douglas, Vernon.

Hotspur. We'll fight with him tonight.

Worcester.   It may not be.

Douglas. You give him then advantage.

Vernon.   Not a whit.

Hotspur. Why say you so? Looks he not for supply?°

Vernon. So do we.

Hotspur.   His is certain, ours is doubtful.

5 *Worcester.* Good cousin, be advised; stir not tonight.

Vernon. Do not, my lord.

Douglas.   You do not counsel well.
You speak it out of fear and cold heart.

Vernon. Do me no slander, Douglas. By my life—
And I dare well maintain it with my life—
10 If well-respected° honor bid me on,
I hold as little counsel with weak fear

---

81 s.d. **Exeunt** (the quarto's "Exeunt," implying that Westmoreland
goes off with Falstaff, may be wrong. Falstaff's last speech sounds
as if Westmoreland had departed, and Falstaff winks at the audience)
IV.iii.3 **supply** reinforcement   10 **well-respected** well-considered

As you, my lord, or any Scot that this day lives.
Let it be seen tomorrow in the battle
Which of us fears.

Douglas.   Yea, or tonight.

Vernon.   Content.

Hotspur. Tonight, say I.   *15*

Vernon. Come, come, it may not be.
I wonder much, being men of such great leading° as
    you are,
That you foresee not what impediments
Drag back our expedition.° Certain horse
Of my cousin Vernon's are not yet come up.   *20*
Your uncle Worcester's horse came but today;
And now their pride and mettle is asleep,
Their courage with hard labor tame and dull,
That not a horse is half the half of himself.

Hotspur. So are the horses of the enemy   *25*
In general journey-bated° and brought low.
The better part of ours are full of rest.

Worcester. The number of the King exceedeth ours.
For God's sake, cousin, stay till all come in.
                    The trumpet sounds a parley.

                Enter Sir Walter Blunt.

Blunt. I come with gracious offers from the King, *30*
If you vouchsafe me hearing and respect.

Hotspur. Welcome, Sir Walter Blunt, and would to God
You were of our determination.°
Some of us love you well; and even those some
Envy your great deservings and good name,   *35*
Because you are not of our quality,°
But stand against us like an enemy.

---

17 **leading** generalship   19 **expedition** i.e., hastening into battle
26 **journey-bated** travel-weakened   33 **determination** party   36 **quality** company

Blunt. And God defend° but still I should stand so,
So long as out of limit° and true rule
⁴⁰   You stand against anointed majesty.
But to my charge.° The King hath sent to know
The nature of your griefs, and whereupon
You conjure from the breast of civil peace
Such bold hostility, teaching his duteous land
⁴⁵   Audacious cruelty. If that the King
Have any way your good deserts forgot,
Which he confesseth to be manifold,
He bids you name your griefs, and with all speed
You shall have your desires with interest,
⁵⁰   And pardon absolute for yourself and these
Herein misled by your suggestion.°

Hotspur. The King is kind, and well we know the King
Knows at what time to promise, when to pay.
My father and my uncle and myself
⁵⁵   Did give him that same royalty he wears;
And when he was not six and twenty strong,
Sick in the world's regard, wretched and low,
A poor unminded outlaw sneaking home,
My father gave him welcome to the shore;
⁶⁰   And when he heard him swear and vow to God
He came but to be Duke of Lancaster,
To sue his livery and beg his peace,°
With tears of innocency and terms of zeal,
My father, in kind heart and pity moved,
⁶⁵   Swore him assistance, and performed it too.
Now when the lords and barons of the realm
Perceived Northumberland did lean to him,
The more and less came in with cap and knee;°
Met him in boroughs, cities, villages,
⁷⁰   Attended him on bridges, stood in lanes,°

---

38 **defend** forbid   39 **limit** i.e., a subject's proper limits   41 **charge**
message   51 **suggestion** instigation   62 **sue . . . peace** sue for the
delivery of his lands (which Richard II had arrogated to the crown)
and make his peace with the king   68 **with cap and knee** i.e., with
cap off and bended knee (in token of allegiance)   70 **lanes** facing
rows

Laid gifts before him, proffered him their oaths,
Gave him their heirs as pages, followed him
Even at the heels in golden multitudes.
He presently, as greatness knows itself,°
Steps me a little higher than his vow   75
Made to my father, while his blood was poor,
Upon the naked shore at Ravenspurgh;
And now, forsooth, takes on him to reform
Some certain edicts and some strait° decrees
That lie too heavy on the commonwealth;   80
Cries out upon abuses, seems to weep
Over his country's wrongs; and by this face,
This seeming brow of justice, did he win
The hearts of all that he did angle for;
Proceeded further—cut me off the heads   85
Of all the favorites that the absent king
In deputation° left behind him here
When he was personal° in the Irish war.

Blunt. Tut! I came not to hear this.

Hotspur.   Then to the point.
In short time after, he deposed the King;   90
Soon after that deprived him of his life;
And in the neck of that° tasked° the whole state;
To make that worse, suff'red his kinsman March
(Who is, if every owner were well placed,
Indeed his king) to be engaged in Wales,   95
There without ransom to lie forfeited;
Disgraced me in my happy victories,
Sought to entrap me by intelligence;°
Rated° mine uncle from the council board;
In rage dismissed my father from the court;   100
Broke oath on oath, committed wrong on wrong;
And in conclusion drove us to seek out
This head° of safety, and withal to pry

---

74 **as greatness knows itself** as greatness begins to feel its strength
79 **strait** strict   87 **In deputation** as deputies   88 **personal** personally   92 **in the neck of that** i.e., next   92 **tasked** taxed
98 **intelligence** spies   99 **Rated** scolded (cf. I.iii.14–20)   103 **head** army

Into his title, the which we find
105 Too indirect° for long continuance.

Blunt. Shall I return this answer to the King?

Hotspur. Not so, Sir Walter. We'll withdraw awhile.
Go to the King; and let there be impawned
Some surety for a safe return again,
110 And in the morning early shall mine uncle
Bring him our purposes; and so farewell.

Blunt. I would you would accept of grace and love.

Hotspur. And may be so we shall.

Blunt.   Pray God you do. [*Exeunt.*]

[Scene IV. *York. The Archbishop's palace.*]

Enter [*the*] *Archbishop of York* [*and*] *Sir Michael.*

Archbishop. Hie, good Sir Michael; bear this sealèd
brief°
With wingèd haste to the Lord Marshal;
This to my cousin Scroop; and all the rest
To whom they are directed. If you knew
5 How much they do import, you would make haste.

Sir Michael. My good lord, I guess their tenor.

Archbishop. Like enough you do.
Tomorrow, good Sir Michael, is a day
Wherein the fortune of ten thousand men
10 Must bide the touch;° for, sir, at Shrewsbury,
As I am truly given to understand,
The King with mighty and quick-raisèd power
Meets with Lord Harry; and I fear, Sir Michael,

---

105 **indirect** (1) not in the direct line (from Richard) (2) morally
oblique   IV.iv.1 **brief** message   10 **bide the touch** stand the test (as
metal is tested by the touchstone to know if it is gold)

What with the sickness of Northumberland,
Whose power was in the first proportion,°   *15*
And what with Owen Glendower's absence thence,
Who with them was a rated sinew° too
And comes not in, overruled by prophecies—
I fear the power of Percy is too weak
To wage an instant trial with the King.   *20*

Sir Michael. Why, my good lord, you need not fear;
There is Douglas and Lord Mortimer.

Archbishop. No, Mortimer is not there.

Sir Michael. But there is Mordake, Vernon, Lord Harry
Percy,
And there is my Lord of Worcester, and a head   *25*
Of gallant warriors, noble gentlemen.

Archbishop. And so there is; but yet the King hath
drawn
The special head° of all the land together—
The Prince of Wales, Lord John of Lancaster,
The noble Westmoreland and warlike Blunt,   *30*
And many moe corrivals° and dear° men
Of estimation and command in arms.

Sir Michael. Doubt not, my lord, they shall be well opposed.

Archbishop. I hope no less, yet needful 'tis to fear;
And, to prevent the worst, Sir Michael, speed.   *35*
For if Lord Percy thrive not, ere the King
Dismiss his power, he means to visit us,
For he hath heard of our confederacy,
And 'tis but wisdom to make strong against him.
Therefore make haste. I must go write again   *40*
To other friends; and so farewell, Sir Michael.
Exeunt.

---

15 **proportion** magnitude   17 **rated sinew** highly valued strength
28 **head** army   31 **moe corrivals** more associates   31 **dear** important

[ACT V

Scene I. *The King's camp, near Shrewsbury.*]

*Enter the King, Prince of Wales, Lord John of
Lancaster, Earl of Westmoreland,° Sir Walter
Blunt, Falstaff.*

King. How bloodily the sun begins to peer
Above yon bulky hill! The day looks pale
At his distemp'rature.°

Prince.   The southern wind
Doth play the trumpet° to his° purposes
And by his hollow whistling in the leaves
Foretells a tempest and a blust'ring day.

King. Then with the losers let it sympathize,
For nothing can seem foul to those that win.

The trumpet sounds. Enter Worcester [and Vernon].

How now, my Lord of Worcester? 'Tis not well
That you and I should meet upon such terms

5

10

V.i.s.d. **Earl of Westmoreland** (in V.ii.28 we learn that Westmoreland has been held as the "surety" of IV.iii.109, but at this point
Shakespeare apparently had not decided who was the hostage)
3 **his distemp'rature** the sun's apparent ailment   4 **play the trumpet**
(1) act the announcer (2) blow as if playing a trumpet   4 **his** the
sun's

As now we meet. You have deceived our trust
And made us doff our easy robes of peace
To crush our old limbs in ungentle steel.
This is not well, my lord; this is not well.
What say you to it? Will you again unknit   15
This churlish knot of all-abhorrèd war,
And move in that obedient orb° again
Where you did give a fair and natural light,
And be no more an exhaled meteor,°
A prodigy of fear, and a portent   20
Of broachèd° mischief to the unborn times?

Worcester. Hear me, my liege.
For mine own part, I could be well content
To entertain the lag-end of my life
With quiet hours, for I protest   25
I have not sought the day of this dislike.

King. You have not sought it! How comes it then?

Falstaff. Rebellion lay in his way, and he found it.

Prince. Peace, chewet,° peace!

Worcester. It pleased your Majesty to turn your looks   30
Of favor from myself and all our house;
And yet I must remember° you, my lord,
We were the first and dearest of your friends.
For you my staff of office did I break
In Richard's time, and posted day and night   35
To meet you on the way and kiss your hand
When yet you were in place and in account
Nothing so strong and fortunate as I.
It was myself, my brother, and his son
That brought you home and boldly did outdare   40
The dangers of the time. You swore to us,
And you did swear that oath at Doncaster,
That you did nothing purpose 'gainst the state,

17 **obedient orb** orbit of obedience   19 **exhaled meteor** wandering
body (not subject to orbit, and thought an omen or "prodigy")
21 **broachèd** opened   29 **chewet** (1) jackdaw, i.e., chatterer (2) meat
pie   32 **remember** remind

Nor claim no further than your new-fall'n° right,
45 The seat of Gaunt, dukedom of Lancaster.
To this we swore our aid. But in short space
It rained down fortune show'ring on your head,
And such a flood of greatness fell on you—
What with our help, what with the absent King,
50 What with the injuries of a wanton time,
The seeming sufferances that you had borne,
And the contrarious winds that held the King
So long in his unlucky Irish wars
That all in England did repute him dead—
55 And from this swarm of fair advantages
You took occasion to be quickly wooed
To gripe° the general sway into your hand;
Forgot your oath to us at Doncaster;
And, being fed by us, you used us so
60 As that ungentle gull,° the cuckoo's bird,°
Useth the sparrow—did oppress our nest,
Grew by our feeding to so great a bulk
That even our love durst not come near your sight
For fear of swallowing; but with nimble wing
65 We were enforced for safety sake to fly
Out of your sight and raise this present head;
Whereby we stand opposèd by such means
As you yourself have forged against yourself
By unkind usage, dangerous° countenance,
70 And violation of all faith and troth
Sworn to us in your younger enterprise.

King. These things, indeed, you have articulate,°
Proclaimed at market crosses, read in churches,
To face° the garment of rebellion
75 With some fine color° that may please the eye
Of fickle changelings and poor discontents,

---

44 **new-fall'n** i.e., by the death of his father, John of Gaunt   57 **gripe** grab   60 **gull, bird** nestling (the cuckoo lays its eggs in other birds' nests, and the young cuckoos when hatched speedily destroy the other nestlings)   69 **dangerous** menacing   72 **articulate** spelled out   74 **face** trim   75 **color** (1) hue (2) rhetorical coloring (hence, pretext)

Which gape and rub the elbow° at the news
Of hurlyburly innovation.°
And never yet did insurrection want
Such water colors to impaint his cause,   *80*
Nor moody beggars, starving for a time
Of pell-mell havoc and confusion.

Prince. In both your armies there is many a soul
  Shall pay full dearly for this encounter,
  If once they join in trial. Tell your nephew   *85*
  The Prince of Wales doth join with all the world
  In praise of Henry Percy. By my hopes,
  This present enterprise set off his head,°
  I do not think a braver gentleman,
  More active-valiant or more valiant-young,   *90*
  More daring or more bold, is now alive
  To grace this latter age with noble deeds.
  For my part, I may speak it to my shame,
  I have a truant been to chivalry;
  And so I hear he doth account me too.   *95*
  Yet this before° my father's majesty—
  I am content that he shall take the odds
  Of his great name and estimation,
  And will, to save the blood on either side,
  Try fortune with him in a single fight.   *100*

King. And, Prince of Wales, so dare we venture thee;
  Albeit,° considerations infinite
  Do make against it. No, good Worcester, no!
  We love our people well; even those we love
  That are misled upon your cousin's part;   *105*
  And, will they take the offer of our grace,°
  Both he, and they, and you, yea, every man
  Shall be my friend again, and I'll be his.
  So tell your cousin, and bring me word
  What he will do. But if he will not yield,   *110*
  Rebuke and dread correction wait on us,°

77 **rub the elbow** i.e., hug themselves with delight   78 **innovation** revolution   88 **set off his head** removed from his record   96 **this before** let me say this in the presence of   102 **Albeit** on the other hand   106 **grace** pardon   111 **wait on us** are in our service

And they shall do their office.° So be gone.
We will not now be troubled with reply.
We offer fair; take it advisedly.

                    Exit Worcester [with Vernon].

115 *Prince.* It will not be accepted, on my life.
The Douglas and the Hotspur both together
Are confident against the world in arms.

King. Hence, therefore, every leader to his charge;
For, on their answer, will we set on them,
120 And God befriend us as our cause is just!

                    Exeunt. Manent° Prince [and] Falstaff.

Falstaff. Hal, if thou see me down in the battle and
bestride me, so!° 'Tis a point of friendship.

Prince. Nothing but a colossus can do thee that friendship. Say thy prayers, and farewell.

125 *Falstaff.* I would 'twere bedtime, Hal, and all well.

Prince. Why, thou owest God a death.°   *[Exit.]*

Falstaff. 'Tis not due yet: I would be loath to pay him
before his day. What need I be so forward with him
that calls not on me? Well, 'tis no matter; honor
130 pricks° me on. Yea, but how if honor prick° me off
when I come on? How then? Can honor set to a leg?
No. Or an arm? No. Or take away the grief of a
wound? No. Honor hath no skill in surgery then?
No. What is honor? A word. What is in that word
135 honor? What is that honor? Air—a trim° reckoning! Who hath it? He that died a Wednesday. Doth
he feel it? No. Doth he hear it? No. 'Tis insensible
then? Yea, to the dead. But will it not live with the
living? No. Why? Detraction° will not suffer it.
140 Therefore I'll none of it. Honor is a mere scutch-
eon°—and so ends my catechism.   *Exit.*

112 **office** duty   120 s.d. **Manent** remain (Latin)   122 **so** i.e., I
shan't object   126 **death** (pronounced like "debt," in which sense
Falstaff takes it)   130 **pricks** spurs   130 **prick** check (as a casualty)
135 **trim** fine (spoken ironically)   139 **Detraction** slander   140–41
scutcheon painted shield with coat of arms identifying a dead nobleman

[Scene II. *The rebel camp, near Shrewsbury.*]

Enter Worcester [and] Sir Richard Vernon.

Worcester. O no, my nephew must not know, Sir
  Richard,
  The liberal and kind offer of the King.

Vernon. 'Twere best he did.

Worcester.   Then are we all undone.
  It is not possible, it cannot be,
  The King should keep his word in loving us.   5
  He will suspect us still and find a time
  To punish this offense in other faults.
  Supposition all our lives shall be stuck full of eyes;°
  For treason is but trusted like the fox,
  Who, never so tame, so cherished and locked up,   10
  Will have a wild trick° of his ancestors.
  Look how we can, or sad or° merrily,
  Interpretation will misquote our looks,
  And we shall feed like oxen at a stall,
  The better cherished still the nearer death.   15
  My nephew's trespass may be well forgot;
  It hath the excuse of youth and heat of blood,
  And an adopted name of privilege°—
  A hare-brained Hotspur, governed by a spleen.
  All his offenses live upon my head   20
  And on his father's. We did train° him on;
  And, his corruption being ta'en° from us,
  We, as the spring of all, shall pay for all.
  Therefore, good cousin, let not Harry know,
  In any case, the offer of the King.   25

V.ii.8 **Supposition . . . eyes** suspicion will always be spying on us
11 **trick** (1) trait (2) wile   12 **or sad or** either sad or   18 **an . . . privilege** a nickname which carries a privilege (to be impulsive) with it
21 **train** (1) draw (2) aim   22 **ta'en** taken (like an infection)

Enter Hotspur [and Douglas].

Vernon. Deliver° what you will, I'll say 'tis so.
Here comes your cousin.

Hotspur.   My uncle is returned.
Deliver up my Lord of Westmoreland.°
Uncle, what news?

30 *Worcester.* The King will bid you battle presently.

Douglas. Defy him by the Lord of Westmoreland.

Hotspur. Lord Douglas, go you and tell him so.

Douglas. Marry, and shall, and very willingly.   *Exit.*

Worcester. There is no seeming mercy in the King.

35 *Hotspur.* Did you beg any? God forbid!

Worcester. I told him gently of our grievances,
Of his oath-breaking, which he mended thus,
By now forswearing that he is forsworn.
He calls us rebels, traitors, and will scourge
40 With haughty arms this hateful name in us.

Enter Douglas.

Douglas. Arm, gentlemen, to arms, for I have thrown
A brave defiance in King Henry's teeth,
And Westmoreland, that was engaged,° did bear it;
Which cannot choose but bring him quickly on.

Worcester. The Prince of Wales stepped forth before
45   the King
And, nephew, challenged you to single fight.

Hotspur. O, would the quarrel lay upon our heads,
And that no man might draw short breath today
But I and Harry Monmouth! Tell me, tell me,
50 How showed his tasking?° Seemed it in contempt?

26 **Deliver** report   28 **Westmoreland** (who has been hostage for the
safe return of Worcester and Vernon)   43 **engaged** held as hostage
50 **tasking** challenging

Vernon. No, by my soul. I never in my life
   Did hear a challenge urged more modestly,
   Unless a brother should a brother dare
   To gentle exercise and proof of arms.
   He gave you all the duties of a man;°   *55*
   Trimmed up your praises with a princely tongue;
   Spoke your deservings like a chronicle;°
   Making you ever better than his praise
   By still dispraising praise valued with you;°
   And, which became him like a prince indeed,   *60*
   He made a blushing cital of° himself,
   And chid his truant youth with such a grace
   As if he mast'red there a double spirit
   Of teaching and of learning instantly.°
   There did he pause; but let me tell the world,   *65*
   If he outlive the envy of this day,
   England did never owe° so sweet a hope,
   So much misconstrued in° his wantonness.

Hotspur. Cousin, I think thou art enamorèd
   On his follies. Never did I hear   *70*
   Of any prince so wild a liberty.°
   But be he as he will, yet once ere night
   I will embrace him with a soldier's arm,
   That° he shall shrink under my courtesy.
   Arm, arm with speed! And, fellows, soldiers, friends,   *75*
   Better consider what you have to do
   Than I, that have not well the gift of tongue,
   Can lift your blood up with persuasion.

Enter a Messenger.

Messenger. My lord, here are letters for you.

Hotspur. I cannot read them now.—   *80*
   O gentlemen, the time of life is short!

---

55 **duties of a man** duties that one man can owe another   57 **like
a chronicle** i.e., with the itemized detail characteristic of a chronicle history   59 **dispraising . . . you** i.e., because it must fall so far
short of your deservings   61 **cital of** reference to   64 **instantly** si-
multaneously   67 **owe** own   68 **in** with respect to   71 **liberty** reck-
less freedom   74 **That** so that

To spend that shortness basely were too long
If life did ride upon a dial's point,
Still ending at the arrival of an hour.°

85 And if we live, we live to tread on kings;
If die, brave death, when princes die with us!
Now for our consciences, the arms are fair,
When the intent of bearing them is just.

Enter another [Messenger].

Messenger. My lord, prepare. The King comes on
apace.

90 *Hotspur.* I thank him that he cuts me from my tale,
For I profess not talking: only this—
Let each man do his best; and here draw I
A sword whose temper I intend to stain
With the best blood that I can meet withal

95 In the adventure of this perilous day.
Now, Esperance! Percy! and set on.
Sound all the lofty instruments of war,
And by that music let us all embrace;
For, heaven to earth,° some of us never shall

100 A second time do such a courtesy.
Here they embrace. The trumpets sound. [Exeunt.]

[Scene III. *Shrewsbury. The battlefield.*]

*The King enters with his power. Alarum to the
battle. [Exeunt.] Then enter Douglas, and Sir
Walter Blunt [disguised as the King].*

Blunt. What is thy name, that in battle thus thou
crossest me?
What honor dost thou seek upon my head?

82–84 **To . . . hour** if life were measured by a clock's hand, closing
after a single hour, it would still be too long if basely spent
99 **heaven to earth** the odds are as great as heaven to earth

Douglas. Know then my name is Douglas,
　And I do haunt thee in the battle thus
　Because some tell me that thou art a king.　　　　　5

Blunt. They tell thee true.

Douglas. The Lord of Stafford dear today hath bought
　Thy likeness, for instead of thee, King Harry,
　This sword hath ended him: so shall it thee,
　Unless thou yield thee as my prisoner.　　　　　10

Blunt. I was not born a yielder, thou proud Scot;
　And thou shalt find a king that will revenge
　Lord Stafford's death.

　　　They fight. Douglas kills Blunt. Then enter
　　　　　　Hotspur.

Hotspur. O Douglas, hadst thou fought at Holmedon
　　thus,
　I never had triumphed upon a Scot.　　　　　15

Douglas. All's done, all's won: here breathless lies the
　　King.

Hotspur. Where?

Douglas. Here.

Hotspur. This, Douglas? No. I know this face full well.
　A gallant knight he was, his name was Blunt;　　　20
　Semblably° furnished like the King himself.

Douglas. A fool° go with thy soul, whither it goes!
　A borrowed title hast thou bought too dear:
　Why didst thou tell me that thou wert a king?

Hotspur. The King hath many marching in his coats.　　25

Douglas. Now, by my sword, I will kill all his coats;
　I'll murder all his wardrobe, piece by piece,
　Until I meet the King.

V.iii.21 **Semblably** similarly　　22 **fool** i.e., the title "fool"

Hotspur.   Up and away!
     Our soldiers stand full fairly for the day.   [*Exeunt.*]

Alarum. Enter Falstaff solus.

30 *Falstaff.* Though I could scape shot-free° at London,
     I fear the shot here. Here's no scoring° but upon the
     pate. Soft! Who are you? Sir Walter Blunt. There's
     honor for you! Here's no vanity!° I am as hot as
     molten lead, and as heavy too. God keep lead out of
35   me. I need no more weight than mine own bowels.
     I have led my rag-of-muffins° where they are pep-
     pered.° There's not three of my hundred and fifty
     left alive, and they are for the town's end, to beg
     during life. But who comes here?

Enter the Prince.

Prince. What, stands thou idle here? Lend me thy
40   sword.
     Many a nobleman lies stark and stiff
     Under the hoofs of vaunting enemies, whose deaths
     are yet unrevenged. I prithee lend me thy sword.

Falstaff. O Hal, I prithee give me leave to breathe
45   awhile. Turk Gregory° never did such deeds in arms
     as I have done this day. I have paid° Percy, I have
     made him sure.

Prince. He is indeed, and living to kill thee.
     I prithee lend me thy sword.

50 *Falstaff.* Nay, before God, Hal, if Percy be alive, thou
     gets not my sword; but take my pistol if thou wilt.

Prince. Give it me. What, is it in the case?

---

30 **shot-free** without paying the bill   31 **scoring** (1) billing (2) striking   33 **Here's no vanity** (spoken ironically: i.e., here *is* "vanity"—
futility, foolishness. But vanity also implies lightness, which is then
set against the "heaviness" of life: cf. "lead," "heavy," "weight")
36–37 **I . . . peppered** (a common practice of officers, who drew the
dead soldiers' pay)   45 **Turk Gregory** (in Shakespeare's time,
"Turk" was a byword for any ruthless man; "Gregory" may refer to
the irascible Pope Gregory VII, or to Elizabeth's enemy, Pope
Gregory XIII. Pope and Turk were regarded as the two great enemies
of Protestant Christendom)   46 **paid** killed

Falstaff. Ay, Hal. 'Tis hot, 'tis hot.° There's that will
sack a city.

> *The Prince draws it out and finds*
> *it to be a bottle of sack.*

Prince. What, is it a time to jest and dally now?   55
> *He throws the bottle at him. Exit.*

Falstaff. Well, if Percy be alive, I'll pierce° him. If he
do come in my way, so; if he do not, if I come in his
willingly, let him make a carbonado° of me. I like
not such grinning honor as Sir Walter hath. Give
me life; which if I can save, so; if not, honor comes   60
unlooked for, and there's an end.   [*Exit.*]

[Scene IV. *Shrewsbury. The battlefield.*]

Alarum. Excursions.° Enter the King, the Prince,
Lord John of Lancaster, Earl of Westmoreland.

King. I prithee, Harry, withdraw thyself, thou bleedest
too much.
Lord John of Lancaster, go you with him.

John. Not I, my lord, unless I did bleed too.

Prince. I beseech your Majesty make up,°
Lest your retirement do amaze° your friends.   5

King. I will do so. My Lord of Westmoreland, lead
him to his tent.

Westmoreland. Come, my lord, I'll lead you to your
tent.

Prince. Lead me, my lord? I do not need your help;
And God forbid a shallow scratch should drive   10

---

53 **hot** i.e., he has fired it so often he has had to put it away to cool
56 **pierce** (pronounced "perse")   58 **carbonado** meat slashed open
for broiling   V.iv.s.d. **Excursions** sorties   4 **make up** move forward   5 **amaze** dismay

The Prince of Wales from such a field as this,
Where stained nobility lies trodden on,
And rebels' arms triumph in massacres!

John. We breathe° too long. Come, cousin Westmoreland,
15   Our duty this way lies. For God's sake, come.
                    [*Exeunt Lancaster and Westmoreland.*]

Prince. By God, thou hast deceived me, Lancaster!
I did not think thee lord of such a spirit.
Before, I loved thee as a brother, John,
But now I do respect thee as my soul.

20 *King.* I saw him hold Lord Percy at the point
With lustier maintenance than I did look for
Of such an ungrown warrior.

Prince. O, this boy lends mettle to us all!   *Exit.*

                    [*Enter Douglas.*]

Douglas. Another king? They grow like Hydra's°
heads.
25   I am the Douglas, fatal to all those
That wear those colors on them. What art thou
That counterfeit'st the person of a king?

King. The King himself, who, Douglas, grieves at heart
So many of his shadows thou hast met,
30   And not the very King. I have two boys
Seek Percy and thyself about the field;
But, seeing thou fall'st on me so luckily,
I will assay thee, and defend thyself.

Douglas. I fear thou art another counterfeit;
35   And yet, in faith, thou bearest thee like a king.
But mine I am sure thou art, whoe'er thou be,
And thus I win thee.

*They fight, the King being in danger. Enter Prince
of Wales.*

14 **breathe** pause   24 **Hydra** a many-headed monster which grew
two heads for each one destroyed

Prince. Hold up thy head, vile Scot, or thou art like
　　Never to hold it up again. The spirits
　　Of valiant Shirley, Stafford, Blunt° are in my arms.　　*40*
　　It is the Prince of Wales that threatens thee,
　　Who never promiseth but he means to pay.
　　　　　　　　　　They fight: Douglas flieth.
　　Cheerly, my lord. How fares your Grace?
　　Sir Nicholas Gawsey hath for succor sent,
　　And so hath Clifton. I'll to Clifton straight.　　*45*

King. Stay and breathe awhile.
　　Thou hast redeemed thy lost opinion,°
　　And showed thou mak'st some tender° of my life,
　　In this fair rescue thou hast brought to me.

Prince. O God, they did me too much injury　　*50*
　　That ever said I heark'ned for your death.
　　If it were so, I might have let alone
　　The insulting hand of Douglas over you,
　　Which would have been as speedy in your end
　　As all the poisonous potions in the world,　　*55*
　　And saved the treacherous labor of your son.

King. Make up to Clifton; I'll to Sir Nicholas Gawsey.
　　　　　　　　　　　　　　Exit.

　　　　　　Enter Hotspur.

Hotspur. If I mistake not, thou art Harry Monmouth.

Prince. Thou speak'st as if I would deny my name.

Hotspur. My name is Harry Percy.　　*60*

Prince. Why, then I see a very valiant rebel of the name.
　　I am the Prince of Wales, and think not, Percy,
　　To share with me in glory any more.
　　Two stars keep not their motion in one sphere,°
　　Nor can one England brook° a double reign　　*65*
　　Of Harry Percy and the Prince of Wales.

---

40 **Shirley, Stafford, Blunt** (those whom Douglas has killed wearing
the King's coats)　47 **opinion** reputation　48 **tender** value　64 **sphere**
orbit　65 **brook** put up with

Hotspur. Nor shall it, Harry, for the hour is come
    To end the one of us; and would to God
    Thy name in arms were now as great as mine!

70 *Prince.* I'll make it greater ere I part from thee,
    And all the budding honors on thy crest
    I'll crop to make a garland for my head.

Hotspur. I can no longer brook thy vanities. *They fight.*

            Enter Falstaff.

Falstaff. Well said, Hal! To it, Hal! Nay, you shall find
75   no boy's play here, I can tell you.

        Enter Douglas. He fighteth with Falstaff, [who]
        falls down as if he were dead. [Exit Douglas.]
             The Prince killeth Percy.

Hotspur. O Harry, thou hast robbed me of my youth!
    —I better brook the loss of brittle life
    — Than those proud titles thou hast won of me.
    ⸜ They wound my thoughts worse than thy sword my
        flesh.
80   But thoughts, the slaves of life, and life, time's fool,°
    And time, that takes survey of all the world,
    Must have a stop. O, I could prophesy,
    But that the earthy and cold hand of death
    Lies on my tongue. No, Percy, thou art dust,
85   And food for—   *[Dies.]*

Prince. For worms, brave Percy. Fare thee well, great
        heart.
    Ill-weaved ambition, how much art thou shrunk!
    When that this body did contain a spirit,
    A kingdom for it was too small a bound;
90   But now two paces of the vilest earth
    Is room enough. This earth that bears thee dead
    Bears not alive so stout° a gentleman.
    If thou wert sensible of courtesy,
    I should not make so dear° a show of zeal.

80 **slaves . . . fool** i.e., because thoughts are dependent on life and
because life is subservient to time   92 **stout** valiant   94 **dear** heart-
felt

But let my favors° hide thy mangled face;   95
And, even in thy behalf, I'll thank myself
For doing these fair rites of tenderness.
Adieu, and take thy praise with thee to heaven.
Thy ignominy sleep with thee in the grave,
But not rememb'red in thy epitaph.   100
                    He spieth Falstaff on the ground.
What, old acquaintance? Could not all this flesh
Keep in a little life? Poor Jack, farewell!
I could have better spared a better man.
O, I should have a heavy miss° of thee
If I were much in love with vanity.°   105
Death hath not struck so fat a deer° today,
Though many dearer,° in this bloody fray.
Emboweled° will I see thee by-and-by;
Till then in blood by noble Percy lie.   *Exit.*

              Falstaff riseth up.

Falstaff. Emboweled? If thou embowel me today, I'll   110
give you leave to powder° me and eat me too tomorrow. 'Sblood, 'twas time to counterfeit, or that
hot termagant° Scot had paid me scot and lot° too.
Counterfeit? I lie; I am no counterfeit. To die is to
be a counterfeit, for he is but the counterfeit of a   115
man who hath not the life of a man; but to counterfeit dying when a man thereby liveth, is to be no
counterfeit, but the true and perfect image of life
indeed. The better part of valor is discretion,° in the
which better part I have saved my life. Zounds, I am   120
afraid of this gunpowder Percy, though he be dead.
How if he should counterfeit too, and rise? By my
faith, I am afraid he would prove the better counterfeit. Therefore I'll make him sure; yea, and I'll swear

95 **favors** (probably Hal's ostrich plumes, his emblem as Prince of
Wales)   104 **heavy miss** "heavy" loss (in two senses)   105 **vanity**
frivolity (and lightness)   106 **deer** (with pun on "dear")   107 **dearer**
nobler, more valuable   108 **Emboweled** disemboweled (for embalm-
ing)   111 **powder** salt   113 **termagant** bloodthirsty   113 **paid me
scot and lot** killed me (literally, paid me in full; "scot" and "lot"
were parish taxes)   119 **The . . . discretion** (Falstaff willfully misin-
terprèts the maxim that valor is the better for being accompanied by
discretion)

125   I killed him. Why may not he rise as well as I? Noth-
      ing confutes me but eyes, and nobody sees me.
      Therefore, sirrah [*stabs him*], with a new wound in
      your thigh, come you along with me.

      *He takes up Hotspur on his back. Enter Prince
      [and] John of Lancaster.*

Prince. Come, brother John; full bravely hast thou
      fleshed
      Thy maiden sword.

130 *John.*   But, soft! whom have we here?
      Did you not tell me this fat man was dead?

Prince. I did; I saw him dead,
      Breathless and bleeding on the ground. Art thou
      alive,
      Or is it fantasy that plays upon our eyesight?
135   I prithee speak. We will not trust our eyes
      Without our ears. Thou art not what thou seem'st.

Falstaff. No, that's certain, I am not a double man;°
      but if I be not Jack Falstaff, then am I a Jack.° There
      is Percy. If your father will do me any honor, so; if
140   not, let him kill the next Percy himself. I look to be
      either earl or duke, I can assure you.

Prince. Why, Percy I killed myself, and saw thee dead!

Falstaff. Didst thou? Lord, Lord, how this world is
      given to lying. I grant you I was down, and out of
145   breath, and so was he; but we rose both at an instant
      and fought a long hour by Shrewsbury clock. If I
      may be believed, so; if not, let them that should re-
      ward valor bear the sin upon their own heads. I'll
      take it upon my death, I gave him this wound in the
150   thigh. If the man were alive and would deny it,
      zounds! I would make him eat a piece of my sword.

John. This is the strangest tale that ever I heard.

Prince. This is the strangest fellow, brother John.

137 **double man** (1) wraith (2) twofold man   138 **Jack** rascal

Come, bring your luggage nobly on your back.
For my part, if a lie may do thee grace,   155
I'll gild it with the happiest terms I have.
                          A retreat is sounded.
The trumpet sounds retreat; the day is ours.
Come, brother, let us to the highest of the field,
To see what friends are living, who are dead.
                Exeunt [Prince Henry and Prince John].

Falstaff. I'll follow,° as they say, for reward. He that   160
rewards me, God reward him. If I do grow great,
I'll grow less; for I'll purge,° and leave sack, and
live cleanly, as a nobleman should do.
                          Exit [bearing off the body].

[Scene V. *Shrewsbury. The battlefield.*]

*The trumpets sound. Enter the King, Prince of
Wales, Lord John of Lancaster, Earl of Westmoreland, with Worcester and Vernon prisoners.*

King. Thus ever did rebellion find rebuke.
Ill-spirited Worcester, did not we send grace,
Pardon, and terms of love to all of you?
And wouldst thou turn our offers contrary?
Misuse the tenor of thy kinsman's trust?   5
Three knights upon our party slain today,
A noble earl, and many a creature else
Had been alive this hour,
If like a Christian thou hadst truly borne
Betwixt our armies true intelligence.°   10

Worcester. What I have done my safety urged me to;
And I embrace this fortune patiently,
Since not to be avoided it falls on me.

---

160 **follow** i.e., as hounds do when the quarry is killed, to receive
their reward   162 **purge** repent   V.v.10 **intelligence** information

King. Bear Worcester to the death, and Vernon too;
15 Other offenders we will pause upon.
                    [*Exeunt Worcester and Vernon, guarded*].
    How goes the field?

Prince. The noble Scot, Lord Douglas, when he saw
    The fortune of the day quite turned from him,
    The noble Percy slain, and all his men
20 Upon the foot of fear, fled with the rest;
    And falling from a hill, he was so bruised
    That the pursuers took him. At my tent
    The Douglas is, and I beseech your Grace
    I may dispose of him.

King.   With all my heart.

25 *Prince.* Then, brother John of Lancaster, to you
    This honorable bounty shall belong.
    Go to the Douglas and deliver him
    Up to his pleasure, ransomless and free.
    His valors shown upon our crests today
30 Have taught us how to cherish such high deeds,
    Even in the bosom of our adversaries.

John. I thank your Grace for this high courtesy,
    Which I shall give away immediately.

King. Then this remains, that we divide our power.
35 You, son John, and my cousin Westmoreland,
    Towards York shall bend you with your dearest
        speed
    To meet Northumberland and the prelate Scroop,
    Who, as we hear, are busily in arms.
    Myself and you, son Harry, will towards Wales
40 To fight with Glendower and the Earl of March.
    Rebellion in this land shall lose his sway,
    Meeting the check of such another day;
    And since this business° so fair is done,
    Let us not leave till all our own be won.   *Exeunt.*

FINIS

43 **business** (trisyllabic)

Textual Note

The text for the present edition as a whole is the first quarto of 1598. This is generally believed to have been set from an earlier edition of the same year (Qo), of which today only four leaves are known—containing the text of the play from I.iii.199 to II.ii.112. Qo, so far as we have it, shows characteristics which relate it closely to an authorial manuscript, probably a corrected working manuscript rather than a fair copy. Q1 may therefore be regarded as still reasonably faithful to what Shakespeare wrote. The later quartos (Q2, 1599; Q3, 1604; Q4, 1608; Q5, 1613), each set from the one preceding, and the Folio (1623), set from Q5, have increasingly less authority.

Apart from spelling and punctuation, which are modernized in this edition, and regularization of speech prefixes, I have followed Q1, and, where it exists, Qo. With one exception (IV.i.12–13), I preserve the lineation of these editions, printing therefore as prose a number of passages so printed in Q1 but now almost invariably divided into lines of verse. It is possible, even probable, that some of these passages were intended to be verse; but the wide differences exhibited by editors in lineating them persuade me to reserve this entertainment for readers who wish to engage in it. I have usually indicated in the footnotes one or more of the traditional patterns of lineation for each passage.

The table below records departures from Qo–Q1. The first reading (*italics*) is that which I have adopted in the text; the second is that of Q1. Almost all of the emendations were made in the quartos or in the First Folio, indicating that in Shakespeare's own day the passages in question were suspect; but because these early texts have no authority, they are not cited as sources.

Division into acts and scenes is here that of the Folio, save that I follow Capell and most other editors (including those of the Globe edition) in dividing the Folio's V.ii into V.ii and V.iii and renumbering the subsequent scenes. In the quartos there is no indication of acts or scenes.

I.i.62 *a dear* deere   69 *blood did* bloud. Did   76 *In faith it is* [the quartos and folios give to the King]

I.ii.82 *similes* smiles   166 *Bardolph, Peto* Haruey, Rossill [these are names that Shakespeare evidently meant originally to assign to Falstaff's associates: see below, II.iv.173–76, 180–81]

I.iii.199–206 [Q0–Q4 do not assign to Hotspur, but give as part of Northumberland's speech]

II.ii.16 *two and twenty* xxii

II.iii.4 *respect* the respect   70 *A roan* Roane

II.iv.34 *precedent* present   37 [assigned to Prince]   173–76 [assigned to Gadshill, Ross (=Russell: see above, I.ii.166), Falstaff, Ross]   180–81 [assigned to Ross]   244 *eel-skin* elsskin   341 *Owen* O   393 *tristful* trustfull

III.i.99 *cantle* scantle   132 *on* an

III.ii.115 *Enlargèd* Enlargd

III.iii.36 *that's* that   59 *tithe* tight   90s.d. *them* him   178 *guests* ghesse   206 *o'* of

IV.i.20 *I, my lord* I my mind   54 *is* tis   107 *dropped* drop   125 *cannot* can   126 *yet* it

IV.iii.21 *horse* horses   28 *ours* our   82 *country's* Countrey

V.i.138 *will it* wil

V.ii.3 *undone* vnder one   25s.d. *Hotspur* Percy

V.iii.22 *A* Ah

V.iv.67 *Nor* Now   75s.d. *who* he   157 *ours* our

The Sources of *Henry IV* [*Part One*]

So far as we know, the sources on which Shakespeare chiefly drew in writing *Henry IV* [*Part One*] were the following: (1) the pages on Henry's reign in Volume III of Raphael Holinshed's compilation of British history, *Chronicles of England, Scotland, and Ireland,* first published in 1577 but later reissued (1586–87) in an enlarged edition, which seems to have been the text actually consulted by Shakespeare; (2) the relevant stanzas in Book III of Samuel Daniel's long poem, *The First Four Books of the Civil Wars between the Two Houses of Lancaster and York* (1595); and (3) *The Famous Victories of Henry the Fifth, Containing the Honorable Battle of Agincourt*—an anonymous play of uncertain date, first printed in 1598, today extant in only one known copy. This has been called in recent years both "a decrepit potboiler"[1] and a work of "extraordinary power of expression," probably an apprentice-piece by Shakespeare.[2]

The relevant parts of Daniel and Holinshed are printed in the following section, together with the whole of the *Famous Victories,* so that every reader may watch for himself the workings of a first-rate dramatic imagination. There are brief comments on this process in the Introduction, but the reader who would understand in practical terms what is meant by "art" in phrases like "the art of

[1] Bullough, Geoffrey. *Narrative and Dramatic Sources of Shakespeare,* vol. 4. New York: Columbia University Press, 1962, p. 168.
[2] Pitcher, S. M. *The Case for Shakespeare's Authorship of the Famous Victories.* New York: University Publishers, 1961, p. 5.

playwriting" will want to compare minutely at least one act of *1 Henry IV* with the materials out of which it was made. In the case of the *Famous Victories,* comparisons with appropriate parts of *2 Henry IV* and *Henry V* will also be illuminating. Spelling and punctuation have been modernized in reprinting these selections, some emendations have been silently made, and the text of the *Famous Victories,* following the lead of J. Q. Adams and S. M. Pitcher, is set as prose.

RAPHAEL HOLINSHED

from *Chronicles of England, Scotland, and Ireland* [1587 Edition]

[Uneasy Lies the Head that Wears a Crown]

. . . One night, as the King was going to bed, he was in
danger to have been destroyed; for some naughty traitor-
ous persons had conveyed into his bed a certain iron made
with smith's craft, like a caltrop, with three long pricks,
sharp and small, standing upright in such sort that when
he had laid him down and that the weight of his body
should come upon the bed, he should have been thrust in
with those pricks and peradventure slain; but as God would,
the King, not thinking of any such thing, chanced yet to
feel and perceive the instrument before he laid him down
and so escaped the danger. Howbeit, he was not so soon
delivered from fear; for he might well have his life in
suspicion and provide for the preservation of the same,
sith perils of death crept into his secret chamber and lay
lurking in the bed of down where his body was to be re-
posed and to take rest. Oh what a suspected state therefore is that of a king holding his regiment with the hatred
of his people, the heartgrudgings of his courtiers, and the
peremptory practices of both together! Could he confi-
dently compose or settle himself to sleep for fear of stran-
gling? Durst he boldly eat and drink without dread of
poisoning? Might he adventure to show himself in great
meetings or solemn assemblies without mistrust of mischief
against his person intended? What pleasure or what felicity
could he take in his princely pomp, which he knew by
manifest and fearful experience to be envied and maligned
to the very death? . . .

[Trouble in Wales and Scotland]

. . . Owen Glendower, according to his accustomed manner, robbing and spoiling within the English borders, caused all the forces of the shire of Hereford to assemble together against them, under the conduct of Edmund Mortimer, Earl of March. But coming to try the matter by battle, whether by treason or otherwise, so it fortuned that the English power was discomfited, the Earl taken prisoner, and above a thousand of his people slain in the place. The shameful villainy used by the Welshwomen towards the dead carcasses was such as honest ears would be ashamed to hear and continent tongues to speak thereof. The dead bodies might not be buried without great sums of money given for liberty to convey them away.

The King was not hasty to purchase the deliverance of the Earl of March, because his title to the crown was well-enough known, and therefore suffered him to remain in miserable prison, wishing both the said Earl and all other of his lineage out of this life, with God and his saints in heaven so they had been out of the way, for then all had been well enough as he thought. But to let these things pass, the King this year sent his eldest daughter Blanch, accompanied with the Earl of Somerset, the Bishop of Worcester, the Lord Clifford, and others, into Almanie [i.e., Germany], which brought her to Colin [i.e., Cologne], and there with great triumph she was married to William, Duke of Bavier [i.e., Bavaria], son and heir to Lewis, the Emperor. About mid of August, the King, to chastise the presumptuous attempts of the Welshmen, went with a great power of men into Wales to pursue the captain of the Welsh rebel Owen Glendower, but in effect he lost his labor; for Owen conveyed himself out of the way into his known lurking places, and (as was thought) through art magic[al], he caused such foul weather of winds, tempest, rain, snow, and hail to be raised for the annoyance of the King's army that the like had not been heard of; in such sort, that the King was constrained to return home, having caused his people yet to spoil and burn first a great part of the country. The same time, the Lord Edmund of

Langley, Duke of York, departed this life and was buried at Langley with his brethren.

The Scots, under the leading of Patric Hepborne of the Hales, the younger, entering into England was overthrown at Nesbit in the marches, as in the Scottish chronicle ye may find more at large. This battle was fought the two and twentieth of June, in this year of our Lord, 1402.

Archibald, Earl Douglas, sore displeased in his mind for this overthrow, procured a commission to invade England, and that to his cost, as ye may likewise read in the Scottish histories. For at a place called Homeldon, they were so fiercely assailed by the Englishmen, under the leading of the Lord Percy, surnamed Henry Hotspur, and George, Earl of March, that with violence of the English shot they were quite vanquished and put to flight, on the Rood Day in harvest, with a great slaughter made by the Englishmen. . . . There were slain of men of estimation: Sir John Swinton, Sir Adam Gordon, Sir John Leviston, Sir Alexander Ramsey of Dalhousie, and three and twenty knights, besides ten thousand of the commons; and of prisoners among others were these: Mordake, Earl of Fife, son to the Governor; Archibald, Earl Douglas, which in the fight lost one of his eyes; Thomas, Earl of Murray; Robert, Earl of Angus; (and as some writers have) the Earls of Athol and Menteith, with five hundred other of meaner degrees. . . .

Edmund Mortimer, Earl of March, prisoner with Owen Glendower, whether for irksomeness of cruel captivity or fear of death or for what other cause, it is uncertain, agreed to take part with Owen against the King of England and took to wife the daughter of the said Owen.

Strange wonders happened (as men reported) at the nativity of this man, for the same night he was born, all his father's horses in the stable were found to stand in blood up to the bellies.

[The Percys' Rebellion]

Henry, Earl of Northumberland, with his brother Thomas, Earl of Worcester, and his son, the Lord Henry Percy, surnamed Hotspur, which were to King Henry in the beginning of his reign both faithful friends and earnest aiders, began now to envy his wealth and felicity; and especially they were grieved because the King demanded of the Earl and his son such Scottish prisoners as were taken at Homeldon and Nesbit: for of all the captives which were taken in the conflicts fought in those two places, there were delivered to the King's possession only Mordake, Earl of Fife, the Duke of Albany's son, though the King did divers and sundry times require deliverance of the residue, and that with great threatenings; wherewith the Percys, being sore offended, for that they claimed them as their own proper prisoners and their peculiar prize, by the counsel of the Lord Thomas Percy, Earl of Worcester, whose study was ever (as some write) to procure malice and set things in a broil, came to the King unto Windsor (upon a purpose to prove him) and there required of him that, either by ransom or otherwise, he would cause to be delivered out of prison Edmund Mortimer, Earl of March, their cousin german, whom (as they reported) Owen Glendower kept in filthy prison, shackled with irons, only for that he took his part and was to him faithful and true.

The King began not a little to muse at this request and not without cause; for indeed it touched him somewhat near, sith this Edmund was son to Roger, Earl of March, son to the Lady Philip, daughter of Lionel, Duke of Clarence, the third son of King Edward the Third; which Edmund, at King Richard's going into Ireland, was proclaimed heir apparent to the crown and realm; whose aunt called Eleanor, the Lord Henry Percy had married; and therefore King Henry could not well hear that any man should be earnest about the advancement of that lineage. The King, when he had studied on the matter, made answer that the Earl of March was not taken prisoner for his cause nor in his service but willingly suffered himself to be taken, because he would not withstand the attempts of Owen Glendower and his [ac]complices, and therefore he would neither ransom him nor relieve him.

The Percys with this answer and fraudulent excuse were not a little fumed, insomuch that Henry Hotspur said openly: "Behold, the heir of the realm is robbed of his right, and yet the robber with his own will not redeem him." So in this fury the Percys departed, minding nothing more than to depose King Henry from the high type of his royalty and to place in his seat their cousin Edmund, Earl of March, whom they did not only deliver out of captivity but also (to the high displeasure of King Henry) entered in league with the foresaid Owen Glendower. Herewith they, by their deputies in the house of the Archdeacon of Bangor, divided the realm amongst them, causing a tripartite indenture to be made and sealed with their seals, by the covenants whereof: all England from Severn and Trent south and eastward was assigned to the Earl of March; all Wales and the lands beyond Severn westward were appointed to Owen Glendower; and all the remnant from Trent northward to the Lord Percy.

This was done (as some have said) through a foolish credit given to a vain prophecy, as though King Henry was the moldwarp, cursed of God's own mouth, and they three were the dragon, the lion, and the wolf, which should divide this realm between them. Such is the deviation (saith Hall [an earlier chronicler]) and not divination of those blind and fantastical dreams of the Welsh prophesiers. King Henry, not knowing of this new confederacy, and nothing less minding than that which after happened, gathered a great army to go again into Wales, whereof the Earl of Northumberland and his son were advertised by the Earl of Worcester, and with all diligence raised all the power they could make, and sent to the Scots which before were taken prisoners at Homeldon for aid of men, promising to the Earl of Douglas the town of Berwick and a part of Northumberland, and to other Scottish lords great lordships and seignories, if they obtained the upper hand. The Scots, in hope of gain and desirous to be revenged of their old griefs, came to the Earl with a great company well appointed.

The Percys, to make their part seem good, devised certain articles by the advice of Richard Scroop, Archbishop of York, brother to the Lord Scroop, whom King Henry had caused to be beheaded at Bristol. These articles being shown to diverse noblemen and other states of the realm, moved them to favor their purpose, insomuch that many of them did not only promise to the Percys aid and succor by words, but also by their writings and seals confirmed the same. Howbeit, when the matter came to trial, the most part of the confederates abandoned them and at the day of the conflict left them alone. Thus after that the conspirators had discovered themselves, the Lord Henry Percy, desirous to proceed in the enterprise, upon trust to be assisted by Owen Glendower, the Earl of March, and others, assembled an army of men-of-arms and archers forth of Cheshire and Wales. Incontinently, his uncle Thomas Percy, Earl of Worcester, that had the government of the Prince of Wales, who as then lay at London in secret manner, conveyed himself out of the Prince's house, and coming to Stafford (where he met his nephew), they increased their power by all ways and means they could devise. The Earl of Northumberland himself was not with them but, being sick, had promised upon his amendment to repair unto them (as some write) with all convenient speed.

These noblemen, to make their conspiracy to seem excusable, besides the articles above mentioned sent letters abroad, wherein was contained that their gathering of an army tended to none other end but only for the safeguard of their own persons and to put some better government in the commonwealth. For whereas taxes and taillages [i.e., imposts] were daily levied under pretense to be employed in defense of the realm, the same were vainly wasted and unprofitably consumed; and where through the slanderous reports of their enemies the King had taken a grievous displeasure with them, they durst not appear personally in the King's presence, until the prelates and barons of the realm had obtained of the King license for them to come and purge themselves before him, by lawful trial of their peers, whose judgment (as they pretended) they would in no wise refuse. Many that saw and heard these letters did commend their diligence and highly praised their assured fidelity and trustiness towards the commonwealth.

But the King, understanding their cloaked drift, devised (by what means he might) to quiet and appease the commons and deface their contrived forgeries; and therefore he wrote an answer to their libels that he marveled much, sith the Earl of Northumberland and the Lord Henry Percy, his son, had received the most part of the sums of money granted to him by the clergy and commonalty for defense of the marches, as he could evidently prove what should move them to complain and raise such manifest slanders. And whereas he understood that the Earls of Northumberland and Worcester and the Lord Percy had by their letters signified to their friends abroad that, by reason of the slanderous reports of their enemies, they durst not appear in his presence without the mediation of the prelates and nobles of the realm, so as they required pledges whereby they might safely come afore him to declare and allege what they had to say in proof of their innocency, he protested by letters sent forth under his seal that they might safely come and go, without all danger or any manner of endamagement to be offered to their persons.

But this could not satisfy those men but that, resolved to go forwards with their enterprise, they marched towards Shrewsbury upon hope to be aided (as men thought) by Owen Glendower and his Welshmen, publishing abroad throughout the countries on each side that King Richard was alive, whom if they wished to see, they willed them to repair in armor unto the castle of Chester, where (without all doubt) he was at that present and ready to come forward. This tale being raised, though it were most untrue, yet it bred variable motions in men's minds, causing them to waver so as they knew not to which part they should stick; and verily divers were well affected towards King Richard, specially such as had tasted of his princely bountifulness, of which there was no small number. And to speak a truth, no marvel it was if many envied the prosperous state of King Henry, sith it was evident enough to the world that he had with wrong usurped the crown, and not only violently deposed King Richard but also cruelly procured his death; for the which, undoubtedly, both he and his posterity tasted such troubles as put them still in danger of their states, till their direct succeeding line was quite rooted out by the contrary faction, as in Henry the Sixth and Edward the Fourth it may appear.

But now to return where we left. King Henry, adver-

tised of the proceedings of the Percys, forthwith gathered
about him such power as he might make, and being earnestly called upon by the Scot, the Earl of March [not Mortimer, but George Dunbar, Earl of March of Scotland], to
make haste and give battle to his enemies, before their
power by delaying of time should still too much increase,
he passed forward with such speed that he was in sight of
his enemies, lying in camp near to Shrewsbury, before they
were in doubt of any such thing; for the Percys thought
that he would have stayed at Burton-upon-Trent till his
council had come thither to him to give their advice what
he were best to do. But herein the enemy was deceived of
his expectation, sith the King had great regard of expedition and making speed for the safety of his own person
whereunto the Earl of March incited him, considering that
in delay is danger and loss in lingering, as the poet in the
like case saith:

> Tolle moras, nocuit semper differre paratis,
> Dum trepidant nullo firmatae robore partes.

By reason of the King's sudden coming in this sort, they
stayed from assaulting the town of Shrewsbury, which enterprise they were ready at that instant to have taken in
hand, and forthwith the Lord Percy (as a captain of high
courage) began to exhort the captains and soldiers to prepare themselves to battle, sith the matter was grown to
that point that by no means it could be avoided, so that
(said he): "This day shall either bring us all to advancement and honor or else, if it shall chance us to be overcome, shall deliver us from the King's spiteful malice and
cruel disdain; for playing the men (as we ought to do),
better it is to die in battle for the commonwealth's cause
than through cowardlike fear to prolong life, which after
shall be taken from us by sentence of the enemy."

Hereupon the whole army, being in number about fourteen thousand chosen men, promised to stand with him
so long as life lasted. There were with the Percys as chief-
tains of this army: the Earl of Douglas, a Scottish man;
the Baron of Kinderton; Sir Hugh Browne and Sir Richard
Vernon, knights; with diverse other stout and right valiant

captains. Now when the two armies were encamped, the one against the other, the Earl of Worcester and the Lord Percy with their [ac]complices sent the articles (whereof I spake before) by Thomas Caiton and Thomas Salvain, esquiers to King Henry, under their hands and seals, which articles in effect charged him with manifest perjury, in that (contrary to his oath received upon the evangelists at Doncaster, when he first entered the realm after his exile) he had taken upon him the crown and royal dignity, imprisoned King Richard, caused him to resign his title and, finally, to be murdered. Diverse other matters they laid to his charge: as levying of taxes and taillages, contrary to his promise; infringing of laws and customs of the realm; and suffering the Earl of March to remain in prison without travailing to have him delivered. All which things they, as procurers and protectors of the commonwealth, took upon them to prove against him, as they protested unto the whole world.

King Henry, after he had read their articles, with the defiance which they annexed to the same, answered the esquiers that he was ready with dint of sword and fierce battle to prove their quarrel false and nothing else than a forged matter, not doubting but that God would aid and assist him in his righteous cause against the disloyal and false forsworn traitors. The next day in the morning early, being the even of Mary Magdalen, they set their battles in order on both sides, and now, whilest the warriors looked when the token of battle should be given, the Abbot of Shrewsbury and one of the clerks of the privy seal were sent from the King unto the Percys to offer them pardon if they would come to any reasonable agreement. By their persuasions, the Lord Henry Percy began to give ear unto the King's offer and so sent with them his uncle, the Earl of Worcester, to declare unto the King the causes of those troubles and to require some effectual reformation in the same.

[The Battle of Shrewsbury, July 21, 1403]

It was reported for a truth that now, when the King had condescended unto all that was reasonable at his hands to be required and seemed to humble himself more than was meet for his estate, the Earl of Worcester (upon his return to his nephew) made relation clean contrary to that the King had said, in such sort that he set his nephew's heart more in displeasure towards the King than ever it was before, driving him by that means to fight whether he would or not; then suddenly [he] blew the trumpets, the King's part crying S[aint] George upon them, the adversaries cried "Esperance Percy," and so the two armies furiously joined. The archers on both sides shot for the best game, laying on such load with arrows that many died and were driven down that never rose again.

The Scots (as some write), which had the fore ward on the Percys' side, intending to be revenged of their old displeasures done to them by the English nation, set so fiercely on the King's fore ward, led by the Earl of Stafford, that they made the same draw back, and had almost broken their adversaries' array. The Welshmen also, which before had lain lurking in the woods, mountains, and marshes, hearing of this battle toward, came to the aid of the Percys and refreshed the wearied people with new succors. The King, perceiving that his men were thus put to distress, what with the violent impression of the Scots and the tempestuous storms of arrows that his adversaries discharged freely against him and his people, it was no need to will him to stir; for suddenly, with his fresh battle, he approached and relieved his men, so that the battle began more fierce than before. Here the Lord Henry Percy and the Earl Douglas, a right stout and hardy captain, not regarding the shot of the King's battle nor the close order of the ranks, pressing forward together bent their whole forces towards the King's person, coming upon him with spears and swords so fiercely that the Earl of March the Scot [again George Dunbar], perceiving their purpose, withdrew the King from that side of the field (as some write) for his great benefit and safeguard (as it appeared), for they gave such a violent onset upon them that stood about the King's standard that, slaying his standard-bearer, Sir Walter Blunt, and overthrowing the standard, they made slaughter of all those that stood about it, as the Earl of

Stafford, that day made by the King Constable of the realm, and diverse other.

The Prince that day holp his father like a lusty young gentleman; for although he was hurt in the face with an arrow, so that diverse noblemen that were about him would have conveyed him forth of the field, yet he would not suffer them so to do, lest his departure from amongst his men might haply have stricken some fear into their hearts; and so, without regard of his hurt, he continued with his men and never ceased either to fight where the battle was most hot or to encourage his men where it seemed most need. This battle lasted three long hours with indifferent fortune on both parts, till at length the King, crying Saint George victory, brake the array of his enemies and adventured so far that (as some write) the Earl Douglas strake him down and at that instant slew Sir Walter Blunt and three others appareled in the King's suit and clothing, saying: "I marvel to see so many kings thus suddenly arise one in the neck of another." The King indeed was raised and did that day many a noble feat of arms, for as it is written, he slew that day with his own hands six and thirty persons of his enemies. The other on his part, encouraged by his doings, fought valiantly and slew the Lord Percy, called Sir Henry Hotspur. To conclude, the King's enemies were vanquished and put to flight, in which flight the Earl of Douglas, for haste, falling from the crag of a high mountain, brake one of his cullions and was taken, and for his valiantness, of the King frankly and freely delivered.

There was also taken the Earl of Worcester, the procurer and setter forth of all this mischief, Sir Richard Vernon, and the Baron of Kinderton, with diverse other. There were slain upon the King's part, besides the Earl of Stafford, to the number of ten knights: Sir Hugh Shirley, Sir John Clifton, Sir John Cokaine, Sir Nicholas Gawsey, Sir Walter Blunt, Sir John Claverley, Sir John Macy of Podington, Sir Hugh Mortimer, and Sir Robert Gawsey, all the which received the same morning the order of knighthood; Sir Thomas Wendesley was wounded to death and so passed out of this life shortly after. There died in all upon the King's side sixteen hundred, and four thousand were griev-

ously wounded. On the contrary side were slain, besides
the Lord Percy, the most part of the knights and esquiers
of the county of Chester, to the number of two hundred,
besides yeomen and footmen; in all there died of those that
fought on the Percys' side about five thousand. This battle
was fought on Mary Magdalen Even, being Saturday. Upon
the Monday following, the Earl of Worcester, the Baron
of Kinderton, and Sir Richard Vernon, knights, were con-
demned and beheaded. The Earl's head was sent to London, there to be set on the bridge.

[Reconciliation of Prince and King, 1411]

... The Lord Henry, Prince of Wales, eldest son to King
Henry, got knowledge that certain of his father's servants
were busy to give informations against him, whereby discord might arise betwixt him and his father; for they put
into the King's head not only what evil rule (according to
the course of youth) the Prince kept, to the offense of
many, but also what great resort of people came to his
house, so that the court was nothing furnished with such
a train as daily followed the Prince. These tales brought no
small suspicion into the King's head, lest his son would
presume to usurp the Crown, he being yet alive, through
which suspicious jealousy it was perceived that he favored
not his son, as in times past he had done.

The Prince, sore offended with such persons as, by slanderous reports, sought not only to spot his good name
abroad in the realm but to sow discord also betwixt him
and his father, wrote his letters into every part of the realm
to reprove all such slanderous devices of those that sought
his discredit. And to clear himself the better, that the world
might understand what wrong he had to be slandered in
such wise, about the feast of Peter and Paul, to wit, the
nine and twentieth day of June, he came to the court with
such a number of noblemen and other his friends that
wished him well, as the like train had been seldom seen re-
pairing to the court at any one time in those days. He was
appareled in a gown of blue satin full of small eyelet holes,
at every hole the needle hanging by a silk thread with which

it was sewed. About his arm he wore a hound's collar set full of SS of gold, and the tirets likewise being of the same metal.

The court was then at Westminster where, he being entered into the hall, not one of his company durst once advance himself further than the fire in the same hall, notwithstanding they were earnestly requested by the lords to come higher; but they, regarding what they had in commandment of the Prince, would not presume to do in any thing contrary thereunto. He himself, only accompanied with those of the King's house, was straight admitted to the presence of the King his father, who being at that time grievously diseased, yet caused himself in his chair to be borne into his privy chamber, where in the presence of three or four persons in whom he had confidence, he commanded the Prince to show what he had to say concerning the cause of his coming.

The Prince, kneeling down before his father, said: "Most redoubted and sovereign lord and father, I am at this time come to your presence as your liege man and as your natural son, in all things to be at your commandment. And where I understand you have in suspicion my demeanor against your Grace, you know very well that if I knew any man within this realm of whom you should stand in fear, my duty were to punish that person, thereby to remove that grief from your heart. Then how much more ought I to suffer death, to ease your Grace of that grief which you have of me, being your natural son and liege man; and to that end I have this day made myself ready by confession and receiving of the sacrament. And therefore I beseech you, most redoubted lord and dear father, for the honor of God, to ease your heart of all such suspicion as you have of me and to dispatch me here before your knees with this same dagger," and withal he delivered unto the King his dagger, in all humble reverence, adding further that his life was not so dear to him that he wished to live one day with his displeasure, "and therefore in thus ridding me out of life and yourself from all suspicion, here in presence of these lords and before God at the day of the general judgment, I faithfully protest clearly to forgive you."

The King, moved herewith, cast from him the dagger and, embracing the Prince, kissed him and with shedding tears confessed that indeed he had him partly in suspicion, though now (as he perceived) not with just cause, and therefore, from thenceforth no misreport should cause him to have him in mistrust, and this he promised of his honor. So by his great wisdom was the wrongful suspicion which his father had conceived against him removed and he restored to his favor. And further, where he could not but grievously complain of them that had slandered him so greatly, to the defacing not only of his honor but also putting him in danger of his life, he humbly besought the King that they might answer their unjust accusation; and in case they were found to have forged such matters upon a malicious purpose, that then they might suffer some punishment for their faults, though not to the full of that they had deserved. The King, seeming to grant his reasonable desire, yet told him that he must tarry a parliament that such offenders might be punished by judgment of their peers; and so for that time he was dismissed, with great love and signs of fatherly affection.

Thus were the father and the son reconciled, betwixt whom the said pickthanks had sown division, insomuch that the son, upon a vehement conceit of unkindness sprung in the father, was in the way to be worn out of favor. Which was the more likely to come to pass by their informations that privily charged him with riot and other uncivil demeanor unseemly for a prince. Indeed, he was youthfully given, grown to audacity, and had chosen him companions agreeable to his age, with whom he spent the time in such recreations, exercises, and delights as he fancied. But yet (it should seem by the report of some writers) that his behavior was not offensive or at least tending to the damage of anybody, sith he had a care to avoid doing of wrong and to tender his affections within the tract of virtue, whereby he opened unto himself a ready passage of good liking among the prudent sort and was beloved of such as could discern his disposition, which was in no degree so excessive as that he deserved in such vehement manner to be suspected. In whose dispraise I find little but to his praise very much. . . .

from *The First Four Books of the Civil Wars
between the Two Houses of Lancaster
and York* [1595]

[Bolingbroke, having become Henry IV, has
military difficulties.]

86

And yet new Hydras lo, new heads appear
T'afflict that peace reputed then so sure,
And gave him much to do, and much to fear,
And long and dangerous tumults did procure,
And those even of his chiefest followers were
Of whom he might presume him most secure,
Who whether not so graced or so preferred
As they expected, these new factions stirred.

87

The Percys were the men, men of great might,
Strong in alliance, and in courage strong
That thus conspire, under pretense to right
The crookèd courses they had suffered long:
Whether their conscience urged them or despite,
Or that they saw the part they took was wrong,
Or that ambition hereto did them call,
Or others envied grace, or rather all.

88

What cause soever were, strong was their plot,
Their parties great, means good, th' occasion fit:
Their practice close, their faith suspected not,
Their states far off and they of wary wit:
Who with large promises draw in the Scot
To aid their cause—he likes, and yields to it,
Not for the love of them or for their good,
But glad hereby of means to shed our blood.

89

Then join they with the Welsh, who fitly trained
And all in arms under a mighty head
Great Glendow'r, who long warred, and much attained,
Sharp conflicts made, and many vanquishèd:
With whom was Edmund Earl of March retained
Being first his prisoner, now confederèd,
A man the King much feared, and well he might
Lest he should look whether his crown stood right.

90

For Richard, for the quiet of the state,
Before he took those Irish wars in hand
About succession doth deliberate,
And finding how the certain right did stand,
With full consent this man did ordinate
The heir apparent in the Crown and land:
Then judge if this the King might nearly touch,
Although his might were small, his right being much.

91

With these the Percys them confederate,
And as three heads they league in one intent,
And instituting a triumvirate
Do part the land in triple government:
Dividing thus among themselves the state,
The Percys should rule all the North from Trent
And Glendow'r Wales: the Earl of March should be
Lord of the South from Trent; and thus they 'gree.

92

Then those two helps which still such actors find—
Pretense of common good, the King's disgrace—
Doth fit their course, and draw the vulgar mind
To further them and aid them in this case:
The King they accused for cruel, and unkind
That did the state, and Crown, and all deface;
A perjured man that held all faith in scorn,
Whose trusted oaths had others made forsworn.

93

Besides the odious detestable act
Of that late murdered king they aggravate,
Making it his that so had willed the fact
That he the doers did remunerate:
And then such taxes daily doth exact
That were against the orders of the state,
And with all these or worse they him assailed
Who late of others with the like prevailed.

94

Thus doth contentious proud mortality
Afflict each other and itself torment:
And thus O thou, mind-tort'ring misery,
Restless ambition, born in discontent,
Turn'st and retossest with iniquity
The unconstant courses frailty did invent:
And foul'st fair order and defil'st the earth
Fost'ring up war, father of blood and dearth.

95

Great seemed the cause, and greatly, too, did add
The peoples' love thereto, these crimes rehearsed,
That many gathered to the troops they had
And many more do flock from coasts dispersed:
But when the King had heard these news so bad,
Th' unlookt for dangerous toil more nearly pierced;
For bent t'wards Wales t'appease those tumults there,
H' is forced divert his course, and them forbear.

96

Not to give time unto th' increasing rage
And gathering fury, forth he hastes with speed,
Lest more delay or giving longer age
To th' evil grown, it might the cure exceed:
All his best men at arms, and leaders sage
All he prepared he could, and all did need;
For to a mighty work thou goest O King,
To such a field that power to power shall bring.

97

There shall young Hotspur with a fury led
Meet with thy forward son as fierce as he:
There warlike Worcester long experiencèd
In foreign arms, shall come t' encounter thee:
There Douglas to thy Stafford shall make head:
There Vernon for thy valiant Blunt shall be:
There shalt thou find a doubtful bloody day,
Though sickness keep Northumberland away.

98

Who yet reserved, though after quit for this,
Another tempest on thy head to raise,
As if still-wrong revenging *Nemesis*
Did mean t' afflict all thy continual days:
And yet this field he happily might miss
For thy great good, and therefore well he stays:
What might his force have done being joined thereto
When that already gave so much to do?

99

The swift approach and unexpected speed
The King had made upon this new-raised force
In th' unconfirmèd troops much fear did breed,
Untimely hind'ring their intended course;
The joining with the Welsh they had decreed
Was hereby stopped which made their part the worse,
Northumberland with forces from the North
Expected to be there, was not set forth.

100

And yet undaunted Hotspur seeing the King
So near approached leaving the work in hand
With forward speed his forces marshaling,
Sets forth his farther coming to withstand:
And with a cheerful voice encouraging
By his great spirit his well emboldened band,
Brings a strong host of firm resolvèd might,
And placed his troops before the King in sight.

101

This day (saith he) O faithful valiant friends,
Whatever it doth give, shall glory give:
This day with honor frees our state, or ends
Our misery with fame, that still shall live,
And do but think how well this day he spends
That spends his blood his country to relieve:
Our holy cause, our freedom, and our right,
Sufficient are to move good minds to fight.

102

Besides th' assurèd hope of victory
That we may even promise on our side
Against this weak-constrainèd company,
Whom force and fear, not will and love doth guide
Against a prince whose foul impiety
The heavens do hate, the earth cannot abide,
Our number being no less, our courage more,
What need we doubt if we but work therefor.

103

This said, and thus resolved even bent to charge
Upon the King, who well their order viewed
And careful noted all the form at large
Of their proceeding, and their multitude:
And deeming better if he could discharge
The day with safety, and some peace conclude,
Great proffers sends of pardon, and of grace
If they would yield, and quietness embrace.

104

But this refused, the King with wrath incensed
Rage against fury doth with speed prepare:
And O, saith he, though I could have dispensed
With this day's blood, which I have sought to spare
That greater glory might have recompensed
The forward worth of these that so much dare,
That we might honor had by th' overthrown,
That th' wounds we make, might not have been our own.

105

Yet since that other men's iniquity
Calls on the sword of wrath against my will,
And that themselves exact this cruelty,
And I constrainèd am this blood to spill:
Then on my masters, on courageously
True-hearted subjects against traitors ill,
And spare them not who seek to spoil us all,
Whose foul confusèd end soon see you shall.

106

Straight moves with equal motion equal rage
The like incensèd armies unto blood,
One to defend, another side to wage
Foul civil war, both vows their quarrel good:
Ah too much heat to blood doth now enrage
Both who the deed provokes and who withstood,
That valor here is vice, here manhood sin,
The forward'st hands doth O least honor win.

107

But now begin these fury-moving sounds
The notes of wrath that music brought from hell,
The rattling drums which trumpets voice confounds,
The cries, th' encouragements, the shouting shrill;
That all about the beaten air rebounds,
Thund'ring confusèd, murmurs horrible,
To rob all sense except the sense to fight:
Well hands may work, the mind hath lost his sight.

108

O war! begot in pride and luxury,
The child of wrath and of dissension,
Horrible good; mischief necessary,
The foul reformer of confusion,
Unjust-just scourge of our iniquity,
Cruel recurrer of corruption:
O that these sin-sick states in need should stand
To be let blood with such a boist'rous hand!

109

And O how well thou hadst been spared this day
Had not wrong-counseled Percy been perverse,
Whose young undangered hand now rash makes way
Upon the sharpest fronts of the most fierce:
Where now an equal fury thrusts to stay
And rebeat-back that force and his disperse,
Then these assail, then those chase back again,
Till stayed with new-made hills of bodies slain.

110

There lo that new-appearing glorious star
Wonder of Arms, the terror of the field,
Young Henry, laboring where the stoutest are,
And even the stoutest forces back to yield,
There is that hand bold'ned to blood and war
That must the sword in woundrous° actions wield:
But better hadst thou learned with others blood
A less expense to us, to thee more good.

111

Hadst thou not there lent present speedy aid
To thy endangered father nearly tired,
Whom fierce encountring Douglas overlaid,
That day had there his troublous life expired:
Heroical courageous Blunt arrayed
In habit like as was the King attired

° **woundrous** (Daniel's pun on ."wound" and "wondress")

And deemed for him, excused that fate with his,
For he had what his lord did hardly miss.

112

For thought a king he would not now disgrace
The person then supposed, but princelike shows
Glorious effects of worth that fit his place,
And fighting dies, and dying overthrows:
Another of that forward name and race
In that hot work his valiant life bestows,
Who bare the standard of the King that day,
Whose colors overthrown did much dismay.

113

And dear it cost, and O much blood is shed
To purchase thee this losing victory
O travailed King: yet hast thou conquerèd
A doubtful day, a mighty enemy:
But O what wounds, what famous worth lies dead!
That makes the winner look with sorrowing eye,
Magnanimous Stafford lost that much had wrought,
And valiant Shirley who great glory got.

114

Such wreck of others' blood thou didst behold,
O furious Hotspur, ere thou lost thine own!
Which now once lost that heat in thine waxed cold,
And soon became thy army overthrown;
And O that this great spirit, this courage bold,
Had in some good cause been rightly shown!
So had not we thus violently then
Have termed that rage, which valor should have been.

ANONYMOUS

The Famous Victories of Henry the Fifth

[Dramatis Personae

King Henry IV
Prince Henry of Monmouth, his son (later
   King Henry V)
Duke of York ⎫
Duke of Exeter ⎬ brothers of Henry IV
Earl of Oxford
Archbishop of Canterbury
The Lord Chief Justice
The Lord Mayor of London
The Sheriff
Ned
Tom ⎫
Sir John Oldcastle, alias Jockey ⎬ friends to Prince Henry
English Captain
English Soldier
Two Receivers
Clerk of the King's Bench
The Jailer
The Thief, Cutbert Cutter, alias Gad's Hill
Derick, a poor carrier

John Cobbler
Robin Pewterer   } the Watch
Lawrence Costermonger }
The Vintner's Boy, Robin
The Porter
King Charles VI, of France
The Dolphin, his son
Duke of Burgundy
Archbishop of Bourges
The Constable
A Herald
A Messenger
A French Captain
Jack Drummer
French Soldiers
A Frenchman

Princess Katherine, daughter of Charles VI
Mistress Cobbler

Lords, Ladies, Attendants

    Scene: England and France]

The Famous Victories of Henry the Fifth
Containing the
Honorable Battle of Agincourt

[Scene I]

Enter the young Prince, Ned, and Tom.

Prince. Come away, Ned and Tom.

Both. Here, my lord.

Prince. Come away, my lads. Tell me, sirs, how much
gold have you got?

Ned. Faith, my lord, I have got five hundred pound.　5

Prince. But tell me, Tom, how much hast thou got?

Tom. Faith, my lord, some four hundred pound.

Prince. Four hundred pounds! Bravely spoken, lads!
But tell me, sirs, think you not that it was a villainous
part of me to rob my father's receivers?　10

Ned. Why, no, my lord; it was but a trick of youth.

Prince. Faith, Ned, thou sayest true. But tell me, sirs,
whereabouts are we?

Tom. My lord, we are now about a mile off London.

Prince. But, sirs, I marvel that Sir John Oldcastle comes　15
not away. Zounds, see where he comes.

Enter Jockey [i.e., John Oldcastle].

How now, Jockey, what news with thee?

John Oldcastle. Faith, my lord, such news as passeth!
For the town of Deptford is risen with hue and cry
20   after your man, which parted from us the last night
and has set upon and hath robbed a poor carrier.

Prince. Zounds, the villain that was wont to spy out our
booties?

John Oldcastle. Ay, my lord, even the very same.

25   *Prince.* Now base-minded rascal to rob a poor carrier!
Well, it skills not; I'll save the base villain's life, ay,
I may. But tell me, Jockey, whereabouts be the re-
ceivers?

John Oldcastle. Faith, my lord, they are hard by; but
30   the best is we are ahorseback and they be afoot, so
we may escape them.

Prince. Well, if the villains come, let me alone with
them! But tell me, Jockey, how much gotst thou from
the knaves? For I am sure I got something, for one
35   of the villains so belammed me about the shoulders
as I shall feel it this month.

John Oldcastle. Faith, my lord, I have got a hundred
pound.

Prince. A hundred pound! Now bravely spoken,
40   Jockey. But come, sirs, lay all your money before
me. Now, by heaven, here is a brave show! But, as
I am true gentleman, I will have the half of this spent
tonight! But, sirs, take up your bags; here comes the
receivers. Let me alone.

Enters two Receivers.°

45   *First Receiver.* Alas, good fellow, what shall we do? I
dare never go home to the court, for I shall be
hanged. But look, here is the young Prince. What
shall we do?

Prince. How now, you villains! What are you?

44 s.d. Receivers i.e., of taxes

First Receiver. Speak you to him.   50

Second Receiver. No, I pray, speak you to him.

Prince. Why, how now, you rascals! Why speak you not?

First Receiver. Forsooth, we be—pray speak you to him.   55

Prince. Zounds, villains, speak, or I'll cut off your heads!

Second Receiver. Forsooth, he can tell the tale better than I.

First Receiver. Forsooth, we be your father's receivers.   60

Prince. Are you my father's receivers? Then I hope ye have brought me some money.

First Receiver. Money? Alas, sir, we be robbed!

Prince. Robbed! How many were there of them?

First Receiver. Marry, sir, there were four of them;   65
and one of them had Sir John Oldcastle's bay hobby, and your black nag.

Prince. Gog's wounds! How like you this, Jockey? Blood, you villains! My father robbed of his money abroad, and we robbed in our stables! But tell me,   70
how many were of them?

First Receiver. If it please you, there were four of them; and there was one about the bigness of you—but I am sure I so belammed him about the shoulders that he will feel it this month.   75

Prince. Gog's wounds! You lammed them fairly—so that they have carried away your money. But come, sirs, what shall we do with the villains?

Both Receivers. I beseech your Grace, be good to us.

Ned. I pray you, my lord, forgive them this once.   80

[*Prince.*] Well, stand up, and get you gone. And look

that you speak not a word of it—for, if there be—
zounds! I'll hang you and all your kin!

Exit [*Receivers*].

Prince. Now, sirs, how like you this? Was not this
bravely done? For now the villains dare not speak a
word of it, I have so feared them with words. Now,
whither shall we go?

All. Why, my lord, you know our old host's at Faversham.

Prince. Our host's at Faversham! Blood, what shall we
do there? We have a thousand pound about us, and
we shall go to a petty ale-house? No, no! You know
the old tavern in Eastcheap; there is good wine—
besides, there is a pretty wench that can talk well;
for I delight as much in their tongues as any part
about them.

All. We are ready to wait upon your Grace.

Prince. Gog's wounds! "Wait"? We will go altogether;
we are all fellows. I tell you, sirs, and the King my
father were dead, we would be all kings. Therefore,
come away!

Ned. Gog's wounds, bravely spoken, Harry!

[*Exeunt omnes.*]

[*Scene II*]

*Enter John Cobbler, Robin Pewterer,
Lawrence Costermonger.*

John. All is well here; all is well, masters.

Lawrence. How say you, neighbor John Cobbler? I
think it best that my neighbor, Robin Pewterer, went
to Pudding Lane End, and we will watch here at
Billingsgate Ward. How say you, neighbor Robin?
How like you this?

Robin. Marry, well, neighbors; I care not much if I go to Pudding Lane's End. But, neighbors, if you hear any ado about me, make haste; and if I hear any ado about you, I will come to you. *Exit Robin.* 10

Lawrence. Neighbor, what news hear you of the young Prince?

John. Marry, neighbor, I hear say he is a toward young prince; for, if he meet any by the highway, he will not let° to—talk with him. I dare not call him thief, 15 but sure he is one of these taking fellows.

Lawrence. Indeed, neighbor, I hear say he is as lively a young prince as ever was.

John. Ay, and I hear say if he use it long, his father will cut him off from the Crown. But, neighbor, say noth- 20 ing of that!

Lawrence. No, no, neighbor, I warrant you!

John. Neighbor, methinks you begin to sleep. If you will, we will sit down; for I think it is about midnight.

Lawrence. Marry, content, neighbor; let us sleep. 25

Enter Derick, roving.

Derick. Who! Who there, who there! *Exit Derick.*

Enter Robin.

Robin. Oh, neighbors, what mean you to sleep, and such ado in the streets?

Both. How now, neighbor, what's the matter?

Enter Derick again.

Derick. Who there! Who there! Who there! 30

John. Why, what ailst thou? Here is no horses.

Derick. O alas, man, I am robbed! Who there! Who there!

15 **let** hesitate (the speaker is about to add "rob", then thinks better of it)

Robin. Hold him, neighbor Cobbler. Why, I see thou
35   art a plain clown.°

Derick. Am I a clown? Zounds, masters, do clowns go
in silk apparel? I am sure all we gentlemen-clowns in
Kent scant go so well. Zounds, you know clowns very
well! Hear you, are you Master Constable? And you
40   be, speak, for I will not take it at his hands.

John. Faith, I am not Master Constable; but I am one
of his bad° officers, for he is not here.

Derick. Is not Master Constable here? Well, it is no matter. I'll have the law at his hands.

45   *John.* Nay, I pray you, do not take the law of us.

Derick. Well, you are one of his beastly officers.

John. I am one of his bad° officers.

Derick. Why, then, I charge thee, look to him!

John. Nay, but hear you, sir; you seem to be an honest
50   fellow, and we are poor men; and now 'tis night, and
we would be loath to have anything ado; therefore,
I pray thee, put it up.

Derick. First, thou sayest true; I am an honest fellow
—and a proper, handsome fellow, too! And you
55   seem to be poor men; therefore I care not greatly.
Nay, I am quickly pacified. But, and you chance to
spy the thief, I pray you lay hold on him.

Robin. Yes, that we will, I warrant you.

Derick. 'Tis a wonderful thing to see how glad the knave
60   is, now I have forgiven him.

John. Neighbors, do you look about you. How now,
who's there?

Enter the Thief.

Thief. Here is a good fellow. I pray you, which is the
way to the old tavern in Eastcheap?

35 **clown** rustic   42, 47 **bad** regularly installed (i.e., "bade")

Derick. Whoop halloo! Now, Gad's Hill, knowest 65
thou me?

Thief. I know thee for an ass.

Derick. And I know thee for a taking fellow upon
Gad's Hill in Kent. A bots light upon ye.

Thief. The whoreson villain would be knocked. 70

Derick. Masters, villain, and ye be men, stand to him,
and take his weapon from him. Let him not pass you!

John. My friend, what make you abroad now? It is too
late to walk now.

Thief. It is not too late for true men to walk. 75

Lawrence. We know thee not to be a true man.

[They seize the Thief.]

Thief. Why, what do you mean to do with me? Zounds!
I am one of the King's liege people.

Derick. Hear you, sir, are you one of the King's liege
people? 80

Thief. Ay, marry am I, sir! What say you to it?

Derick. Marry, sir, I say you are one of the King's
filching people.

John. Come, come. let's have him away.

Thief. Why, what have I done? 85

Robin. Thou hast robbed a poor fellow, and taken
away his goods from him.

Thief. I never saw him before.

Derick. Masters, who comes here?

Enter the Vintner's Boy.

Boy. How now, goodman Cobbler. 90

John. How now, Robin, what makes thou abroad at
this time of night?

Boy. Marry, I have been at the Counter;° I can tell
such news as never you have heard the like!

95 *John.* What is that, Robin? What is the matter?

Boy. Why, this night, about two hours ago, there came
the young Prince, and three or four more of his companions, and called for wine good store; and then
they sent for a noise of musicians, and were very
100 merry for the space of an hour; then, whether their
music liked them not, or whether they had drunk
too much wine or no, I cannot tell, but our pots flew
against the walls; and then they drew their swords
and went into the street and fought, and some took
105 one part and some took another; but for the space
of half an hour there was such a bloody fray as
passeth! And none could part them until such time
as the Mayor and Sheriff were sent for; and then, at
the last, with much ado, they took them; and so the
110 young Prince was carried to the Counter; and then,
about one hour after, there came a messenger from
the Court in all haste from the King for my Lord
Mayor and the Sheriff—but for what cause I know
not.

115 *John.* Here is news, indeed, Robert!

Lawrence. Marry, neighbor, this news is strange, indeed! I think it best, neighbor, to rid our hands of
this fellow first.

Thief. What mean you to do with me?

120 *John.* We mean to carry you to the prison, and there
to remain till the sessions day.

Thief. Then, I pray you, let me go to the prison where
my master is.

John. Nay, thou must go to the country prison, to New-
125 gate. Therefore, come away.

Thief. [*To Derick*] I prithee, be good to me, honest
fellow.

93 **Counter** London prison under jurisdiction of the Lord Mayor

Derick. Ay, marry, will I; I'll be very charitable to
thee, for I will never leave thee—till I see thee on
the gallows.   130

[*Exeunt omnes.*]

[*Scene III*]

*Enter Henry the Fourth [attended], with the
Earl of Exeter, and the Lord of Oxford.*

Oxford. And please your Majesty, here is my Lord
Mayor and the Sheriff of London to speak with your
Majesty.

King. Admit them to our presence.

Enter the Mayor and the Sheriff.

King. Now, my good Lord Mayor of London, the   *5*
cause of my sending for you at this time is to tell
you of a matter which I have learned of my council.
Herein I understand that you have committed my
son to prison without our leave and license. What!
Although he be a rude youth, and likely to give occa-   10
sion, yet you might have considered that he is a
prince, and my son, and not to be haled to prison by
every subject.

Mayor. May it please your Majesty to give us leave to
tell our tale?   15

King. Or else God forbid! Otherwise, you might think
me an unequal judge, having more affection to my
son than to any rightful judgment.

Mayor. Then I do not doubt but we shall rather deserve commendations at your Majesty's hands than   20
any anger.

King. Go to, say on.

Mayor. Then, if it please your Majesty, this night be-

twixt two and three of the clock in the morning my
25 lord the young Prince, with a very disordered company, came to the old tavern in Eastcheap; and
whether it was that their music liked them not, or
whether they were overcome with wine, I know not,
but they drew their swords, and into the street they
30 went; and some took my lord the young Prince's
part, and some took the other; but betwixt them
there was such a bloody fray for the space of half
an hour that neither watchmen nor any other could
stay them; till my brother, the Sheriff of London,
35 and I were sent for; and, at the last, with much ado,
we stayed them. But it was long first, which was a
great disquieting to all your loving subjects thereabouts. And then, my good lord, we knew not
whether your Grace had sent them to try us whether
40 we would do justice, or whether it were of their own
voluntary will or not, we cannot tell. And, therefore,
in such a case, we knew not what to do; but, for our
own safeguard, we sent him to ward; where he
wanteth nothing that is fit for his Grace and your
45 Majesty's son. And thus, most humbly beseeching
your Majesty to think of our answer—

King. Stand aside until we have further deliberated on
your answer.

                              Exit Mayor [*with Sheriff*].
Ah, Harry, Harry, now thrice-accursed Harry, that
50 hath gotten a son which with grief will end his
father's days! Oh, my son, a prince thou art, ay, a
prince indeed—and to deserve imprisonment! And
well have they done, and like faithful subjects. [*To
his Attendants*] Discharge them, and let them go.

55 *Exeter.* I beseech your Grace, be good to my lord the
young Prince.

King. Nay, nay, 'tis no matter; let him alone.

Oxford. Perchance the Mayor and the Sheriff have been
too precise in this matter.

King. No, they have done like faithful subjects. I will go   60
myself to discharge them and let them go.

Exit omnes.

[Scene IV]

*Enter Lord Chief Justice, Clerk of the Office,
Jailer, John Cobbler, Derick, and the Thief.*

Judge. Jailer, bring the prisoner to the bar.

Derick. Hear you, my lord; I pray you, bring the bar
to the prisoner.

Judge. Hold thy hand up at the bar.

Thief. Here it is, my lord.   5

Judge. Clerk of the Office, read his indictment.

Clerk. What is thy name?

Thief. My name was known before I came here, and
shall be when I am gone, I warrant you.

Judge. Ay, I think so; but we will know it better be-   10
fore thou go.

Derick. Zounds, and you do but send to the next jail,
we are sure to know his name; for this is not the first
prison he hath been in, I'll warrant you.

Clerk. What is thy name?   15

Thief. What need you to ask, and have it in writing?

Clerk. Is not thy name Cutbert Cutter?

Thief. What the devil need you ask, and know it so
well?

Clerk. Why then, Cutbert Cutter, I indict thee, by the   20
name of Cutbert Cutter, for robbing a poor carrier
the 20th day of May last past, in the fourteenth year

of the reign of our sovereign lord King Henry the
Fourth, for setting upon a poor carrier upon Gad's
25   Hill, in Kent, and having beaten and wounded the
said carrier, and taken his goods from him—

Derick. Oh, masters, stay there! Nay, let's never belie
the man, for he hath not beaten and wounded me
also, but he hath beaten and wounded my pack, and
30   hath taken the great raze° of ginger that Bouncing
Bess with the jolly buttocks should have had. That
grieves me most.

Judge. Well, what sayest thou? Art thou guilty, or not
guilty?

35   *Thief.* Not guilty, my lord.

Judge. By whom wilt thou be tried?

Thief. By my lord the young Prince, or by myself,
whether you will.

Enter the young Prince, with Ned and Tom.

Prince. Come away, my lads. Gog's wounds, ye villain,
40   what make you here? I must go about my business
myself and you must stand loitering here?

Thief. Why, my lord, they have bound me, and will not
let me go.

Prince. Have they bound thee, villain? Why, how now,
45   my lord?

Judge. I am glad to see your Grace in good health.

Prince. Why, my lord, this is my man. 'Tis marvel you
knew him not long before this. I tell you, he is a
man of his hands.

50   *Thief.* Ay, Gog's wounds, that I am! Try me, who dare.

Judge. Your Grace shall find small credit by acknowl-
edging him to be your man.

Prince. Why, my lord, what hath he done?

30 **raze** root

Judge. And it please your Majesty, he hath robbed a
poor carrier.   55

Derick. Hear you, sir; marry, it was one Derick, goodman Hobling's man, of Kent.

Prince. What! Was't you, buttonbreech? Of my word,
my lord, he did it but in jest.

Derick. Hear you, sir, is it your man's quality to rob   60
folks in jest? In faith, he shall be hanged in earnest.

Prince. Well, my lord, what do you mean to do with
my man?

Judge. And please your Grace, the law must pass on
him according to justice; then he must be executed.   65

Prince. Why, then, belike you mean to hang my man?

Judge. I am sorry that it falls out so.

Prince. Why, my lord, I pray you, who am I?

Judge. And it please your Grace, you are my lord the
young Prince, our king that shall be after the decease   70
of our sovereign lord King Henry the Fourth, whom
God grant long to reign!

Prince. You say true, my lord. And you will hang my
man?

Judge. And it like your Grace, I must needs do justice.   75

Prince. Tell me, my lord, shall I have my man?

Judge. I cannot, my lord.

Prince. But will you not let him go?

Judge. I am sorry that his case is so ill.

Prince. Tush, case me no casings! Shall I have my man?   80

Judge. I cannot, nor I may not, my lord.

Prince. Nay, and "I shall not," say—and then I am
answered?

Judge. No.

85   *Prince.* No! Then I will have him.

             He giveth him a box on the ear.

Ned. Gog's wounds, my lord, shall I cut off his head?

Prince. No. I charge you, draw not your swords. But
     get you hence. Provide a noise of musicians. Away,
     begone!

                         Exeunt Ned and Tom.

90   *Judge.* Well, my lord, I am content to take it at your
     hands.

Prince. Nay, and you be not, you shall have more!

Judge. Why, I pray you, my lord, who am I?

Prince. You, who knows not you? Why, man, you are
95   Lord Chief Justice of England.

Judge. Your Grace hath said truth; therefore, in strik-
     ing me in this place you greatly abuse me; and not
     me only but also your father, whose lively person
     here in this place I do represent. And therefore to
100 teach you what prerogatives mean, I commit you to
     the Fleet until we have spoken with your father.

Prince. Why, then, belike you mean to send me to the
     Fleet!

Judge. Ay, indeed; and therefore, carry him away.

             Exeunt Henry V with the Officers.
105 Jailer, carry the prisoner to Newgate again until the
     next 'sizes.

Jailer. At your commandment, my lord, it shall be
     done.

         [Exeunt all except] Derick and John Cobbler.

[Scene V]

Derick. Zounds, masters, here's ado when princes must
     go to prison! Why, John, didst ever see the like?

John. O Derick, trust me, I never saw the like!

Derick. Why, John, thou mayst see what princes be in choler. A judge a box on the ear! I'll tell thee, John, O John, I would not have done it for twenty shillings.

John. No, nor I. There had been no way but one with us—we should have been hanged.

Derick. Faith, John, I'll tell thee what; thou shalt be my Lord Chief Justice, and thou shalt sit in the chair; and I'll be the young Prince, and hit thee a box on the ear; and then thou shalt say, "To teach you what prerogatives mean, I commit you to the Fleet."

John. Come on; I'll be your judge! But thou shalt not hit me hard?

Derick. No, no.

                    [John Cobbler takes the Judge's seat.]

John. What hath he done?

Derick. Marry, he hath robbed Derick.

John. Why, then, I cannot let him go.

Derick. I must needs have my man.

John. You shall not have him!

Derick. Shall I not have my man? Say No, and you dare! How say you? Shall I not have my man?

John. No, marry, shall you not!

Derick. Shall I not, John?

John. No, Derick.

Derick. Why, then, take you that [*boxing his ear*] till more come! Zounds, shall I not have him?

John. Well, I am content to take this at your hand. But, I pray you, who am I?

Derick. Who art thou? Zounds, dost not know thyself?

John. No.

Derick. Now away, simple fellow. Why, man, thou art John the Cobbler.

35 *John*. No, I am my Lord Chief Justice of England.

Derick. Oh, John, mass, thou sayst true, thou art indeed.

John. Why, then, to teach you what prerogatives mean, I commit you to the Fleet.

40 *Derick*. Well, I will go; but, i'faith, you gray-beard knave, I'll course° you.

Exit. And straight enters again.
Oh, John, come, come out of thy chair. Why, what a clown wert thou to let me hit thee a box on the ear! And now thou seest they will not take me to the Fleet.
45 I think that thou art one of these Worenday° clowns.

John. But I marvel what will become of thee.

Derick. Faith, I'll be no more a carrier.

John. What wilt thou do, then?

Derick. I'll dwell with thee, and be a cobbler.

50 *John*. With me? Alas, I am not able to keep thee. Why, thou wilt eat me out of doors.

Derick. Oh, John! No, John; I am none of these great slouching fellows that devour these great pieces of beef and brews.° Alas, a trifle serves me—a wood-
55 cock, a chicken, or a capon's leg, or any such little thing serves me.

John. A capon! Why, man, I cannot get a capon once a year—except it be at Christmas, at some other man's house; for we cobblers be glad of a dish of
60 roots.

Derick. Roots, why, are you so good at rooting? Nay, cobbler, we'll have you ringed.°

John. But, Derick,

41 **course** keep pace with   45 **Worenday** workaday (?)   54 **brews**
beef broth   62 **ringed** i.e., in the nose, like a pig

Though we be so poor,
Yet will we have in store   *65*
A crab in the fire,
With nut-brown ale
That is full stale,°
Which will a man quail
And lay in the mire.   *70*

Derick. A bots on you! And be but for your ale, I'll
dwell with you. Come, let's away as fast as we can.
                                        Exeunt.

[Scene VI]

Enter the young Prince, with Ned and Tom.

Prince. Come away, sirs. Gog's wounds, Ned, didst
thou not see what a box on the ear I took my Lord
Chief Justice?

Tom. By Gog's blood, it did me good to see it. It made
his teeth jar in his head!   *5*

Enter Sir John Oldcastle.

Prince. How now, Sir John Oldcastle, what news with
you?

John Oldcastle. I am glad to see your Grace at liberty.
I was come, I, to visit you in prison.

Prince. To visit me! Didst thou not know that I am a   *10*
prince's son? Why, 'tis enough for me to look into
a prison, though I come not in myself. But here's
such ado nowadays—here's prisoning, here's hanging, whipping, and the devil and all. But I tell you,
sirs, when I am King we will have no such things.   *15*
But, my lads, if the old King, my father, were dead,
we would be all kings.

68 stale strong

John Oldcastle. He is a good old man; God take him to his mercy the sooner!

20   *Prince.* But, Ned, so soon as I am King, the first thing I will do shall be to put my Lord Chief Justice out of office, and thou shalt be my Lord Chief Justice of England.

Ned. Shall I be Lord Chief Justice? By Gog's wounds,
25   I'll be the bravest Lord Chief Justice that ever was in England!

Prince. Then, Ned, I'll turn all these prisons into fence-schools, and I will endue thee with them, with lands to maintain them withal. Then I will have a bout
30   with my Lord Chief Justice. Thou shalt hang none but pick-purses, and horse-stealers, and such base-minded villains; but that fellow that will stand by the highway side courageously with his sword and buckler and take a purse—that fellow, give him
35   commendations! Beside that, send him to me, and I will give him an annual pension out of my ex-chequer to maintain him all the days of his life.

John Oldcastle. Nobly spoken, Harry! We shall never have a merry world till the old King be dead.

40   *Ned.* But whither are you going now?

Prince. To the court; for I hear say my father lies very sick.

Tom. But I doubt he will not die.

Prince. Yet will I go thither; for the breath shall be no
45   sooner out of his mouth but I will clap the crown on my head.

John Oldcastle. Will you go to the court with that cloak so full of needles?

Prince. Cloak, eyelet-holes, needles, and all was of
50   mine own devising; and therefore I will wear it.

Tom. I pray you, my lord, what may be the meaning thereof?

Prince. Why, man, 'tis a sign that I stand upon thorns
till the crown be on my head.

John Oldcastle. Or that every needle might be a prick   55
to their hearts that repine at your doings?

Prince. Thou sayst true, Jockey. But there's some will
say the young Prince will be "a well toward young
man"—and all this gear,° that I had as leave they
would break my head with a pot as to say any such   60
thing. But we stand prating here too long; I must
needs speak with my father. Therefore, come away!
                    [*They cross the stage, and rap.*]

[*Enter a Porter.*]

Porter. What a rapping keep you at the King's court-
gate?

Prince. Here's one that must speak with the King.   65

Porter. The King is very sick, and none must speak
with him.

Prince. No? You rascal, do you not know me?

Porter. You are my lord, the young Prince.

Prince. Then go and tell my father that I must, and will,   70
speak with him.

Ned. Shall I cut off his head?

Prince. No, no. Though I would help you in other
places, yet I have nothing to do here. What, you are
in my father's court.   75

Ned. I will write him in my tables; for so soon as I am
made Lord Chief Justice I will put him out of his
office.   *The trumpet sounds.*

Prince. Gog's wounds, sirs, the King comes. Let's all
stand aside.   80

Enter the King, with the Lord of Exeter.

King. And is it true, my lord, that my son is already
sent to the Fleet? Now, truly, that man is more fitter

59 **gear** nonsense

to rule the realm than I; for by no means could I
rule my son, and he, by one word, hath caused him
85 to be ruled. Oh, my son, my son, no sooner out of
one prison but into another? I had thought once
whiles I had lived to have seen this noble realm of
England flourish by thee, my son; but now I see it
goes to ruin and decay.   *He weepeth.*

Enters Lord of Oxford.

90 *Oxford.* And please your Grace, here is my lord your
son that cometh to speak with you. He saith he must,
and will, speak with you.

King. Who? My son Harry?

Oxford. Ay, and please your Majesty.

95 *King.* I know wherefore he cometh. But look that none
come with him.

Oxford. A very disordered company, and such as make
very ill rule in your Majesty's house.

King. Well, let him come; but look that none come
100 with him.   *He goeth.*

Oxford. And please your Grace, my lord the King
sends for you.

Prince. Come away, sirs, let's go all together.

Oxford. And please your Grace, none must go with
105 you.

Prince. Why, I must needs have them with me; otherwise I can do my father no countenance: therefore,
come away.

Oxford. The King your father commands there should
110 none come.

Prince. Well, sirs, then be gone—and provide me three
noise of musicians.   *Exeunt Knights.*

*Enters the Prince, with a dagger in his hand,
[to the King, attended].*

King. Come, my son; come on, a God's name! I know
wherefore thy coming is. Oh, my son, my son, what
cause hath ever been that thou shouldst forsake me,   *115*
and follow this vile and reprobate company, which
abuseth youth so manifestly? Oh, my son, thou
knowest that these thy doings will end thy father's
days.   *He weeps.*
Ay, so, so, my son, thou fearest not to approach the   *120*
presence of thy sick father in that disguised sort. I
tell thee, my son, that there is never a needle in thy
cloak but it is a prick to my heart, and never an
eyelet-hole but it is a hole to my soul; and wherefore
thou bringest that dagger in thy hand I know not, but   *125*
by conjecture.   ·   *He weeps.*

Prince. My conscience accuseth me. Most sovereign
lord, and well-beloved father, to answer first to the
last point, that is, whereas you conjecture that this
hand and this dagger shall be armed against your   *130*
life, no! Know, my beloved father, far be the
thoughts of your son—"son," said I? an unworthy
son for so good a father!—but far be the thoughts
of any such pretended mischief. And I most humbly
render it [*giving him the dagger*] to your Majesty's   *135*
hand. And live, my lord and sovereign, forever! And
with your dagger-arm show like vengeance upon the
body of—"that, your son," I was about to say, and
dare not; ah, woe is me therefore!—that, your wild°
slave. 'Tis not the crown that I come for, sweet   *140*
father, because I am unworthy. And those vile and
reprobate companions—I abandon and utterly abolish their company forever! Pardon, sweet father,
pardon, the least thing and most desire. And this
ruffianly cloak I here tear from my back, and sacri-   *145*
fice it to the devil, which is master of all mischief.
Pardon me, sweet father, pardon me! Good my
Lord of Exeter, speak for me. Pardon me, pardon,
good father! Not a word? Ah, he will not speak one
word! Ah, Harry, now thrice-unhappy Harry! But   *150*
what shall I do? I will go take me into some solitary

139 **wild** (the quarto has *wilde* = vilde = vile? cf. the King's previous speech)

place, and there lament my sinful life; and, when I
have done, I will lay me down and die.   *Exit.*

King. Call him again! Call my son again!

[*Enter the Prince.*]

155 *Prince.* And doth my father call me again? Now,
Harry, happy be the time that thy father calleth thee
again! [*He kneels.*]

King. Stand up, my son; and do not think thy father
but at the request of thee, my son, I will pardon thee.
160 And God bless thee, and make thee his servant.

Prince. Thanks, good my lord. And no doubt but this
day, even this day, I am born new again.
King. Come, my son and lords, take me by the hands.
                              Exeunt omnes.

[*Scene VII*]

Enter Derick [*shouting at Mistress Cobbler
within*].

Derick. Thou art a stinking whore, and a whoreson
stinking whore! Dost think I'll take it at thy hands?

Enter John Cobbler, running.

John. Derick, Derick, Derick, hearest 'a? Do, Derick,
never while thou livest use that! Why, what will my
5 neighbors say and thou go away so?

Derick. She's an arrant whore; and I'll have the law on
you, John.

John. Why, what hath she done?

Derick. Marry, mark thou, John. I will prove it, that
10 I will!

John. What wilt thou prove?

Derick. That she called me in to dinner—John, mark
the tale well, John—and when I was set, she brought
me a dish of roots and a piece of barrel-butter°
therein! And she is a very knave, and thou a drab   15
if thou take her part.

John. Hearest 'a, Derick? Is this the matter? Nay, if
it be no worse we will go home again, and all shall
be amended.

Derick. Oh, John, hearest 'a, John? Is all well?   20

John. Ay, all is well.

Derick. Then I'll go home before, and break all the
glass windows.   [*Exeunt Derick and John.*]

[*Scene VIII*]

Enter the King with his Lords.

King. Come, my lords. I see it boots me not to take
any physic, for all the physicians in the world cannot cure me; no, not one. But, good my lords, remember my last will and testament concerning my
son; for truly, my lords, I do not think but he will   5
prove as valiant and victorious a king as ever reigned
in England.

Both. Let heaven and earth be witness between us if we
accomplish not thy will to the uttermost.

King. I give you most unfeigned thanks, good my lords.   10
Draw the curtains, and depart my chamber awhile;
and cause some music to rock me asleep.
                    He sleepeth. Exeunt Lords.

Enter the Prince.

Prince. Ah, Harry, thrice-unhappy, that hath neglect
so long from visiting of thy sick father! I will go.

14 **barrel-butter** butter heavily salted (to preserve it)

15 Nay, but why do I not go to the chamber of my sick
father to comfort the melancholy soul of his body?
His soul, said I? Here is his body, indeed, but his
soul is whereas it needs no body. Now, thrice-
accursed Harry, that hath offended thy father so
20 much! And could not I crave pardon for all? O my
dying father! Cursed be the day wherein I was born,
and accursed be the hour wherein I was begotten!
But what shall I do? If weeping tears, which come
too late, may suffice the negligence neglected to
25 some,° I will weep day and night until the fountain
be dry with weeping.   Exit [taking the crown.]

Enter Lord[s] of Exeter and Oxford.

Exeter. Come easily, my lord, for waking of the King.

King. [*Waking*] Now, my lords?

Oxford. How doth your Grace feel yourself?

30 *King.* Somewhat better after my sleep. But, good my
lords, take off my crown. Remove my chair a little
back, and set me right.

Both. And please your Grace, the crown is taken away.

King. The crown taken away! Good my Lord of
35 Oxford, go see who hath done this deed.
                                    [*Exit Oxford.*]
No doubt 'tis some vile traitor that hath done it to
deprive my son. They that would do it now would
seek to scrape and scrawl for it after my death.

Enter Lord of Oxford with the Prince.

Oxford. Here, and please your Grace, is my lord the
40 young Prince with the crown.

King. Why, how now, my son? I had thought the last
time I had you in schooling I had given you a lesson
for all; and do you now begin again? Why, tell me,
my son, dost thou think the time so long that thou

24–25 **suffice . . . some** atone for my neglect toward some (but "too
some" may be an error for "too soon," intended to match "too late"
in line 24)

wouldst have it before the breath be out of my   45
mouth?

Prince. Most sovereign lord and well-beloved father, I
came into your chamber to comfort the melancholy
soul of your body; and finding you at that time past
all recovery, and dead, to my thinking—God is my   50
witness—and what should I do, but with weeping
tears lament the death of you, my father? And after
that, seeing the crown, I took it. And tell me, my
father, who might better take it than I, after your
death? But, seeing you live, I most humbly render   55
it into your Majesty's hands; and the happiest man
alive that my father live. And live, my lord and
father, forever!

King. Stand up, my son. Thine answer hath sounded
well in mine ears; for I must need confess that I was   60
in a very sound sleep, and altogether unmindful of
thy coming. But come near, my son, and let me put
thee in possession whilst I live, that none deprive
thee of it after my death.

Prince. Well may I take it at your Majesty's hands; but   65
it shall never touch my head so long as my father
lives.   *He taketh the crown.*

King. God give thee joy, my son. God bless thee, and
make thee his servant, and send thee a prosperous
reign! For God knows, my son, how hardly I came   70
by it, and how hardly I have maintained it.

Prince. Howsoever you came by it I know not; but now
I have it from you, and from you I will keep it. And
he that seeks to take the crown from my head, let
him look that his armor be thicker than mine, or I   75
will pierce him to the heart, were it harder than brass
or bullion.

King. Nobly spoken, and like a king! Now trust me, my
lords, I fear not but my son will be as warlike and
victorious a prince as ever reigned in England.   80

Both Lords. His former life shows no less.

King. Well, my lords, I know not whether it be for
sleep, or drawing near of drowsy summer of death,
but I am very much given to sleep. Therefore, good
85   my lords, and my son, draw the curtains; depart my
chamber; and cause some music to rock me asleep.
                    Exeunt omnes. The King dieth.

[*Scene IX*]

Enter the Thief.

Thief. Ah, God, I am now much like to a bird which
hath escaped out of the cage; for so soon as my Lord
Chief Justice heard that the old King was dead he
was glad to let me go for fear of my lord the young
5   Prince. But here come some of his companions. I
will see if I can get anything of them for old acquaintance.

Enter Knights, ranging.

Tom. Gog's wounds, the King is dead!

John Oldcastle. Dead! Then, Gog's blood, we shall be
10   all kings!

Ned. Gog's wounds, I shall be Lord Chief Justice of
England.

Tom. [*To the Thief*] Why, how! Are you broken out
of prison?

15   *Ned.* Gog's wounds, how the villain stinks!

John Oldcastle. Why, what will become of thee now?
Fie upon him, how the rascal stinks!

Thief. Marry, I will go and serve my master again.

Tom. Gog's blood, dost think that he will have any
20   such scabbed knave as thou art? What, man, he is
a king now.

Ned. [*Giving him money*] Hold thee. Here's a couple
of angels for thee. And get thee gone, for the King
will not be long before he come this way. And hereafter I will tell the King of thee.   *Exit Thief.*   25

John Oldcastle. Oh, how it did me good to see the King
when he was crowned! Methought his seat was like
the figure of heaven, and his person was like unto
a god.

Ned. But who would have thought that the King would   30
have changed his countenance so?

John Oldcastle. Did you not see with what grace he
sent his embassage into France to tell the French
King that Harry of England hath sent for the crown,
and Harry of England will have it?   35

Tom. But 'twas but a little to make the people believe
that he was sorry for his father's death.
                    The trumpet sounds.

Ned. Gog's wounds, the King comes! Let's all stand
aside.

Enter the King with the Archbishop [*of Canterbury*], *and the Lord of Oxford.*

John Oldcastle. How do you, my lord?   40

Ned. How now, Harry? Tut, my lord, put away these
dumps. You are a king, and all the realm is yours.
What, man, do you not remember the old sayings?
You know I must be Lord Chief Justice of England.
Trust me, my lord, methinks you are very much   45
changed. And 'tis but with a little sorrowing, to
make folks believe the death of your father grieves
you—and 'tis nothing so.

King. I prithee, Ned, mend thy manners, and be more
modester in thy terms; for my unfeigned grief is not   50
to be ruled by thy flattering and dissembling talk.
Thou sayst I am changed; so I am, indeed; and so
must thou be, and that quickly, or else I must cause
thee to be changed.

55 *John Oldcastle*. Gog's wounds, how like you this?
Zounds, 'tis not so sweet as music.

Tom. I trust we have not offended your Grace no way.

King. Ah, Tom, your former life grieves me, and makes
me to abandon and abolish your company forever.
60 And therefore, not upon pain of death to approach
my presence by ten miles space. Then, if I hear well
of you, it may be I will do somewhat for you; otherwise, look for no more favor at my hands than at
any other man's. And, therefore, begone! We have
65 other matters to talk on.   *Exeunt Knights*.

Now, my good Lord Archbishop of Canterbury,
what say you to our embassage into France?

Archbishop. Your right to the French crown of France
came by your great grandmother Isabel, wife to King
70 Edward the Third, and sister to Charles, the French
king. Now, if the French king deny it, as likely
enough he will, then must you take your sword in
hand and conquer the right. Let the usurped Frenchman know, although your predecessors have let it
75 pass, you will not; for your countrymen are willing
with purse and men to aid you. Then, my good lord,
as it hath been always known that Scotland hath been
in league with France by a sort of pensions which
yearly come from thence, I think it therefore best to
80 conquer Scotland; and then I think that you may go
more easily into France. And this is all that I can
say, my good lord.

King. I thank you, my good Lord Archbishop of Canterbury. What say you, my good Lord of Oxford?

85 *Oxford*. And please your Majesty, I agree to my Lord
Archbishop, saving in this: "He that will Scotland
win must first with France begin," according to the
old saying. Therefore, my good lord, I think it best
first to invade France; for in conquering Scotland
90 you conquer but one; and conquer France and conquer both.

Enter Lord of Exeter.

Exeter. And please your Majesty, my Lord Ambassador is come out of France.

King. Now trust me, my lord, he was the last man that
we talked of. I am glad that he is come to resolve   95
us of our answer. Commit him to our presence.

Enter Duke of York.

York. God save the life of my sovereign lord the King!

King. Now, my good lord the Duke of York, what news
from our brother, the French king?

York. And please your Majesty, I delivered him my   100
embassage, whereof I took some deliberation. But
for the answer, he hath sent my Lord Ambassador
of Bourges, the Duke of Burgundy, Monsieur le
Cole, with two hundred and fifty horsemen to bring
the embassage.   105

King. Commit my Lord Archbishop of Bourges into
our presence.

Enter Archbishop of Bourges.

King. Now, my Lord Archbishop of Bourges, we do
learn by our Lord Ambassador that you have our
message to do from our brother, the French king.   110
Here, my good lord, according to our accustomed
order, we give you free liberty and license to speak
with good audience.

Archbishop. God save the mighty King of England! My
lord and master, the most Christian king, Charles   115
the Seventh, the great and mighty King of France,
as a most noble and Christian king not minding to
shed innocent blood, is rather content to yield somewhat to your unreasonable demands—that, if fifty
thousand crowns a year, with his daughter, the said   120
Lady Katherine, in marriage, and some crowns
which he may well spare not hurting of his king-

dom, he is content to yield so far to your unreasonable desire.

125 *King.* Why, then, belike your lord and master thinks to
puff me up with fifty thousands crowns a year? No!
Tell thy lord and master that all the crowns in France
shall not serve me, except the crown and kingdom
itself! And perchance hereafter I will have his daugh-
130 ter.

Archbishop. If it please your Majesty, my Lord Prince
Dolphin greets you well with this present.
                    He delivereth a tun of tennis balls.

King. What, a gilded tun! I pray you, my Lord of
York, look what is in it.

135 *York.* And it please your Grace, here is a carpet, and a
tun of tennis balls.

King. A tun of tennis balls! I pray you, good my Lord
Archbishop, what might the meaning thereof be?

Archbishop. And it please you, my lord, a messenger,
140 you know, ought to keep close his message—and
specially an ambassador.

King. But I know that you may declare your message
to a king; the Law of Arms allows no less.

Archbishop. My lord, hearing of your wildness before
145 your father's death, sent you this, my good lord,
meaning that you are more fitter for a tennis court
than a field, and more fitter for a carpet than the
camp.

King. My Lord Prince Dolphin is very pleasant with
150 me! But tell him that instead of balls of leather we
will toss him balls of brass and iron—yea, such balls
as never were tossed in France. The proudest tennis
court shall rue it! Ay, and thou, Prince of Bourges,
shalt rue it! Therefore, get thee hence; and tell him
155 thy message quickly, lest I be there before thee.
Away, priest! Begone!

Archbishop. I beseech your Grace to deliver me your
safe conduct under your broad seal manual.°

King. Priest of Bourges, know that the hand and seal
of a king, and his word, is all one. And instead of my   160
hand and seal I will bring him my hand and sword.
And tell thy lord and master that I, Harry of England, said it; and I, Harry of England, will perform
it! My Lord of York, deliver him our safe conduct
under our broad seal manual.   165

      Exeunt Archbishop and the Duke of York.

Now, my lords, to arms, to arms! For I vow by
heaven and earth that the proudest Frenchman in
all France shall rue the time that ever these tennis
balls were sent into England. My lord, I will that
there be provided a great navy of ships with all speed   170
at Southampton, for there I mean to ship my men;
for I would be there before him, if it were possible.
Therefore come—but stay! I had almost forgot the
chiefest thing of all with chafing with this French
ambassador. Call in my Lord Chief Justice of Eng-   175
land.

    Enters Lord Chief Justice of England.

Exeter. Here is the King, my lord.

Justice. God preserve your Majesty!

King. Why, how now, my lord, what is the matter?

Justice. I would it were unknown to your Majesty.   180

King. Why, what ail you?

Justice. Your Majesty knoweth my grief well.

King. Oh, my lord, you remember you sent me to the
Fleet, did you not?

Justice. I trust your Grace have forgotten that.   185

King. Ay, truly, my lord; and for revengement I have
chosen you to be my Protector over my realm, until

158 **manual** inscribed by hand

it shall please God to give me speedy return out of
France.

190 *Justice.* And if it please your Majesty, I am far unworthy of so high dignity.

King. Tut, my lord, you are not unworthy, because I
think you worthy; for you that would not spare me,
I think, will not spare another. It must needs be so.
195 And therefore, come, let us be gone, and get our
men in a readiness.   *Exeunt omnes.*

[Scene X]

Enter a Captain, John Cobbler, and his Wife.

Captain. Come, come; there's no remedy. Thou must
needs serve the King.

John. Good master Captain, let me go. I am not able
to go so far.

5 *Wife.* I pray you, good master Captain, be good to my
husband.

Captain. Why, I am sure he is not too good to serve the
King.

John. Alas, no—but a great deal too bad; therefore, I
10 pray you, let me go.

Captain. No, no; thou shalt go.

John. Oh, sir, I have a great many shoes at home to
cobble.

Wife. I pray you, let him go home again.

15 *Captain.* Tush, I care not. Thou shalt go.

John. Oh, wife, and you had been a loving wife to me
this had not been; for I have said many times that I

would go away, and now I must go—against my will.
                                        He weepeth.

Enter Derick [with a pot-lid for a shield].

Derick. How now, ho! *Basillus manus,*° for an old cod-
   piece! Master Captain, shall we away? Zounds, how   *20*
   now, John? What, a-crying? What make you and
   my dame there? [*To the Wife*] I marvel whose head
   you will throw the stools at now we are gone.

Wife. I'll tell you! Come, ye cloghead! What do you
   with my pot-lid? Here you, will you have it rapped   *25*
   about your pate?   *She beateth him with her pot-lid.*

Derick. Oh good dame!   *Here he shakes her.*
   And I had my dagger here I would worry you all to
   pieces—that I would!

Wife. Would you so? I'll try that.   *She beateth him.* *30*

Derick. Master Captain, will you suffer her? Go to,
   dame! I will go back as far as I can; but, and you
   come again—I'll clap the law on your back, that's
   flat! I'll tell you, Master Captain, what you shall do:
   press her for a soldier! I warrant you she will do as   *35*
   much good as her husband and I too.

Enters the Thief.

   Zounds, who comes yonder?

Captain. How now, good fellow; dost thou want a master?

Thief. Ay, truly, sir.   *40*

Captain. Hold thee, then. I press thee for a soldier to
   serve the King in France.

Derick. How now, Gads! What, dost know us, thinkest?

Thief. Ay, I knew thee long ago.

Derick. Hear you, Master Captain.   *45*

19 **Basillus manus** (corruption of *besa las manos* = kiss the hands,
say good-bye)

Captain. What sayst thou?

Derick. I pray you, let me go home again.

Captain. Why, what wouldst thou do at home?

Derick. Marry, I have brought two shirts with me, and
50   I would carry one of them home again; for I am sure
he'll steal it from me, he is such a filching fellow.

Captain. I warrant thee he will not steal it from thee.
Come, let's away.

Derick. Come, Master Captain, let's away. Come, fol-
55   low me.

John. Come, wife, let's part lovingly.

Wife. Farewell, good husband.

Derick. Fie, what a kissing and crying is here! Zounds,
do you think he will never come again? Why, John,
60   come away! Dost think that we are so base-minded
to die among Frenchmen? Zounds, we know not
whether they will lay us in their church or no. Come,
Master Captain, let's away.

Captain. I cannot stay no longer; therefore, come away.
                              Exeunt omnes.

[Scene XI]

*Enter the [French] King, Prince Dolphin, and
Lord High Constable of France.*

King. Now, my Lord High Constable, what say you to
our embassage into England?

Constable. And it please your Majesty, I can say nothing until my lords ambassadors be come home. But
5   yet methinks your Grace hath done well to get your
men in so good a readiness for fear of the worst.

King. Ay, my lord, we have some in a readiness; but if
the King of England make against us we must have
thrice so many more.

Dolphin. Tut, my lord; although the King of England   *10*
be young and wild-headed, yet never think he will be
so unwise to make battle against the mighty King of
France.

King. Oh, my son, although the King of England be
young and wild-headed, yet never think but he is   *15*
ruled by his wise councillors.

Enter Archbishop of Bourges.

Archbishop. God save the life of my sovereign lord the
King!

King. Now, my good Lord Archbishop of Bourges,
what news from our brother, the English king?   *20*

Archbishop. And please your Majesty, he is so far from
your expectation that nothing will serve him but the
crown and kingdom itself. Besides, he bade me haste
quickly lest he be there before me. And, so far as I
hear, he hath kept promise; for they say he is already   *25*
landed at Kidocks in Normandy upon the River
Seine, and laid his siege to the garrison-town of Harfleur.

King. You have made great haste in the meantime, have
you not?   *30*

Dolphin. I pray you, my lord, how did the King of England take my presents?

Archbishop. Truly, my lord, in very ill part. For these
your balls of leather he will toss you balls of brass
and iron. Trust me, my lord, I was very afraid of him,   *35*
he is such a haughty and high-minded prince. He is
as fierce as a lion.

Constable. Tush, we will make him as tame as a lamb,
I warrant you.

Enters a Messenger.

Messenger. God save the mighty King of France!   *40*

King. Now, messenger, what news?

Messenger. And it please your Majesty, I come from
  your poor distressed town of Harfleur, which is so
  beset on every side, if your Majesty do not send pres-
45 ent aid the town will be yielded to the English king.

King. Come, my lords, come! Shall we stand still till
  our country be spoiled under our noses? My lords,
  let the Normans, Brabanters, Picards, and Danes be
  sent for with all speed. And you, my Lord High Con-
50 stable, I make General over all my whole army;
  Monsieur le Colle, Master of the Bows, Seigneur
  Devens, and all the rest, at your appointment.

Dolphin. I trust your Majesty will bestow some part of
  the battle on me. I hope not to present any otherwise
55 than well.

King. I tell thee, my son, although I should get the victory, and thou lose thy life, I should think myself
  quite conquered, and the Englishmen to have the victory.

60 *Dolphin.* Why, my lord and father, I would have the
  petty king of England to know that I dare encounter
  him in any ground of the world.

King. I know well, my son; but at this time I will have
  it thus. Therefore, come away.   *Exeunt omnes.*

[*Scene XII*]

Enters Henry the Fifth, with his Lords.

King. Come, my lords of England. No doubt this good
  luck of winning this town is a sign of an honorable
  victory to come! But, good my lord, go and speak
  to the captains with all speed, to number the host of
5 the Frenchmen, and by that means we may the better know how to appoint the battle.

York. And it please your Majesty, there are many of
  your men sick and diseased, and many of them die
  for want of victuals.

King. And why did you not tell me of it before? If we   *10*
    cannot have it for money we will have it by dint of
    sword; the Law of Arms allows no less.

Oxford. I beseech your Grace to grant me a boon.

King. What is that, my good lord?

Oxford. That your Grace would give me the vanguard   *15*
    in the battle.

King. Trust me, my Lord of Oxford, I cannot; for I
    have already given it to my uncle, the Duke of York.
    Yet I thank you for your good will.

> *A trumpet sounds.*

How now, what is that?   *20*

York. I think it be some herald of arms.

> *Enters a Herald.*

Herald. King of England, my Lord High Constable and
    others of the noblemen of France sends me to defy
    thee as open enemy to God, our country, and us;
    and hereupon they presently bid thee battle.   *25*

King. Herald, tell them that I defy them as open ene-
    mies to God, my country, and me, and as wrongful
    usurpers of my right. And whereas thou sayst they
    presently bid me battle, tell them, that I think they
    know how to please me. But, I pray thee, what place   *30*
    hath my lord Prince Dolphin here in battle?

Herald. And it please your Grace, my Lord and King,
    his father, will not let him come into the field.

King. Why, then, he doth me great injury. I thought
    that he and I should have played at tennis together;   *35*
    therefore I have brought tennis balls for him—but
    other manner of ones than he sent me. And, Herald,
    tell my Lord Prince Dolphin that I have inured my
    hands with other kind of weapons than tennis balls
    ere this time of day, and that he shall find it, ere it   *40*
    be long. And so, adieu, my friend. And tell my
    lord that I am ready when he will.   *Exit Herald.*

Come, my lords. I care not and I go to our captains;
and I'll see the number of the French army myself.
45   Strike up the drum!   *Exeunt omnes.*

[*Scene XIII*]

Enter French Soldiers.

First Soldier. Come away, Jack Drummer! Come away
all, and me will tell you what me will do. Me will tro
one chance on the dice who shall have the King of
England and his lords.

5   *Second Soldier.* Come away, Jack Drummer, and tro
your chance; and lay down your drum.

Enter Drummer.

Drummer. Oh, the brave apparel that the English-mans
hay broth° over! I will tell you what me ha done. Me
ha provided a hundreth trunks, and all to put the
10   fine 'parel of the English-mans in.

First Soldier. What do thou mean by "trunks"?

Second Soldier. A shest, man, a hundred shests.

First Soldier. Awee, awee, awee. Me will tell you what:
me ha put five shildren out of my house, and all too
15   little to put the fine apparel of the English-mans in.

Drummer. Oh, the brave, the brave apparel that we
shall have anon! But come, and you shall see what
me will tro at the king's drummer and fife. Ha, me
ha no good luck. Tro you.

20   *Third Soldier.* Faith, me will tro at the Earl of Northumberland, and my Lord o' Willoughby, with his
great horse, snorting, farting—oh brave horse!

First Soldier. Ha! By'r Lady, you ha reasonable good
luck. Now I will tro at the King himself. Ha! Me
25   have no good luck.

8 **hay broth** i.e., have brought

Enters a Captain.

Captain. How now, what make you here so far from
the camp?

Second Soldier. Shall me tell our captain what we have
done here?

Drummer. Awee, awee.   30
                    Exeunt Drummer and one Soldier.

Second Soldier. I will tell you what we have done. We
have been troing our chance on the dice; but none
can win the King.

Captain. I think so. Why, he is left behind for me! And
I have set three or four chair-makers a-work to make   35
a new disguised chair to set that womanly King of
England in, that all the people may laugh and scoff
at him.

Second Soldier. Oh brave captain!

Captain. I am glad, and yet with a kind of pity, to see   40
the poor King—why, who ever saw a more flourish-
ing army in France in one day than here is? Are not
here all the peers of France? Are not here the Normans, with their fiery handguns and flaunching° curtleaxes?° Are not here the barbarians, with their   45
bard° horses and launching spears? Are not here the
Picards, with their cross-bows and piercing darts?
The Henneys° with their cutting glaives° and sharp
carbuncles?° Are not here the lance-knights of Burgundy? And, on the other side, a sight of poor Eng-   50
lish scabs! Why, take an English-man out of his warm
bed and his stale drink but one month, and, alas,
what will become of him? But give the Frenchman a

---

44 **flaunching** (a word of uncertain origin and meaning, which is
perhaps here intended to mean "flaming," but has been confused
or conflated with the armorial and heraldic term, "flanch" = any
subdevice borne on an escutcheon)   44–45 **curtleaxes** cutlasses
46 **bard** barded, armed with metal plates   48 **Henneys** men of
Hainault   48 **glaives** broadswords   49 **carbuncles** eight-rayed blazon (escarboucle) on the French shields, which often had a spike
at its center

radish root, and he will live with it all the days of his
55   life.   *Exit.*

Second Soldier. Oh, the brave apparel that we shall
    have of the English-mans.   *Exit.*

[Scene XIV]

Enters the King of England and his Lords.

King. Come, my lords and fellows of arms. What com-
    pany is there of the Frenchmen?

Oxford. If it please your Majesty, our captains have
    numbered them, and, so near as they can judge, they
5   are about threescore thousand horsemen and forty
    thousand footmen.

King. They threescore thousand horsemen, and we but
    two thousand! They forty thousand footmen, and we
    twelve thousand! They are a hundred thousand, and
10   we forty thousand! Ten to one! My lords and loving
    countrymen, though we be few, and they many, fear
    not. Your quarrel is good, and God will defend you.
    Pluck up your hearts, for this day we shall either
    have a valiant victory, or a honorable death! Now,
15   my lords, I will that my uncle, the Duke of York,
    have the vanguard in the battle; the Earl of Derby,
    the Earl of Oxford, the Earl of Kent, the Earl of
    Nottingham, the Earl of Huntingdon I will have be-
    side the army, that they may come fresh upon them;
20   and I myself, with the Duke of Bedford, the Duke of
    Clarence, and the Duke of Gloucester will be in the
    midst of the battle. Furthermore, I will that my Lord
    of Willoughby and the Earl of Northumberland, with
    their troops of horsemen, be continually running like
25   wings on both sides of the army—my Lord of North-
    umberland on the left wing. Then I will that every
    archer provide him a stake of a tree, and sharp it at
    both ends; and, at the first encounter of the horse-

men, to pitch their stakes down into the ground before them, that they may gore themselves upon them;   *30*
and then, to recoil back, and shoot wholly altogether,
and so discomfit them.

Oxford. And it please your Majesty, I will take that in
charge, if your Grace be therewith content.

King. With all my heart, my good Lord of Oxford. And   *35*
go and provide quickly.

Oxford. I thank your Highness.   *Exit.*

King. Well, my lords, our battles are ordained, and the
French making of bonfires, and at their banquets.
But let them look, for I mean to set upon them.   *40*
　　　　　　　　　　　The trumpet sounds.
Soft, here comes some other French message.

Enters Herald.

Herald. King of England, my Lord High Constable and
other of my lords, considering the poor estate of thee
and thy poor countrymen, sends me to know what
thou wilt give for thy ransom. Perhaps thou mayst   *45*
agree better cheap° now than when thou art conquered.

King. Why then, belike, your High Constable sends to
know what I will give for my ransom? Now trust me,
Herald, not so much as a tun of tennis balls—no,   *50*
not so much as one poor tennis ball! Rather shall
my body lie dead in the field to feed crows than ever
England shall pay one penny ransom for my body.

Herald. A kingly resolution!

King. No, Herald; 'tis a kingly resolution and the reso-   *55*
lution of a king. Here, take this for thy pains.
　　　　　　　　　　　　　Exit Herald.

King. But stay, my lords; what time is it?

All. Prime, my lord.

46 **agree better cheap** make a better bargain

King. Then is it good time, no doubt, for all England
60   prayeth for us. What, my lords! Methinks you look
       cheerfully upon me. Why, then, with one voice, and
       like true English hearts, with me throw up your caps,
       and for England cry, "Saint George!" And God and
       Saint George help us!

                            Strike Drummer. Exeunt omnes.

                            [*Scene XV*]

*The Frenchmen cry within, "Saint Denis! Saint Denis!
Mount Joy! Saint Denis!"*

                            The battle.

              Enters King of England and his Lords.

King. Come, my lords, come! By this time our swords
       are almost drunk with French blood. But, my lords,
       which of you can tell me how many of our army be
       slain in the battle?

5   *Oxford.* And it please your Majesty, there are of the
       French army slain above ten thousand twenty-six
       hundred, whereof are princes and nobles bearing
       banners; besides, all the nobility of France are taken
       prisoners. Of your Majesty's army are slain none but
10   the good Duke of York, and not above five or six
       and twenty common soldiers.

King. For the good Duke of York, my uncle, I am
       heartily sorry, and greatly lament his misfortune.
       Yet the honorable victory which the Lord hath given
15   us doth make me much rejoice. But, stay! Here
       comes another French message.   *Sound trumpet.*

              Enters a Herald, and kneeleth.

Herald. God save the life of the most mighty conqueror,
       the honorable King of England!

King. Now, Herald, methinks the world is changed with

you now. What! I am sure it is a great disgrace for 20
a herald to kneel to the King of England! What is
thy message?

Herald. My lord and master, the conquered King of
France, sends thee long health, with hearty greeting.

King. Herald, his greetings are welcome; but I thank 25
God for my health. Well, Herald, say on.

Herald. He hath sent me to desire your Majesty to give
him leave to go into the field to view his poor countrymen, that they may all be honorably buried.

King. Why, Herald, doth thy lord and master send to 30
me to bury the dead? Let him bury them, a God's
name! But, I pray thee, Herald, where is my Lord
High Constable, and those that would have had my
ransom?

Herald. And it please your Majesty, he was slain in the 35
battle.

King. Why, you may see—you will make yourselves
sure before the victory be won. But, Herald, what
castle is this so near adjoining to our camp?

Herald. And it please your Majesty, 'tis called the 40
Castle of Agincourt.

King. Well then, my lords of England, for the more
honor of our Englishmen, I will that this be forever
called The Battle of Agincourt.

Herald. And it please your Majesty, I have a further 45
message to deliver to your Majesty.

King. What is that, Herald? Say on.

Herald. And it please your Majesty, my lord and master
craves to parley with your Majesty.

King. With a good will—so some of my nobles view the 50
place for fear of treachery and treason.

Herald. Your Grace needs not to doubt that.

King. Well, tell him, then, I will come.   *Exit Herald.*
Now, my lords, I will go into the field myself to view
55   my countrymen, and to have them honorably buried;
for the French king shall never surpass me in courtesy whiles I am Harry, King of England. Come on,
my lords.   *Exeunt omnes.*

[Scene XVI]

Enters John Cobbler and Robin Pewterer.

Robin. Now, John Cobbler, didst thou see how the King
    did behave himself?

John. But, Robin, didst thou see what a policy the King
    had? To see how the Frenchmen were killed with
5   the stakes of the trees!

Robin. Ay, John, there was a brave policy!

Enters an English Soldier, roaming.

Soldier. What are you, my masters?

Both. Why, we be Englishmen.

Soldier. Are you Englishmen? Then change your lan-
10   guage, for the King's tents are set afire, and all they
    that speak English will be killed.   [*Exit.*]

John. What shall we do, Robin? Faith, I'll shift, for I
    can speak broken French.

Robin. Faith, so can I. Let's hear how thou canst speak.

15 *John. Commodevales,*° *Monsieur?*

Robin. That's well. Come, let's be gone.   [*Exeunt.*]

15 **Commodevales** *Comment allez* [*-vous*]? How are you?

[Scene XVII]

Drum and trumpet sounds.

Enters Derick, roaming. After him a Frenchman,
and takes him prisoner.

Derick. Oh, good *Mounser!*°

Frenchman. Come, come, you *villeaco.*°

Derick. Oh, I will, sir, I will.

Frenchman. Come quickly, you peasant!

Derick. I will, sir. What shall I give you?   5

Frenchman. Marry, thou shalt give me one, two, tre,
four hundred crowns.

Derick. Nay, sir, I will give you more; I will give you
as many crowns as will lie on your sword.

Frenchman. Wilt thou give me as many crowns as will   10
lie on my sword?

Derick. Ay, marry, will I. Ay, but you must lay down
your sword, or else they will not lie on your sword.

Here the Frenchman lays down his sword, and the
Clown [Derick] takes it up, and hurls him down.

Derick. Thou villain! darest thou look up?

Frenchman. Oh, good *Monsieur, comparteve!*° Mon-   15
sieur, pardon me!

Derick. O you villain! Now you lie at my mercy. Dost
thou remember since thou lammedst me in thy short
ell?° O villain! Now I will strike off thy head.

Here, whiles he turns his back, the Frenchman runs his
ways.   20

Derick. What, is he gone? Mass, I am glad of it. For, if
he had stayed, I was afraid he would have stirred

---

1 **Mounser** *Monsieur*   2 **villeaco** *villanaccio* (?) = rustic   15 **comparteve** *compat[iss]ez vous* (?) = have pity   18-19 **lammedst . . .
ell** gave me a short measure

again, and then I should have been spilt. But I will
away to kill more Frenchmen.   [*Exit.*]

[*Scene XVIII*]

*Enters King of France, King of England, and
Attendants.*

King of England. Now, my good brother of France, my
   coming into this land was not to shed blood, but for
   the right of my country; which, if you can deny, I
   am content peaceably to leave my siege and to depart
5 out of your land.

King of France. What is it you demand, my loving
   brother of England?

King of England. My secretary hath it written. Read it.

Secretary. Item, that immediately Henry of England be
10   crowned King of France.

King of France. A very hard sentence, my good brother
   of England.

King of England. No more but right, my good brother
   of France!

15 *King of France.* Well, read on.

Secretary. Item, that after the death of the said Henry
   the crown remain to him and his heirs forever.

King of France. Why then, you do not only mean to
   dispossess me, but also my son!

20 *King of England.* Why, my good brother of France, you
   have had it long enough. And as for Prince Dolphin,
   it skills not though he sit beside the saddle. Thus I
   have set it down, and thus it shall be!

King of France. You are very peremptory, my good
25   brother of England.

King of England. And you as perverse, my good brother
   of France.

King of France. Why then, belike all that I have here is yours!

King of England. Ay, even as far as the kingdom of   30
France reaches.

King of France. Ay, for by this hot beginning we shall scarce bring it to a calm ending.

King of England. It is as you please. Here is my resolution.   35

King of France. Well, my brother of England, if you will give me a copy we will meet you again tomorrow.

King of England. With a good will, my good brother of France. Secretary, deliver him a copy.
         Exit King of France and all their Attendants.

King of England. My lords of England, go before, and   40
I will follow you.   *Exeunt Lords.*
Speaks to himself. Ah, Harry, thrice-unhappy Harry!
Hast thou now conquered the French king, and begins a fresh supply with his daughter? But with what
face canst thou seek to gain her love which hath   45
sought to win her father's crown? Her father's crown,
said I? No, it is mine own.

   Ay, but I love her, and must crave her—
   Nay, I love her, and will have her!

Enters Lady Katherine and her Ladies.

King of England. But here she comes. How now, fair   50
Lady Katherine of France, what news?

Katherine. And it please your Majesty, my father sent
me to know if you will debate any of these unreasonable demands which you require.

King of England. Now trust me, Kate, I commend thy   55
father's wit greatly in this; for none in the world
could sooner have made me debate it, if it were possible. But tell me, sweet Kate, canst thou tell how to
love?

60 *Katherine*. I cannot hate, my good lord; therefore, far
        unfit were it for me to love.

King of England. Tush, Kate! but tell me in plain terms,
        canst thou love the King of England? I cannot do as
        these countries do that spend half their time in woo-
65   ing. Tush, wench, I am none such. But, wilt thou go
        over to England?

Katherine. I would to God that I had your Majesty as
        fast in love as you have my father in wars! I would
        not vouchsafe so much as one look until you had
70   abated all these unreasonable demands.

King of England. Tush, Kate! I know thou wouldst not
        use me so hardly. But tell me, canst thou love the
        King of England?

Katherine. How should I love him that hath dealt so
75   hardly with my father?

King of England. But I'll deal as easily with thee as thy
        heart can imagine, or tongue can require. How sayst
        thou? What! will it be?

Katherine. If I were of my own direction I could give
80   you answer; but seeing I stand at my father's direc-
        tion, I must first know his will.

King of England. But shall I have thy good will in the
        mean season?

Katherine. Whereas I can put your Grace in no assur-
85   ance, I would be loath to put you in any despair.

King of England. Now, before God, it is a sweet wench!

She goes aside, and speaks as followeth.

Katherine. I may think myself the happiest in the world
        that is beloved of the mighty King of England!

King of England. Well, Kate, are you at host° with me?
90   Sweet Kate, tell thy father from me that none in the

89 **at host** in accord

world could sooner have persuaded me to it than
thou; and so tell thy father from me.

Katherine. God keep your Majesty in good health.
                                        Exit Katherine.

King of England. Farewell, sweet Kate. In faith, it is a
sweet wench! But if I knew I could not have her   95
father's good will, I would so rouse the towers over
his ears that I would make him be glad to bring her
me upon his hands and knees.   *Exit King.*

[*Scene XIX*]

Enters Derick with his girdle full of shoes.

Derick. How, now! Zounds, it did me good to see how
I did triumph over the Frenchmen!

*Enters John Cobbler, roving, with a pack
full of apparel.*

John. Whoop, Derick! How dost thou?

Derick. What, John! *Comedevales?* Alive yet?

John. I promise thee, Derick, I scaped hardly; for I was   5
within half a mile when one was killed!

Derick. Were you so?

John. Ay, trust me. I had like been slain.

Derick. But, once killed—why it—'tis nothing. I was
four or five times slain.   10

John. Four or five times slain. Why, how couldst thou
have been alive now?

Derick. O John, never say so! For I was called "the
bloody soldier" amongst them all.

John. Why, what didst thou?   15

Derick. Why, I will tell thee, John. Every day when I
went into the field I would take a straw and thrust

it into my nose and make my nose bleed; and then
I would go into the field. And when the captain saw
20   me, he would say, "Peace, a bloody soldier!" and
bid me stand aside. Whereof I was glad. But mark
the chance, John: I went and stood behind a tree—
but mark, then, John—I thought I had been safe;
but on a sudden there steps to me a lusty, tall
25   Frenchman; now he drew, and I drew; now I lay
here, and he lay there; now I set this leg before, and
turned this backward—and skipped quite over a
hedge; and he saw me no more there that day! And
was not this well done, John?

30 *John.* Mass, Derick, thou hast a witty head.

Derick. Ay, John, thou mayst see, if thou hadst taken
my counsel. But what hast thou there? I think thou
hast been robbing the Frenchmen.

John. In faith, Derick, I have gotten some reparel to
35   carry home to my wife.

Derick. And I have got some shoes; for I'll tell thee
what I did: when they were dead, I would go take
off all their shoes.

John. Ay, but Derick, how shall we get home?

40 *Derick.* Nay, zounds, and they take thee they will hang
thee. O, John, never do so! If it be thy fortune to be
hanged, be hanged in thy own language, whatsoever
thou dost!

John. Why, Derick, the wars is done; we may go home
45   now.

Derick. Ay, but you may not go before you ask the
King leave. But I know a way to go home and ask
the King no leave.

John. How is that, Derick?

50 *Derick.* Why, John, thou knowest the Duke of York's
funeral must be carried into England, dost thou not?

John. Ay, that I do.

Derick. Why, then, thou knowest we'll go with it.

John. Ay, but Derick, how shall we do for to meet
  them?   55

Derick. Zounds, if I make not shift to meet them, hang
  me! Sirrah, thou knowest that in every town there
  will be ringing, and there will be cakes and drink.
  Now I will go to the clerk and sexton, and keep
  a-talking and say, "Oh, this fellow rings well!" And   60
  thou shalt go and take a piece of cake. Then I'll ring,
  and thou shalt say, "Oh, this fellow keeps a good
  stint!" And then I will go drink to thee all the way.
  But I marvel what my dame will say when we come
  home, because we have not a French word to cast   65
  at a dog by the way.

John. Why, what shall we do, Derick?

Derick. Why, John, I'll go before and call my dame
  whore; and thou shalt come after and set fire on the
  house. We may do it, John, for I'll prove it—because   70
  we be soldiers.   *The trumpets sound.*

John. Derick, help me to carry my shoes and boots.
                    [*Exeunt Derick and John.*]

[Scene XX]

*Enters King of England, Lord of Oxford and
Exeter, then the King of France, Prince Dolphin,
and the Duke of Burgundy, [Princess Katherine]
and Attendants.*

King of England. Now, my good brother of France,
  I hope by this time you have deliberated of your
  answer.

King of France. Ay, my well-beloved brother of England. We have viewed it over with our learned coun-   5
  cil, but cannot find that you should be crowned
  King of France.

King of England. What, not King of France? Then
nothing. I must be King. But, my loving brother of
France, I can hardly forget the late injuries offered
me when I came last to parley; the Frenchmen had
better 'a raked the bowels out of their fathers' carcasses than to have fired my tents. And if I knew thy
son Prince Dolphin, for one, I would so rouse him
as he was never so roused!

King of France. I dare swear for my son's innocency in
this matter. But if this please you, that immediately
you be proclaimed and crowned Heir and Regent
of France, not King, because I myself was once
crowned king——

King of England. Heir and Regent of France? That is
well. But that is not all that I must have.

King of France. The rest my secretary hath in writing.

Secretary. [*Reads*] Item, that Henry, King of England,
be crowned Heir and Regent of France during the
life of King Charles; and after his death the crown
with all rights to remain to King Henry of England,
and to his heirs forever.

King of England. Well, my good brother of France,
there is one thing I must needs desire.

King of France. What is that, my good brother of
England?

King of England. That all your nobles must be sworn
to be true to me.

King of France. Whereas they have not stuck with
greater matters, I know they will not stick with such
a trifle. Begin you, my Lord Duke of Burgundy.

King of England. Come, my Lord of Burgundy; take
your oath upon my sword.

Burgundy. I, Philip, Duke of Burgundy, swear to
Henry, King of England, to be true to him, and to
become his liege man; and that if I, Philip, hear of

any foreign power coming to invade the said Henry,
or his heirs, then I, the said Philip, to send him word,
and aid him with all the power I can make. And
thereunto I take my oath.   *He kisseth the sword.*   *45*

King of England. Come, Prince Dolphin, you must
swear, too.   *He kisseth the sword.*
Well, my brother of France, there is one thing more
I must needs require of you.   *50*

King of France. Wherein is it that we may satisfy your
Majesty?

King of England. A trifle, my good brother of France;
I mean to make your daughter Queen of England, if
she be willing, and you therewith content. How sayst   *55*
thou, Kate? Canst thou love the King of England?

Katherine. How should I love thee, which is my father's
enemy?

King of England. Tut, stand not upon these points. 'Tis
you must make us friends. I know, Kate, thou art   *60*
not a little proud that I love thee. What, wench, the
King of England?

King of France. Daughter, let nothing stand betwixt
the King of England and thee. Agree to it.

Katherine. [*Aside*] I had best whilst he is willing, lest   *65*
when I would he will not—I rest at your Majesty's
command.

King of England. Welcome, sweet Kate! But, my
brother of France, what say you to it?

King of France. With all my heart I like it. But when   *70*
shall be your wedding day?

King of England. The first Sunday of the next month,
God willing.   *Sound trumpets. Exeunt omnes.*

FINIS

Commentaries

SAMUEL JOHNSON

from *The Plays of William Shakespeare*

None of Shakespeare's plays are more read than the *First and Second Parts of Henry the Fourth*. Perhaps no author has ever in two plays afforded so much delight. The great events are interesting, for the fate of kingdoms depends upon them; the slighter occurrences are diverting and, except one or two, sufficiently probable; the incidents are multiplied with wonderful fertility of invention, and the characters diversified with the utmost nicety of discernment and the profoundest skill in the nature of man.

The Prince, who is the hero both of the comic and tragic part, is a young man of great abilities and violent passions, whose sentiments are right, though his actions are wrong; whose virtues are obscured by negligence, and whose understanding is dissipated by levity. In his idle hours he is rather loose than wicked; and when the occasion forces out his latent qualities, he is great without effort and brave without tumult. The trifler is roused into a hero, and the hero again reposes in the trifler. This character is great, original, and just.

Percy is a rugged soldier, choleric, and quarrelsome, and has only the soldier's virtues, generosity and courage.

But Falstaff, unimitated, unimitable Falstaff, how shall I describe thee? Thou compound of sense and vice; of sense which may be admired but not esteemed, of vice which may be despised but hardly detested. Falstaff is a character loaded with faults, and with those faults which naturally produce contempt. He is a thief and a glutton, a coward and a boaster, always ready to cheat the weak and prey upon the poor; to terrify the timorous and insult the defenseless. At once obsequious and malignant, he satirizes in their absence those whom he lives by flattering. He is familiar with the Prince only as an agent of vice, but of this familiarity he is so proud as not only to be supercilious and haughty with common men but to think his interest of importance to the Duke of Lancaster. Yet the man thus corrupt, thus despicable, makes himself necessary to the Prince that despises him, by the most pleasing of all qualities, perpetual gaiety, by an unfailing power of exciting laughter, which is the more freely indulged as his wit is not of the splendid or ambitious kind but consists in easy escapes and sallies of levity, which make sport but raise no envy. It must be observed that he is stained with no enormous or sanguinary crimes, so that his licentiousness is not so offensive but that it may be borne for his mirth.

The moral to be drawn from this representation is that no man is more dangerous than he that, with a will to corrupt, hath the power to please; and that neither wit nor honesty ought to think themselves safe with such a companion when they see Henry seduced by Falstaff.   [1765]

SAMUEL TAYLOR COLERIDGE

from *H. C. Robinson's Memoranda*

Falstaff Coleridge also considered as an instance of the
predominance of intellectual power. He is content to be
thought both a liar and a coward in order to obtain influence over the minds of his associates. His aggravated lies
about the robbery are conscious and purposed, not inad-
vertent untruths. On my observing that this account seemed
to justify [George Frederick] Cooke's representation, according to which a foreigner imperfectly understanding the
character would fancy Falstaff to be the designing knave
who actually does outwit the Prince, Coleridge answered
that in his *own* estimation Falstaff is the superior who cannot easily be convinced that the Prince has escaped him;
but that as in other instances Shakespeare has shown us
the defeat of mere intellect by a noble feeling, the Prince
being the superior moral character who rises above his in-
sidious companion.

from *Seven Lectures*

Falstaff was no coward, but pretended to be one merely
for the sake of trying experiments on the credulity of man-
kind: he was a liar with the same object, and not because

Both selections by Coleridge come from *Shakespearean Criticism* by
Samuel Taylor Coleridge, 2nd ed., ed. Thomas Middleton Raysor. 2 vols.
New York: E. P. Dutton and Company, Inc., 1960; London: J. M. Dent
& Sons, Ltd., 1961. The first passage is Robinson's memorandum of one
of Coleridge's conversations of 1810; the second passage is J. P. Collier's
memorandum of a conversation of 1811. In the first, abbreviations have
been expanded.

he loved falsehood for itself. He was a man of such pre-
eminent abilities, as to give him a profound contempt for
all those by whom he was usually surrounded, and to lead
to a determination on his part, in spite of their fancied
superiority, to make them his tools and dupes. He knew,
however low he descended, that his own talents would raise
him and extricate him from any difficulty. While he was
thought to be the greatest rogue, thief, and liar, he still had
that about him which could render him not only respectable, but absolutely necessary to his companions. It was
in characters of complete moral depravity, but of first-rate
wit and talents, that Shakespeare delighted; and Coleridge
instanced Richard the Third, Falstaff, and Iago.

JOHN DOVER WILSON

from *The Fortunes of Falstaff*

Henry IV, a play much neglected by both actors and critics, offers to our view the broadest, the most varied, and in some ways the richest champaign in Shakespeare's extensive empire. Much of this, and not the least alluring stretches, must be ignored in what follows, or barely glanced at; Glendower's domain[1] in Part One, for example. Many characters can hardly be touched; I shall have little to say about Ancient Pistol or Mistress Quickly, Hotspur or Prince John. The more subtle aspects of the play, its poetry, its dramatic light and shade, what may be called its atmospheric effects; all matters of first importance to anyone concerned in tracing the development of Shakespeare's art in the crucial and largely unexplored period that divides *Richard II* from *Hamlet:* these also lie beyond my present scope. The task I have set before me is at once narrow and simple. I am attempting to discover what Professor Charlton has called "the deliberate plan of Shakespeare's play" and, if such a plan existed, how far he succeeded in carrying it into execution.

My title, *The Fortunes of Falstaff,* will suggest the method to be followed. I propose to look for the outlines of Shakespeare's scheme by tracing the career of the knight of Eastcheap. This does not mean that I think him of

---

[1] I refer to III.i of Part One, which was headed "The Archbishop of Bangor's House in Wales" by Theobald and later editors, though without any warrant in Shakespeare. Glendower behaves like a host throughout the scene, which is clearly a family party.

From *The Fortunes of Falstaff* by John Dover Wilson. London: Cambridge University Press, 1943, pp. 15–35; New York: The Macmillan Company, 1944. Reprinted by permission of Cambridge University Press.

greater structural consequence than Prince Hal. On the contrary, Falstaff's career is dependent upon Hal's favor, and Hal's favor is determined by that young man's attitude towards his responsibilities as heir to the throne of England. Yet if the Prince's choice spans the play like a great arch, it is Falstaff and his affairs that cover most of the ground.

The title I have selected has, moreover, the convenience of comprising the fortunes, or misfortunes, of the fat rogue outside the pages of Shakespeare. There are, for instance, his prenatal adventures. He tells us that he "was born about three of the clock in the afternoon, with a white head and something of a round belly"; but all the world now knows that he was walking the boards in an earlier, pre-Shakespearian, incarnation, as a comic travesty of Sir John Oldcastle, the famous Lollard leader, who was historically a friend and fellow-soldier of Prince Hal in the reign of Henry IV, but was burnt as a heretic by the same prince when he became King Henry V. He still retained the name Oldcastle, as is also well known, in the original version of Shakespeare's play; until the company discovered, or were forcibly reminded, that the wife of the proto-Protestant martyr they were guying on the public stage was the revered ancestress of the Cobhams, powerful lords at Elizabeth's court. Worse still, one of these lords was not only of strongly Protestant bent, but also, as Lord Chamberlain, actually Shakespeare's official controller. Hasty changes in the prompt-book became necessary. How far they extended beyond a mere alteration of names can never be determined, though it seems possible that references to some of Oldcastle's historical or legendary characteristics would require modification. It is even more likely (as Alfred Ainger was, I believe, the first to point out)[2] that traces of Lollardry may still be detected in Falstaff's frequent resort to scriptural phraseology and in his affectation of an uneasy conscience. Of this I shall have something to say later.

First of all, however, I wish to deal with Falstaff's ancestral fortunes of a different kind. As he shares these to a large extent with Prince Hal, a consideration of them

[2] V. Alfred Ainger, *Lectures and Essays*, 1905, vol. i, pp. 140–55.

should prove helpful in bringing out the main lines of the plot which it is our object to discover.

RIOT AND THE PRODIGAL PRINCE

Falstaff may be the most conspicuous, he is certainly the most fascinating, character in *Henry IV*, but all critics are agreed, I believe, that the technical center of the play is not the fat knight but the lean prince. Hal links the low life with the high life, the scenes at Eastcheap with those at Westminster, the tavern with the battlefield; his doings provide most of the material for both parts, and with him too lies the future, since he is to become Henry V, the ideal king, in the play that bears his name; finally, the mainspring of the dramatic action is the choice I have already spoken of, the choice he is called upon to make between vanity and government, taking the latter in its accepted Tudor meaning, which includes chivalry or prowess in the field, the theme of Part One, and justice, which is the theme of Part Two. Shakespeare, moreover, breathes life into these abstractions by embodying them, or aspects of them, in prominent characters, who stand, as it were, about the Prince, like attendant spirits; Falstaff typifying Vanity in every sense of the word, Hotspur Chivalry, of the old anarchic kind, and the Lord Chief Justice the Rule of Law or the new ideal of service to the state.[3]

Thus considered, Shakespeare's *Henry IV* is a Tudor version of a time-honored theme, already familiar for decades, if not centuries, upon the English stage. Before its final secularization in the first half of the sixteenth century, our drama was concerned with one topic, and one only: human salvation. It was a topic that could be represented in either of two ways: (i) historically, by means of miracle plays, which in the Corpus Christi cycles unrolled

[3] In what follows I develop a hint in Sir Arthur Quiller-Couch's *Shakespeare's Workmanship*, 1918, p. 148: "The whole of the business [in *Henry IV*] is built on the old Morality structure, imported through the Interlude. Why, it might almost be labeled, after the style of a Morality title, *Contentio inter Virtutem et Vitium de anima Principis.*"

before spectators' eyes the whole scheme of salvation from the Creation to the Last Judgment; or (ii) allegorically, by means of morality plays, which exhibited the process of salvation in the individual soul on its road between birth and death, beset with the snares of the World or the wiles of the Evil One. In both kinds the forces of iniquity were allowed full play upon the stage, including a good deal of horseplay, provided they were brought to nought, or safely locked up in Hell, at the end. Salvation remains the supreme interest, however many capers the Devil and his Vice may cut on Everyman's way thither, and always the powers of darkness are withstood, and finally overcome, by the agents of light. But as time went on the religious drama tended to grow longer and more elaborate, after the encyclopedic fashion of the Middle Ages, and such development invited its inevitable reaction. With the advent of humanism and the early Tudor court, morality plays became tedious and gave place to lighter and much shorter moral interludes dealing, not with human life as a whole, but with youth and its besetting sins.

An early specimen, entitled *Youth*[4] and composed about 1520, may be taken as typical of the rest. The plot, if plot it can be called, is simplicity itself. The little play opens with a dialogue between Youth and Charity. The young man, heir to his father's land, gives insolent expression to his self-confidence, lustihood, and contempt for spiritual things. Whereupon Charity leaves him, and he is joined by Riot,[5] that is to say wantonness, who presently introduces him to Pride and Lechery. The dialogue then becomes boisterous, and continues in that vein for some time, much no doubt to the enjoyment of the audience. Yet, in the end, Charity reappears with Humility; Youth repents; and the interlude terminates in the most seemly fashion imaginable.

[4] *The Enterlude of Youth*, ed. by W. Bang and R. B. McKerrow, Louvain, 1905.
[5] Riot="wanton, loose, or wasteful living; debauchery, dissipation, extravagance" (*O.E.D.*). Cf. the Prodigal Son, who "wasted his substance with riotous living" (Luke xv: 13).

No one, I think, reading this lively playlet, no one certainly who has seen it performed, as I have seen it at the Malvern Festival, can have missed the resemblance between Riot and Falstaff. The words he utters, as he bounces on to the stage at his first entry, give us the very note of Falstaff's gaiety:

> Huffa! Huffa! Who calleth after me?
> I am Riot full of jollity.
> My heart is as light as the wind,
> And all on riot is my mind,
> Wheresoever I go.

And the parallel is even more striking in other respects. Riot, like Falstaff, escapes from tight corners with a quick dexterity; like Falstaff, commits robbery on the highway; like Falstaff, jests immediately afterwards with his young friend on the subject of hanging; and like Falstaff, invites him to spend the stolen money at a tavern, where, he promises, "We will drink diuers wine" and "Thou shalt haue a wench to kysse Whansoeuer thou wilte"; allurements which prefigure the Boar's Head and Mistress Doll Tearsheet.

But Youth at the door of opportunity, with Age or Experience, Charity or Good Counsel, offering him the yoke of responsibility, while the World, the Flesh, and the Devil beckon him to follow them on the primrose way to the everlasting bonfire, is older than even the medieval religious play. It is a theme to which every generation gives fresh form, while retaining its eternal substance. Young men are the heroes of the Plautine and Terentian comedy which delighted the Roman world; and these young men, generally under the direction of a clever slave or parasite, disport themselves, and often hoodwink their old fathers, for most of the play, until they too settle down in the end. The same theme appears in a very different story, the parable of the Prodigal Son. And the similarity of the two struck humanist teachers of the early sixteenth century with such force that, finding Terence insufficiently edifying for their pupils to act, they developed a "Christian

Terence" by turning the parable into Latin plays, of which many examples by different authors have come down to us.[6] In these plot and structure are much the same. The opening scene shows us Acolastus, the prodigal, demanding his portion, receiving good counsel from his father, and going off into a far country. Then follow three or four acts of entertainment almost purely Terentian in atmosphere, in which he wastes his substance in riotous living and falls at length to feeding with the pigs. Finally, in the last act he returns home, penniless and repentant, to receive his pardon. This ingenious blend of classical comedy and humanistic morality preserves, it will be noted, the traditional ratio between edification and amusement, and distributes them in the traditional manner. So long as the serious note is duly emphasized at the beginning and end of the play, almost any quantity of fun, often of the most unseemly nature, was allowed and expected during the intervening scenes.

All this, and much more of a like character, gave the pattern for Shakespeare's *Henry IV*. Hal associates Falstaff in turn with the Devil of the miracle play, the Vice of the morality, and the Riot of the interlude, when he calls him "that villainous abominable misleader of Youth, that old white-bearded Satan,"[7] "that reverend Vice, that grey Iniquity, that father Ruffian, that Vanity in years,"[8] and "the tutor and the feeder of my riots."[9] "Riot," again, is the word that comes most readily to King Henry's lips when speaking of his prodigal son's misconduct.[10] And, as heir to the Vice, Falstaff inherits by reversion the functions and attributes of the Lord of Misrule, the Fool, the Buffoon, and the Jester, antic figures the origins of which are lost in

---

[6] V. C. H. Herford, *The Literary Relations between England and Germany in the Sixteenth Century*, 1886, pp. 84–95.

[7] Part One, II.iv.462; cf. line 446: "Thou art violently carried away from grace, there is a devil haunts thee in the likeness of an old fat man."

[8] *Ibid.* II.iv.452.

[9] Part Two, V.v.63.

[10] Cf. Part One, I.i.84: "Riot and dishonor stain the brow / Of my young Harry"; Part Two, IV.iv.62: "His headstrong riot hath no curb," IV.v.135: "When that my care could not withhold thy riots, / What wilt thou do when riot is thy care?"

the dark backward and abysm of folk-custom.[11] We shall find that Falstaff possesses a strain, and more than a strain, of the classical *miles gloriosus* as well. In short, the Falstaff-Hal plot embodies a composite myth which had been centuries a-making, and was for the Elizabethans full of meaning that has largely disappeared since then: which is one reason why we have come so seriously to misunderstand the play.

Nor was Shakespeare the first to see Hal as the prodigal. The legend of Harry of Monmouth began to grow soon after his death in 1422; and practically all the chroniclers, even those writing in the fifteenth century, agree on his wildness in youth and on the sudden change that came upon him at his accession to the throne. The essence of Shakespeare's plot is, indeed, already to be found in the following passage about King Henry V taken from Fabyan's *Chronicle* of 1516:

> This man, before the death of his fader, applyed him unto all vyce and insolency, and drewe unto hym all ryottours and wylde disposed persones; but after he was admytted to the rule of the lande, anone and suddenly he became a newe man, and tourned al that rage into sobernesse and wyse sadnesse, and the vyce into constant vertue. And for he wolde contynewe the vertue, and not to be reduced thereunto by the familiarytie of his olde nyse company, he therefore, after rewards to them gyuen, charged theym upon payne of theyr lyues, that none of theym were so hardy to come within x. myle of such place as he were lodgyd, after a day by him assigned.[12]

There appears to be no historical basis for any of this,

---

[11] In particular, the exact significance of the Vice is exasperatingly obscure. Cf. the discussion by Sir E. K. Chambers (*Medieval Stage*, vol. ii, pp. 203–5), who concludes "that whatever the name may mean . . . the character of the vice is derived from that of the domestic fool or jester." I hazard the suggestion that it was originally the title or name of the Fool who attended upon the Lord of Misrule; *v.* Feuillerat, *Revels of the time of Edward VI*, p. 73: "One vyces dagger & a ladle with a bable pendante . . . deliuerid to the Lorde of Mysrules foole."

[12] Fabyan's *Chronicle*, 1516, p. 577.

and Kingsford has plausibly suggested that its origin may be "contemporary scandal which attached to Henry through his youthful association with the unpopular Lollard leader," Sir John Oldcastle. "It is noteworthy," he points out, "that Henry's political opponents were Oldcastle's religious persecutors; and also that those writers who charge Henry with wildness as Prince find his peculiar merit as King in the maintaining of Holy Church and destroying of heretics. A supposed change in his attitude on questions of religion may possibly furnish a partial solution for his alleged 'change suddenly into a new man.' "[13] The theory is the more attractive that it would account not only for Hal's conversion but also for Oldcastle's degradation from a Protestant martyr and distinguished soldier to what Ainger calls "a broken-down Lollard, a fat old sensualist, retaining just sufficient recollection of the studies of his more serious days to be able to point his jokes with them."

Yet when all is said, the main truth seems to be that the fifteenth and early sixteenth centuries, the age of allegory in poetry and morality in drama, needed a Prodigal Prince, whose miraculous conversion might be held up as an example by those concerned (as what contemporary political writer was not?) with the education of young noblemen and princes. And could any more alluring fruits of repentance be offered such pupils than the prowess and statesmanship of Henry V, the hero of Agincourt, the mirror of English kingship for a hundred years? In his miracle play, *Richard II,* Shakespeare had celebrated the traditional royal martyr;[14] in his morality play, *Henry IV,* he does the like with the traditional royal prodigal.

He made the myth his own, much as musicians adopt and absorb a folk-tune as the theme for a symphony. He glorified it, elaborated it, translated it into what were for the Elizabethans modern terms, and exalted it into a heaven of delirious fun and frolic; yet never, for a moment, did he twist it from its original purpose, which was serious, moral,

[13] C. L. Kingsford, *The First English Life of King Henry the Fifth,* 1911, pp. xlii, xliii.

[14] *V.* pp. xvi-xix, lviii-lix of my Introduction to *Richard II,* 1939 ("The New Shakespeare").

didactic. Shakespeare plays no tricks with his public. He did not, like Euripides, dramatize the stories of his race and religion in order to subvert the traditional ideals those stories were first framed to set forth. Prince Hal is the prodigal, and his repentance is not only to be taken seriously, it is to be admired and commended. Moreover, the story of the prodigal, secularized and modernized as it might be, ran the same course as ever and contained the same three principal characters: the tempter, the younker, and the father with property to bequeath and counsel to give. It followed also the fashion set by miracle, morality and the Christian Terence by devoting much attention to the doings of the first-named. Shakespeare's audience enjoyed the fascination of Prince Hal's "white-bearded Satan" for two whole plays, as perhaps no character on the world's stage had ever been enjoyed before. But they knew, from the beginning, that the reign of this marvelous Lord of Misrule must have an end, that Falstaff must be rejected by the Prodigal Prince when the time for reformation came. And they no more thought of questioning or disapproving of that finale than their ancestors would have thought of protesting against the Vice being carried off to Hell at the end of the interlude.

The main theme, therefore, of Shakespeare's morality play is the growing-up of a madcap prince into the ideal king, who was Henry V; and the play was made primarily—already made by some dramatist before Shakespeare took it over—in order to exhibit his conversion and to reveal his character unfolding towards that end, as he finds himself faced more and more directly by his responsibilities. It is that which determines its very shape. Even the "fearful symmetry" of Falstaff's own person was welded upon the anvil of that purpose. It is probably because the historical Harry of Monmouth "exceeded the meane stature of men," as his earliest chronicler tells us; "his necke . . . longe, his body slender and leane, his boanes smale,"[15]—because in Falstaff's words he actually was a starveling, an eel-skin, a tailor's yard, and all the rest of it—that the idea of Falstaff himself as "a huge hill of flesh" first came to

15 Kingsford, *op. cit.* p. 16.

Shakespeare.[16] It was certainly, at any rate in part, in order to explain and palliate the Prince's love of rioting and wantonness that he set out to make Falstaff as enchanting as he could.[17] And he succeeded so well that the young man now lies under the stigma, not of having yielded to the tempter, but of disentangling himself, in the end, from his toils. After all, Falstaff *is* "a devil . . . in the likeness of an old fat man," and the Devil has generally been supposed to exercise limitless attraction in his dealings with the sons of men. A very different kind of poet, who imagined a very different kind of Satan, has been equally and similarly mis-understood by modern critics, who no longer believing in the Prince of Darkness have ceased to understand him. For, as Professor R. W. Chambers reminded us in his last pub-lic utterance,[18] when Blake declared that Milton was "of the Devil's party without knowing it," he overlooked the fact, and his many successors have likewise overlooked the fact, that, if the fight in Heaven, the struggle in Eden, the defeat of Adam and Eve, and the victory of the Second Adam in *Paradise Regained,* are to appear in their true proportions, we must be made to realize how immeasurable, how indomitable, is the spirit of the Great Enemy. It may also be noted that Milton's Son of God has in modern times been charged with priggishness no less freely than Shakespeare's son of Bolingbroke.

[16] Ainger tries to persuade himself that there was a tradition associating the Lollard, Oldcastle, with extreme fatness; but his editor, Beeching, is obliged to admit in a footnote that he is not aware of any references to this fatness before Shakespeare; *v.* Ainger, *op. cit.* pp. 126–30.

[17] Cf. H. N. Hudson, *Shakespeare: his Life, Art and Characters* (ed. 1888), vol. ii, p. 83: "It must be no ordinary companionship that yields entertainment to such a spirit [as Prince Hal's] even in his loosest mo-ments. Whatever bad or questionable elements may mingle with his mirth, it must have some fresh and rich ingredients, some sparkling and generous flavor, to make him relish it. Anything like vulgar rowdyism cannot fail of disgusting him. His ears were never organized to that sort of music. Here then we have a sort of dramatic necessity for the character of Fal-staff. To answer the purpose it was imperative that he should be just such a marvelous congregation of charms and vices as he is." See also A. H. Tolman, *Falstaff and other Shakespearian Topics,* 1925, and W. W. Lawrence, *Shakespeare's Problem Comedies,* 1931, p. 64 (an interesting contrast between Hal and Falstaff, Bertram and Parolles).

[18] *Poets and their Critics: Langland and Milton* (British Academy Warton Lecture), 1941, pp. 29–30.

Shakespeare, I say, translated his myth into a language and endued it with an atmosphere that his contemporaries would best appreciate. First, Hal is not only youth or the prodigal, he is the young prodigal *prince,* the youthful heir to the throne. The translation, then, already made by the chroniclers, if Kingsford be right, from sectarian terms into those more broadly religious or moral, now takes us out of the theological into the political sphere. This is seen most clearly in the discussion of the young king's remarkable conversion by the two bishops at the beginning of *Henry V.* King Henry, as Bradley notes, "is much more obviously religious than most of Shakespeare's heroes,"[19] so that one would expect the bishops to interpret his change of life as a religious conversion. Yet they say nothing about religion except that he is "a true lover of the holy church" and can "reason in divinity"; the rest of their talk, some seventy lines, is concerned with learning and statecraft. In fact, the conversation of these worldly prelates demonstrates that the conversion is not the old repentance for sin and amendment of life, which is the burden, as we have seen, of Fabyan and other chroniclers, but a repentance of the renaissance type, which transforms an idle and wayward prince into an excellent soldier and governor. Even King Henry IV, at the bitterest moments of the scenes with his son, never taxes him with sin, and his only use of the word refers to sins that would multiply in the country, when

> the fifth Harry from curbed licence plucks
> The muzzle of restraint.[20]

If Hal had sinned, it was not against God, but against chivalry, against justice, against his father, against the interests of the Crown, which was the keystone of England's political and social stability. Instead of educating himself for the burden of kingship, he had been frittering away his time, and making himself cheap, with low companions

> that daff the world aside
> And bid it pass.

19 *Oxford Lectures,* p. 256.
20 Part Two, IV. v. 131.

In a word, a word that Shakespeare applies no less than six times to his conduct, he is guilty of vanity. And vanity, though not in the theological category of the seven deadly sins, was a cardinal iniquity in a young prince or nobleman of the sixteenth and seventeenth centuries; almost as heinous, in fact, as idleness in an apprentice.

I am not suggesting that this represents Shakespeare's own view. Of Shakespeare's views upon the problems of conduct, whether in prince or commoner, we are in general ignorant, though he seems to hint in both *Henry IV* and *Henry V* that the Prince of Wales learnt some lessons at least from Falstaff and his crew, Francis and his fellow-drawers, which stood him in good stead when he came to rule the country and command troops in the field. But it is the view that his father and his own conscience take of his mistreadings; and, as the spectators would take it as well, we must regard it as the thesis to which Shakespeare addressed himself.

When, however, he took audiences by storm in 1597 and 1598 with his double *Henry IV* he gave them something much more than a couple of semi-mythical figures from the early fifteenth century, brought up to date politically. He presented persons and situations at once fresh and actual. Both Hal and Falstaff are denizens of Elizabethan London. Hal thinks, acts, comports himself as an heir to the Queen might have done, had she delighted her people by taking a consort and giving them a Prince of Wales; while Falstaff symbolizes, on the one hand, all the feasting and good cheer for which Eastcheap stood, and reflects, on the other, the shifts, subterfuges, and shady tricks that decayed gentlemen and soldiers were put to if they wished to keep afloat and gratify their appetites in the London underworld of the late sixteenth century. It is the former aspects of the old scoundrel that probably gave most pleasure to those who first saw him on the stage; and, as they are also those that we moderns are most likely to miss, I make no apology for devoting most of the rest of this chapter to an exposition of them.

SWEET BEEF

Riot invites Youth, it will be remembered, to drink wine at a tavern, and tavern scenes are common in other interludes, especially those of the Prodigal Son variety. But Shakespeare's tavern is more than a drink-shop, while his Riot is not only a "huge bombard of sack" but also a "roasted Manningtree ox with the pudding in his belly."

The site of the Boar's Head tavern in Eastcheap is now as deep-sunk in the ooze of human forgetfulness as that of the palace of Haroun. But it was once a real hostelry, and must have meant much to Londoners of the reigns of Elizabeth and James. Records are scanty, but the very fact that Shakespeare makes it Falstaff's headquarters suggests that it was the best tavern in the city. And the further fact that he avoids mentioning it directly, though quibbling upon the name more than once,[21] suggests, on the one hand, that he kept the name off the stage in order to escape complications with the proprietors of the day, and on the other that he could trust his audience to jump to so obvious an identification without prompting. In any event, no other tavern in Eastcheap is at all likely to have been intended, and as Eastcheap is referred to six times in various scenes, there can be little real doubt that what Falstaff once calls "the King's tavern"[22] is the famous Boar's Head, the earliest known reference to which occurs in a will dating from the reign of Richard II.[23] Whether there is anything or not in Skeat's conjecture that the Glutton in *Piers Plowman*

21 *V.* Part One, II.iv.110: "That damned brawn"; Part Two, I.i.19: "Harry Monmouth's brawn"; II.ii.143: "Doth the old boar feed in the old frank? / At the old place, my lord, in Eastcheap"; and II.iv.224: "Thou whoreson little tidy Bartholomew boar-pig."

22 Part One, II.ii.55. This designation perhaps implies a claim to royal patronage on the proprietor's part, possibly connected with the quasi-historical incident known as the Hurling in Eastcheap, an affray which arose among their retinue while Hal's brothers, the princes John and Thomas, were taking supper at a tavern (unnamed) in Eastcheap, on St. John's Eve, 1410, as is related by Stow (*v.* Kingsford, *op. cit.* p. xxxix).

23 *V.* "East Cheap" in Sugden's *Topographical Dictionary to the Works of Shakespeare.*

made it the scene of his exploits like Falstaff,[24] it was a well-known house of entertainment more than two hundred years before Shakespeare introduced it into his play, and had come therefore by his day to be regarded as a historic hostelry, for which reason it was probably already associated in popular imagination with the floating legends of the wild young prince. What, however, seems to have escaped the attention of modern writers is that the house, with a name that symbolized good living and good fellowship above that of any other London tavern, was almost certainly even better known for good food than for good drink.

Eastcheap, there is plenty of evidence to show, was then, and had long been, the London center at once of butchers and cookshops. Lydgate, writing in the reign of Henry V, puts the following words in the mouth of his *London Lyckpenny:*

> Then I hyed me into Estchepe;
> One cryes "rybbes of befe and many a pye";
> Pewter pots they clattered on a heap;
> There was a harp, pype, and minstrelsy.

The street was famed, in short, not only for meat and drink, but also for the "noise" of musicians, which belonged to "the old Tauerne in Eastcheap" in *The Famous Victories,* and which "Mistress Tearsheet would fain hear" in Part Two of *Henry IV.*[25] As for "rybbes of befe," though we never see or hear of Falstaff eating, or desiring to eat, anything except Goodwife Keech's dish of prawns[26] and the capon, anchovies and halfpenny worth of bread recorded with "an intolerable deal of sack" in the bill found upon him while asleep,[27] Shakespeare nonetheless contrives to associate him perpetually with appetizing food by means of the imagery that plays about his person. For the epithets

24 *V.* note on Piers Plowman, Passus v, line 313, ed. Skeat (Clarendon Press).
25 Part Two, II.iv.
26 *Ibid.* II.i.94ff.
27 Part One, II.iv.536–43.

and comparisons which Hal and Poins apply to him, or he himself makes use of, though at times connected with his consumption of sack, are far more often intended to recall the chief stock-in-trade of the victuallers and butchers of Eastcheap, namely meat of all kinds, and meat both raw and roast.

Falstaff is once likened to a "huge bombard,"[28] once to a "hogshead,"[29] once to a "tun,"[30] and twice to a "hulk," that is, to a cargo boat; the nature of the cargo being specified by Doll, who protests to Mistress Quickly, "There's a whole merchant's venture of Bourdeaux stuff in him, you have not seen a hulk better stuffed in the hold."[31] But beyond these there is little or nothing about him in the vintner's line. When, on the other hand, Shakespeare promises the audience, through the mouth of his Epilogue in Part Two, to continue the story, with Sir John in it, "if you be not too much cloyed with fat meat," the phrase sums up the prevailing image, constant in reference though ever-varying in form, which the physical characteristics of Falstaff presented to his mind's eye, and which he in turn was at pains to keep before the mind's eye of his public. Changes in London, and even more, changes in the language, have obliterated all this for the modern reader, so that what was intended, from the first, as little more than a kind of shimmering half-apprehended jest playing upon the surface of the dialogue, must now be recovered as a piece of archaeology, that is, as something long dead. The laughter has gone out of it; yet I shall be disappointed if the reader does not catch himself smiling now and again at what follows.

"Call in Ribs, call in Tallow" is Hal's cue for Falstaff's entry in the first great Boar's Head scene; and what summons to the choicest feast in comedy could be more apt? For there is the noblest of English dishes straightaway: Sir John as roast Sir Loin-of-Beef, gravy and all. "Tallow," a word often applied to him, generally in opprobrium, is

28 *Ibid.* II.iv.450.
29 Part Two, II.iv.59.
30 Part One, II.iv.447.
31 Part Two, II.iv.59–61.

not rightly understood, unless two facts be recalled: first, that it meant to the Elizabethans liquid fat, as well as dripping or suet or animal fat rendered down; second, that human sweat, partly owing perhaps to the similarity of the word to "suet," was likewise thought of as fat, melted by the heat of the body. The most vivid presentation of Falstaff served up hot, so to say, is the picture we get of him sweating with fright in Mistress Page's dirty linen basket, as it was emptied by her servants into the Thames; and though *The Merry Wives* does not strictly belong to the Falstaff canon, the passage may be quoted here as giving the clue to passages in *Henry IV* itself. For however different in character the Windsor Falstaff may be from his namesake of Eastcheap, he possesses the same body, the body that on Gad's Hill "sweats to death, and *lards* the lean earth, as he walks along."[32]

"And then," he relates to the disguised Ford,

> to be stopped in, like a strong distillation, with stinking clothes that fretted in their own grease! Think of that, a man of my kidney! think of that—that am as subject to heat, as butter; a man of continual dissolution and thaw; it was a miracle to 'scape suffocation. And in the height of this bath, when I was more than half stewed in grease, like a Dutch dish, to be thrown into the Thames, and cooled, glowing-hot, in that surge, like a horse-shoe. Think of that—hissing hot: think of that, Master Brook![33]

The "greasy tallow-catch,"[34] again, to which the Prince compares him, much to the bewilderment of commentators, betokens, I believe, nothing more mysterious than a dripping-pan to catch the fat as the roasting joint turned upon the spit before the fire. Or take the following scrap of dialogue:

[32] Part One, II.ii.109–10.
[33] *Merry Wives of Windsor*, III.v.103–12.
[34] Part One, II.iv.227.

L. CHIEF JUSTICE. What, you are as a candle, the better
part burnt out.
FALSTAFF. A wassail candle, my lord, all tallow—if I
did say of wax, my growth would approve the truth.
L. CHIEF JUSTICE. There is not a white hair on your
face, but should have his effect of gravity.
FALSTAFF. His effect of gravy, gravy, gravy.[35]

Falstaff's repeated "gravy" is a quibble, of course. But it
is not just a feeble jest upon his table manners, as seems
to be usually assumed: it follows upon the mention of
"tallow" and refers to the drops of sweat that never cease
to stand upon his face. In fact, to use a seventeenth-century
expression, applicable to one bathed in perspiration, he
may be said perpetually to "stew in his own gravy."[36]

Indeed, he glories in the fact. Was it not, according to
the physiological notions of the time, the very warrant of
his enormous vitality? Never is he more angered to the
heart than when the Prince likens him one day to a dry
withered old apple-john. His complexion is merely sanguine; heat and moisture mingle to form the element he
moves in; except in moods of mock-repentance he leaves
to baser earth the cold and dry of melancholy.[37]

Once we have the trick of it, all sorts of other allusions
and playful terms of abuse are seen to belong to the same
category, while the analogy between that vast carcass, as
a whole or in its parts, and roasts of various kinds is capable
of almost infinite elaboration. "Chops," for instance, as
he is twice called,[38] carries the double significance of "fat
cheeks" and "cutlets"; "guts," the Elizabethan word for
"tripe," is an epithet that occurs no less than five times;[39]
and "sweet beef" as a term of endearment[40] requires no
explaining. Nor is he only served up as beef; pork, still
more appropriate to the Boar's Head, though brought in

---

35 Part Two, I.ii.155–61.
36 V. O.E.D. "gravy."
37 V. p. 224, *Edinburgh University Journal*, Summer 1942 (article on
"Shakespeare's Universe").
38 Part One, I.ii.140; Part Two, II.iv.211.
39 Part One, II.iv.226, 259, 451; *ibid*. III.iii.156–59.
40 Part One, III.iii.183.

less often, provides some magnificent examples. The term "brawn," which means a large pig fattened for the slaughter, is applied to him on two occasions;[41] on his return from Wales the Prince, enquiring of Bardolph, "Is your master here in London? . . . Where sups he? doth the old boar feed in the old frank?"[42] refers to the familiar inn sign; Falstaff himself declares that he walks the streets followed by the diminutive page "like a sow that hath overwhelmed all her litter but one";[43] last, and best of all, when Doll salutes him between her "flattering busses" as her "whoreson little tidy Bartholomew boar-pig,"[44] she is alluding to the tender sweet-fleshed little sucking-pigs which formed the chief delicacy at Bartholomew Fair.

The mention of Bartholomew Fair, the most popular annual festivity of Elizabethan and Jacobean London, may be linked with two other comparisons, which take us beyond the confines of Eastcheap and help to bestow on Falstaff that "touch of infinity" which Bradley discovers in him, associating him, as they do, with feasting on a vast and communal scale. The first, already quoted above, is the Prince's description of him as a "Manningtree ox with the pudding in his belly,"[45] in other words, as an ox roasted whole and stuffed with sausages, after the fashion of the annual fairs at Manningtree, an Essex town famed for the exceeding fatness of its beasts. But the extremest inch of possibility is reached by Poins when he asks Bardolph "How doth the Martlemas, your master?"[46] Martlemas, or the feast of St Martin, on 11 November, was in those days of scarce fodder the season at which most of the beasts had to be killed off and salted for the winter, and therefore the season for great banquets of fresh meat. Thus it had been for centuries, long before the coming of Christianity,[47] and thus it remained down to the introduction of the cropping of turnips in the eighteenth century. In calling him

41 Part One, II.iv.110; Part Two, I.i.19.
42 Part Two, II.ii.143.
43 Ibid. I.i.11-12.
44 Ibid. II.iv.224-25.
45 Part One, II.iv.452.
46 Part Two, II.ii.100.
47 V. Sir E. K. Chambers, Medieval Stage, ch. xi, "The Beginning of Winter."

a "Martlemas" Poins is at once likening Falstaff's enormous
proportions to the prodigality of fresh-killed meat which the
feast brought, and acclaiming his identity with Riot and
Festivity in general.[48] But perhaps the best comment upon
Falstaff as Martlemas comes from Spenser's procession of
the seasons in the Book of Mutabilitie. His November
might almost be Falstaff himself, though the dates prove
that the two figures must be independent:

> Next was Nouember, he full grosse and fat,
> As fed with lard, and that right well might seeme;
> For, he had been a fatting hogs of late,
> That yet his browes with sweat did reek and steem,
> And yet the season was full sharp and breem.[49]

One might go to the other end of the scale and point out that
the objects Falstaff chooses as a contrast to his person, objects excessively thin, wizened or meager, are likewise often
taken from the food shops. There is, for instance, the shotten herring, the soused gurnet, the bunch of radish, the rabbit-sucker or poulter's hare, and wittiest of all perhaps, the
carbonado—the rasher of bacon, we should say—which he
will only allow Hotspur to make of him, if he is foolish
enough to come in his way.[50] But enough to have shown
that by plying his audience with suggestions of the choicest
food that London and Eastcheap had to offer, whenever the
person of Falstaff is mentioned, Shakespeare lays as it were
the physical foundations of his Falstaff myth.

The prodigiously incarnate Riot, who fills the Boar's
Head with his jollity, typifies much more, of course, than
the pleasures of the table. He stands for a whole globe of
happy continents, and his laughter is "broad as ten thousand beeves at pasture."[51] But he is Feasting first, and his
creator never allows us to forget it. For in this way he not
only perpetually associates him in our minds with appetizing images, but contrives that as we laugh at his wit our souls

48 I owe this point to the late Lord Ernle: writing in *Shakespeare's England* (vol. i, p. 356), he notes: "To Shakespeare's mind the prodigious
plenty of Martlemas suggested Falstaff in its proportions."
49 *The Faerie Queene*, Bk. vii, canto vii, st. 40.
50 Part One, V.iii.59.
51 George Meredith, *The Spirit of Shakespeare*.

shall be satisfied as with marrow and fatness. No one has given finer expression to this satisfaction than Hazlitt, and I may fitly round off the topic with words of his:

> Falstaff's wit is an emanation of a fine constitution; an exuberance of good humor and good nature; an overflowing of his love of laughter and good fellowship; a giving vent to his heart's ease, and overcontentment with himself and others. He would not be in character if he were not so fat as he is; for there is the greatest keeping in the boundless luxury of his imagination and the pampered self-indulgence of his physical appetites. He manures and nourishes his mind with jests, as he does his body with sack and sugar. He carves out his jokes, as he would a capon or a haunch of venison, where there is *cut and come again;* and pours out upon them the oil of gladness. His tongue drops fatness, and in the chambers of his brain "it snows of meat and drink." He keeps perpetually holiday and open house, and we live with him in a round of invitations to a rump and dozen. . . . He never fails to enrich his discourse with allusions to eating and drinking, but we never see him at table. He carries his own larder about with him, and is himself "a tun of man."[52]

MONSIEUR REMORSE

Like all great Shakespearian characters Falstaff is a bundle of contradictions. He is not only Riot but also Repentance. He can turn an eye of melancholy upon us, assume the role of puritan sanctimony, and when it pleases him, even threaten amendment of life. It is, of course, *mock*-repentance, carried through as part of the untiring "play extempore" with which he keeps the Prince, and us, and himself, entertained from beginning to end of the drama. And yet it is not mere game; Shakespeare makes it more interesting by persuading us that there is a strain of sincerity in it; and it almost completely disappears in Part Two, when the rogue

[52] *Characters of Shakespear's Plays* (Hazlitt's *Works,* ed. A. R. Waller and A. Glover, 1902, vol. i, p. 278).

finds himself swimming on the tide of success. There is a good deal of it in Part One, especially in the earliest Falstaff scenes.

> But, Hal, I prithee, trouble me no more with vanity.
> I would to God thou and I knew where a commodity of good names were to be bought.
> Thou hast done much harm upon me, Hal—God for-give thee for it: before I knew thee, Hal, I knew noth-ing, and now am I, if a man should speak truly, little better than one of the wicked: I must give over this life, and I will give it over: by the Lord, an I do not, I am a villain. I'll be damned for never a king's son in Chris-tendom.[53]

One of his favorite poses is that of the innocent, beguiled by a wicked young heir apparent; he even makes it the bur-den of his apologia to the Lord Chief Justice at their first encounter. It serves too when things go wrong, when reso-lute men who have taken £1000 on Gad's Hill are left in the lurch by cowardly friends, or when there's lime in a cup of sack:

> There is nothing but roguery to be found in villainous man, yet a coward is worse than a cup of sack with lime in it. A villainous coward! Go thy ways, old Jack, die when thou wilt, if manhood, good manhood, be not for-got upon the face of the earth, then am I a shotten herring. . . . There lives not three good men unhanged in England, and one of them is fat, and grows old. God help the while! a bad world, I say. I would I were a weaver—I could sing psalms or anything.[54]

But beside this talk of escaping from a wicked world and the toils of a naughty young prince, there is also the pose of personal repentance. At his first entry Poins hails him as Monsieur Remorse, an indication that this is one of his recognized roles among Corinthians and lads of mettle. And we may see him playing it at the opening of Act III, Scene 3, when there is no Hal present to require entertaining.

[53] Part One, I.ii.84–87, 95–102.
[54] *Ibid.* II.iv.124–33.

Well, I'll repent, and that suddenly, while I am in some liking. I shall be out of heart shortly, and then I shall have no strength to repent. An I have not forgotten what the inside of a church is made of, I am a peppercorn, a brewer's horse. The inside of a church! Company, villainous company, hath been the spoil of me.

Such passages, together with the habit of citing Scripture, may have their origin, I have said, in the puritan, psalmsinging, temper of Falstaff's prototype—that comic Lollard, Sir John Oldcastle in the old *Henry IV*.[55] But, if so, the motif, adapted and developed in Shakespeare's hands, has come to serve a different end. In this play of the Prodigal Prince it is Hal who should rightly exhibit moods of repentance; and on the face of it, it seems quite illogical to transfer them to Falstaff, the tempter. Yet there are reasons why Hal could not be thus represented. In the first place, as already noted, repentance in the theological sense, repentance for sin, is not relevant to his case at all, which is rather one of a falling away from political virtues, from the duties laid upon him by his royal vocation. And in the second place, since Henry V is the ideal king of English history, Shakespeare must take great care, even in the days of his "wildness," to guard him from the breath of scandal. As has been well observed by a recent editor: "His riots are mere frolics. He does not get drunk and is never involved in any scandal with a woman."[56] And there is a third reason, this time one of dramatic technique not of morals, why the repentance of the Prince must be kept in the background as much as possible, viz. that as the only satisfactory means of rounding off the two parts, it belongs especially to the last act of the play.

[55] *V. supra*, p. 16 and ch. iv note 20.
[56] *V.* p. xi of *1 Henry IV*, ed. by G. L. Kittredge (Ginn & Co.). I fancy Hal is just a little tipsy at the beginning of Part One, II.iv, but the point is, in general, sound enough, and the more striking that the chroniclers do not hide the fact that Prince Henry was given to sexual intemperance; *v.* Kingsford, *op. cit.* p. 17: "he exercised meanelie the feates of Venus and of Mars, and other pastimes of youth, for so longe as the Kinge his father liued."

Yet Monsieur Remorse is a good puppet in the property box of the old morality, and may be given excellent motions in the fingers of a skilful showman, who is laying himself out, in this play especially, to make fun of the old types. Why not shape a comic part out of it, and hand it over to Falstaff, who as the heir of traditional medieval "antics" like the Devil, the Vice, the Fool, Riot and Lord of Misrule, may very well manage one more? Whether or not Shakespeare argued it out thus, he certainly added the ingredient of melancholy, and by so doing gave a piquancy to the sauce which immensely enhances the relish of the whole dish. If only modern actors who attempt to impersonate Falstaff would realize it!

Falstaff, then, came to stand for the repentance, as well as the riotous living, of the Prodigal Son. And striking references to the parable, four of them, seem to show that his creator was fully aware of what he was doing. "What, will you make a younker of me? shall I not take mine ease in mine inn but I shall have my pocket picked?"[57] Sir John indignantly demands of Mistress Quickly, on discovering, or pretending to discover, the loss of his grandfather's seal ring. The word "younker" calls up a scene from some well-known representation of the parable, in picture or on the stage, a scene to which Shakespeare had already alluded in the following lines from *The Merchant of Venice:*

> How like a younker or a prodigal
> The scarféd bark puts from her native bay,
> Hugged and embracéd by the strumpet wind!
> How like a prodigal doth she return,
> With over-weathered ribs and ragged sails,
> Lean, rent, and beggared by the strumpet wind![58]

Equally vivid is Falstaff's description of the charge of foot he led into battle at Shrewsbury as so "dishonorable ragged" that "you would think that I had a hundred and

57 Part One, III.iii.82–84. "The alternative title for the Prodigal Son was the 'younger,' as the alternative for the good brother was the 'elder' " (Richmond Noble, *Shakespeare's Biblical Knowledge*, p. 277).
58 *The Merchant of Venice*, II.vi.14–19; cf. *3 Henry VI*, II.i.24: "Trimmed like a younker, prancing to his love."

fifty tattered prodigals, lately come from swine-keeping, from eating draff and husks."[59] And seeing that he calls them in the same speech "slaves as ragged as Lazarus in the painted cloth, where the Glutton's dogs licked his sores," we may suppose that, here too, he is speaking right painted cloth, from whence he had studied his Bible;[60] an inference which seems borne out by his third reference, this time from Part Two. Having, you will remember, already honored Mistress Quickly by becoming indebted to her for a hundred marks, that is for over £65, he graciously condescends to borrow £10 more from her. And when she protests that to raise the sum she must be fain to pawn both her plate and the tapestry of her dining chambers, he replies: "Glasses, glasses, is the only drinking—and for thy walls, a pretty drollery or the story of the Prodigal or the German hunting in waterwork is worth a thousand of these bed-hangers and these fly-bitten tapestries."[61] This is not just the patter of the confidence-trickster; Falstaff, we must believe, had a real liking for the Prodigal Son story, or why should that tactful person, mine Host of the Garter Inn, have gone to the trouble of having it painted, "fresh and new," about the walls of the chamber that he let to the greasy philanderer who assumed the part of Sir John, in Windsor.[62] Not being a modern critic, the good man could not know that his guest was an impostor.

But jollification and mock-repentance do not exhaust Falstaff's roles. For most of *Henry IV* he plays the soldier, taking a hand in a couple of campaigns, the first culminating in the death of Hotspur at Shrewsbury, and the other in the encounter between Prince John and the Archbishop of York at Gaultree Forest, where the rebels are finally overthrown. In both of these he performs the useful dramatic function of supplying the light relief, and in so doing he exhibits himself as at once the supreme comic soldier of English literature and a variation of a timeworn theme, the *miles gloriosus* of Plautus.

59 Part One, IV.ii.31–34.
60 Cf. *As You Like It*, III.ii.271–72: "I answer you right painted cloth, from whence you have studied your questions."
61 Part Two, II.i.143–47.
62 *The Merry Wives of Windsor*, IV.v.7.

Suggested References

The number of possible references is vast and grows alarmingly. (The *Shakespeare Quarterly* devotes a substantial part of one issue each year to a list of the previous year's work, and *Shakespeare Survey*—an annual publication—includes a substantial review of recent scholarship, as well as an occasional essay surveying a few decades of scholarship on a chosen topic.) Though no works are indispensable, those listed below have been found helpful.

1. Shakespeare's Times

Byrne, M. St. Clare. *Elizabethan Life in Town and Country*. Rev. ed. New York: Barnes & Noble, Inc., 1961. Chapters on manners, beliefs, education, etc., with illustrations.

Craig, Hardin. *The Enchanted Glass: the Elizabethan Mind in Literature*. New York and London: Oxford University Press, 1936. The Elizabethan intellectual climate.

Nicoll, Allardyce (ed.). *The Elizabethans*. London: Cambridge University Press, 1957. An anthology of Elizabethan writings, especially valuable for its illustrations from paintings, title pages, etc.

Shakespeare's England. 2 vols. Oxford: The Clarendon Press, 1916. A large collection of scholarly essays on a wide variety of topics (e.g., astrology, costume, gardening, horsemanship), with special attention to Shakespeare's references to these topics.

Tillyard, E. M. W. *The Elizabethan World Picture*. London: Chatto & Windus, 1943; New York: The Macmillan Company, 1944. A brief account of some Elizabethan ideas of the universe.

Wilson, John Dover (ed.). *Life in Shakespeare's England*. 2nd ed. New York: The Macmillan Company, 1913. An anthology of Elizabethan writings on the countryside, superstition, education, the court, etc.

2. Shakespeare

Bentley, Gerald E. *Shakespeare: A Biographical Handbook.* New Haven, Conn.: Yale University Press, 1961. The facts about Shakespeare, with virtually no conjecture intermingled.

Bradby, Anne (ed.). *Shakespeare Criticism, 1919–1935.* London: Oxford University Press, 1936. A small anthology of excellent essays on the plays.

Bush, Geoffrey Douglas. *Shakespeare and the Natural Condition.* Cambridge, Mass.: Harvard University Press; London: Oxford University Press, 1956. A short, sensitive account of Shakespeare's view of "Nature," touching most of the works.

Chambers, E. K. *William Shakespeare: A Study of Facts and Problems.* 2 vols. London: Oxford University Press, 1930. An invaluable, detailed reference work; not for the casual reader.

Chute, Marchette. *Shakespeare of London.* New York: E. P. Dutton & Co., Inc., 1949. A readable biography fused with portraits of Stratford and London life.

Clemen, Wolfgang H. *The Development of Shakespeare's Imagery.* Cambridge, Mass.: Harvard University Press, 1951. (Originally published in German, 1936.) A temperate account of a subject often abused.

Craig, Hardin. *An Interpretation of Shakespeare.* Columbia, Missouri: Lucas Brothers, 1948. A scholar's book designed for the layman. Comments on all the works.

Dean, Leonard F. (ed.). *Shakespeare: Modern Essays in Criticism.* New York: Oxford University Press, 1957. Mostly mid-twentieth-century critical studies, covering Shakespeare's artistry.

Granville-Barker, Harley. *Prefaces to Shakespeare.* 2 vols. Princeton, N.J.: Princeton University Press, 1946–47. Essays on ten plays by a scholarly man of the theater.

Harbage, Alfred. *As They Liked It.* New York: The Macmillan Company, 1947. A sensitive, long essay on Shakespeare, morality, and the audience's expectations.

Harbage, Alfred (ed.). *Shakespeare: The Tragedies. A Collection of Critical Essays.* Englewood Cliffs, N.J.: Prentice-Hall, Inc., 1964. A discriminating selection of recent criticism.

Ridler, Anne Bradby (ed.). *Shakespeare Criticism, 1935–1960*. New York and London: Oxford University Press, 1963. An excellent continuation of the anthology edited earlier by Miss Bradby (see above).

Smith, D. Nichol (ed.). *Shakespeare Criticism*. New York: Oxford University Press, 1916. A selection of criticism from 1623 to 1840, ranging from Ben Jonson to Thomas Carlyle.

Spencer, Theodore. *Shakespeare and the Nature of Man*. New York: The Macmillan Company, 1942. Shakespeare's plays in relation to Elizabethan thought.

Stoll, Elmer Edgar. *Shakespeare and Other Masters*. Cambridge, Mass.: Harvard University Press; London: Oxford University Press, 1940. Essays on tragedy, comedy, and aspects of dramaturgy, with special reference to some of Shakespeare's plays.

Traversi, D. A. *An Approach to Shakespeare*. Rev. ed. New York: Doubleday & Co., Inc., 1956. An analysis of the plays, beginning with words, images, and themes, rather than with characters.

Van Doren, Mark. *Shakespeare*. New York: Henry Holt & Company, Inc., 1939. Brief, perceptive readings of all of the plays.

Waith, Eugene M. (ed.). *Shakespeare: The Histories: A Collection of Critical Essays*. Englewood Cliffs, N.J.: Prentice-Hall, Inc., 1965. A convenient anthology of recent essays.

Whitaker, Virgil K. *Shakespeare's Use of Learning*. San Marino, Calif.: Huntington Library, 1953. A study of the relation of Shakespeare's reading to his development as a dramatist.

3. Shakespeare's Theater

Adams, John Cranford. *The Globe Playhouse*. Rev. ed. New York: Barnes & Noble, Inc., 1961. A detailed conjecture about the physical characteristics of the theater Shakespeare often wrote for.

Beckerman, Bernard. *Shakespeare at the Globe, 1599–1609*. New York: The Macmillan Company, 1962. On the playhouse and on Elizabethan dramaturgy, acting, and staging.

Chambers, E. K. *The Elizabethan Stage*. 4 vols. New York: Oxford University Press, 1923. Reprinted with corrections, 1945. A valuable reference work on theaters, theatrical companies, and staging at court.

Harbage, Alfred. *Shakespeare's Audience*. New York: Columbia University Press; London: Oxford University Press, 1941. A study of the size and nature of the theatrical public.

Hodges, C. Walter. *The Globe Restored*. London: Ernest Benn, Ltd., 1953; New York: Coward-McCann, Inc., 1954. A well-illustrated and readable attempt to reconstruct the Globe Theatre.

Kernodle, George R. *From Art to Theatre: Form and Convention in the Renaissance*. Chicago: University of Chicago Press, 1944. Pioneering and stimulating work on the symbolic and cultural meanings of theater construction.

Nagler, A. M. *Shakespeare's Stage*. Tr. by Ralph Manheim. New Haven, Conn.: Yale University Press, 1958. An excellent brief introduction to the physical aspect of the playhouse.

Nicoll, Allardyce (ed.). *Shakespeare Survey 12*. London: Cambridge University Press, 1959. Devoted largely to the Elizabethan theater.

Smith, Irwin. *Shakespeare's Globe Playhouse*. New York: Charles Scribner's Sons, 1957. Chiefly indebted to J. C. Adams' controversial book, with additional material and scale drawings for model-builders.

Venezky, Alice S. *Pageantry on the Shakespearean Stage*. New York: Twayne Publishers, Inc., 1951. An examination of spectacle in Elizabethan drama.

4. Miscellaneous Reference Works

Abbott, E. A. *A Shakespearean Grammar*. New edition. New York: The Macmillan Company, 1877. An examination of differences between Elizabethan and modern grammar.

Bartlett, John. *A New and Complete Concordance . . . to . . . Shakespeare*. New York: The Macmillan Company, 1894. An index to most of Shakespeare's words.

Bullough, Geoffrey. *Narrative and Dramatic Sources of Shakespeare*. 5 vols. Vols. 6 and 7 in preparation. New York: Columbia University Press; London: Routledge & Kegan Paul, Ltd., 1957–. A collection of many of the books Shakespeare drew upon.

Greg, W. W. *The Shakespeare First Folio*. New York and London: Oxford University Press, 1955. A detailed yet readable history of the first collection (1623) of Shakespeare's plays.

Kökeritz, Helge. *Shakespeare's Names*. New Haven, Conn.: Yale University Press, 1959; London: Oxford University Press, 1960. A guide to the pronunciation of some 1,800 names appearing in Shakespeare.

———. *Shakespeare's Pronunciation*. New Haven, Conn.: Yale University Press; London: Oxford University Press, 1953. Contains much information about puns and rhymes.

Linthicum, Marie C. *Costume in the Drama of Shakespeare and His Contemporaries*. New York and London: Oxford University Press, 1936. On the fabrics and dress of the age, and references to them in the plays.

Muir, Kenneth. *Shakespeare's Sources*. London: Methuen & Co., Ltd., 1957. Vol. 2 in preparation. The first volume, on the comedies and tragedies, attempts to ascertain what books were Shakespeare's sources, and what use he made of them.

Onions, C. T. *A Shakespeare Glossary*. London: Oxford University Press, 1911; 2nd ed., rev., with enlarged addenda, 1953. Definitions of words (or senses of words) now obsolete.

Partridge, Eric. *Shakespeare's Bawdy*. Rev. ed. New York: E. P. Dutton & Co., Inc.; London: Routledge & Kegan Paul, Ltd., 1955. A glossary of bawdy words and phrases.

Shakespeare Quarterly. See headnote to Suggested References.

Shakespeare Survey. See headnote to Suggested References.

Smith, Gordon Ross. *A Classified Shakespeare Bibliography 1936–1958*. University Park, Pa.: Pennsylvania State University Press, 1963. A list of some 20,000 items on Shakespeare.

5. *Henry IV* [*Part One*]

Auden, W. H. *The Dyer's Hand and Other Essays*. New York: Random House, Inc.; London: Faber & Faber, Ltd., 1962, pp. 182–208.

Barber, C. L. *Shakespeare's Festive Comedy*. Princeton, N.J.: Princeton University Press; London: Oxford University Press, 1959.

Bradley, A. C. *Oxford Lectures on Poetry*. New York: The Macmillan Company, 1909.

Brooks, Cleanth and R. B. Heilman. *Understanding Drama*. New York: Henry Holt, 1945; London: George G. Harrap & Company, 1947.

Charlton, H. B. "Falstaff," *Shakespearian Comedy*. 4th ed. London: Methuen and Co., Ltd., 1938.

Dickinson, Hugh. "The Reformation of Prince Hal," *Shakespeare Quarterly*, XII (1961), 33–46.

Doran, Madeleine. "Imagery in *Richard II* and in *Henry IV*," *Modern Language Review*, XXXVII (1942), 113–22.

Evans, Gareth Lloyd. "The Comical-tragical-historical Method—*Henry IV*," *Stratford-upon-Avon Studies 3: Early Shakespeare*. J. R. Brown and B. Harris (eds.). London: Edward Arnold, Ltd., 1961.

Hemingway, Samuel B. "On Behalf of That Falstaff," *Shakespeare Quarterly*, III (1952), 307–11.

Jenkins, Harold. *The Structural Problem in Shakespeare's "Henry the Fourth."* London: Methuen and Co., Ltd., 1956. Reprinted in the Signet Classic edition of *Henry IV* [*Part Two*].

Kris, Ernst. "Prince Hal's Conflict," *Psychoanalytic Quarterly*, XVII (1948), 487–505.

McLuhan, Herbert Marshall. "*Henry IV*, a Mirror for Magistrates," *University of Toronto Quarterly*, XVII (1948), 152–60.

Spivack, Bernard. "Falstaff and the Psychomachia," *Shakespeare Quarterly*, VIII (1957), 449–59.

Sprague, Arthur Colby. "Gadshill Revisited," *Shakespeare Quarterly*, IV (1953), 125–37.

Stoll, Elmer Edgar. *Shakespeare Studies: Historical and Comparative in Method.* New York: The Macmillan Company, 1927.

Tillyard, E. M. W. *Shakespeare's History Plays.* London: Chatto and Windus, 1944; New York: The Macmillan Company, 1946.

Traversi, D. A. *Shakespeare: from "Richard II" to "Henry V."* Stanford: Stanford University Press, 1957; London: Hollis & Carter, Ltd., 1958.

Unger, Leonard. *The Man in the Name.* Minneapolis: University of Minnesota Press, 1956.

Waldock, A. J. A. "The Men in Buckram," *Review of English Studies,* XXIII (1947), 16–23.

Wilson, John Dover. *The Fortunes of Falstaff.* London: Cambridge University Press, 1943; New York: The Macmillan Company, 1944. A selection from this book is reprinted in the present edition.

The SIGNET Classic Shakespeare

- [ ] **ALL'S WELL THAT ENDS WELL**, Sylvan Barnet, ed., Tufts University. (#CD296—50¢)
- [ ] **ANTONY AND CLEOPATRA**, Barbara Everett, ed., Cambridge University. (#CQ741—95¢)
- [ ] **AS YOU LIKE IT**, Albert Gilman, ed., Boston University. (#CQ933—95¢)
- [ ] **THE COMEDY OF ERRORS**, Harry Levin, Harvard. (#CQ761—95¢)
- [ ] **CORIOLANUS**, Reuben Brower, ed., Harvard. (#CQ806—95¢)
- [ ] **CYMBELINE**, Richard Hosley, ed., University of Arizona. (#CQ763—95¢)
- [ ] **HAMLET**, Edward Hubler, ed., Princeton University. (#CQ771—95¢)
- [ ] **HENRY IV, Part II**, Norman H. Holland, ed., M.I.T. (#CQ856—95¢)
- [ ] **HENRY V**, John Russell Brown, ed., University of Birmingham. (#CQ858—95¢)
- [ ] **HENRY VI, Part I**, Lawrence V. Ryan, ed., Stanford. (#CD333—50¢)
- [ ] **HENRY VI, Part II**, Arthur Freeman, ed., Boston. (#CD336—50¢)
- [ ] **HENRY VI, Part III**, Milton Crane, ed., George Washington University. (#CT383—75¢)
- [ ] **HENRY VIII**, Samuel Schoenbaum, ed., Northwestern University. (#CQ850—95¢)
- [ ] **JULIUS CAESAR**, William and Barbara Rosen, eds., University of Connecticut. (#CQ826—95¢)
- [ ] **KING JOHN**, William H. Matchett, ed., University of Washington. (#CD330—50¢)
- [ ] **KING LEAR**, Russel Fraser, ed., Princeton University. (#CQ795—95¢)
- [ ] **LOVE'S LABOR LOST**, John Arthos, ed., University of Michigan. (#CQ848—95¢)

C

- [ ] **THE MERRY WIVES OF WINDSOR, William Green,** ed., Queens College. (#CD318—50¢)
- [ ] **A MIDSUMMER NIGHT'S DREAM, Wolfgang Clemen,** ed., University of Munich. (#CQ823—95¢)
- [ ] **MUCH ADO ABOUT NOTHING, David Stevenson,** ed., Hunter College. (#CQ830—95¢)
- [ ] **OTHELLO, Alvan Kernan,** ed., Yale University. (#CQ756—95¢)
- [ ] **RICHARD II, Kenneth Muir,** ed., University of Liverpool. (#CQ808—95¢)
- [ ] **RICHARD III, Mark Eccles,** ed., University of Wisconsin. (#CQ831—95¢)
- [ ] **ROMEO AND JULIET, Joseph Bryant,** ed., University of North Carolina. (#CQ796—95¢)
- [ ] **THE TAMING OF THE SHREW, Robert Heilman,** ed., University of Washington. (#CQ792—95¢)
- [ ] **THE TEMPEST, Roberg Langbaum,** ed., University of Virginia. (#CQ825—95¢)
- [ ] **TIMON OF ATHENS, Maurice Charney,** ed., Rutgers. (#CD289—50¢)
- [ ] **TITUS ANDRONICUS, Sylvan Barnet,** ed., Tufts. (#CD197—50¢)
- [ ] **TROILUS AND CRESSIDA, Daniel Seltzer,** ed., Harvard. (#CT589—75¢)
- [ ] **TWELFTH NIGHT, Herschel Clay Baker,** ed., Harvard. (#CQ748—95¢)
- [ ] **THE TWO GENTLEMEN OF VERONA, Bertrand Evans,** ed., University of California. (#CQ805—95¢)
- [ ] **THE WINTER'S TALE, Frank Kermode,** ed., University of Bristol. (#CQ793—95¢)
- [ ] **THE SONNETS, William Burto,** ed., Introduction by W. H. Auden. (#CQ827—95¢)

THE NEW AMERICAN LIBRARY, INC.,
P.O. Box 999, Bergenfield, New Jersey 07621

Please send me the SIGNET CLASSIC BOOKS I have checked above. I am enclosing $_____(check or money order—no currency or C.O.D.'s). Please include the list price plus 25¢ a copy to cover handling and mailing costs. (Prices and numbers are subject to change without notice.)

Name_____

Address_____

City_____State_____Zip Code_____
Allow at least 3 weeks for delivery

MENTOR Books of Plays

Edited by Sylvan Barnet,
Morton Berman and William Burto

☐ **EIGHT GREAT TRAGEDIES.** The great dramatic literature of the ages, eight memorable tragedies by Aeschylus, Euripides, Sophocles, Shakespeare, Ibsen, Strindberg, Yeats, and O'Neill. With essays on tragedy by Aristotle, Emerson and others.　　　　　(#MJ1510—$1.95)

☐ **EIGHT GREAT COMEDIES.** Complete texts of eight masterpieces of comic drama by Aristophanes, Machiavelli, Shakespeare, Molière, John Gay, Wilde, Chekhov, and Shaw. Includes essays on comedy by four distinguished critics and scholars.　　　(#ME1340—$1.75)

☐ **THE GENIUS OF THE EARLY ENGLISH THEATRE.** Complete plays including three anonymous plays—"Abraham and Isaac," "The Second Shepherd's Play," and "Everyman," and Marlowe's "Doctor Faustus," Shakespeare's "Macbeth," Jonson's "Volpone," and Milton's "Samson Agonistes," with critical essays.
　　　　　　　　　　　　　　　　(#MJ1455—$1.95)

𝒪

The SIGNET CLASSIC Poetry Series

☐ **THE SELECTED POETRY OF BROWNING.** Edited by
George Ridenour   (#CY789—$1.25)

☐ **THE SELECTED POETRY OF BYRON.** Edited by W. H.
Auden   (#CW905—$1.50)

☐ **THE SELECTED POETRY OF DONNE.** Edited by Marius
Bewley   (#CW833—$1.50)

☐ **THE SELECTED POETRY OF DRYDEN.** Edited by John
Arthos   (#CW493—$1.50)

☐ **THE SELECTED POETRY OF KEATS.** Edited by Paul de
Man   (#CW901—$1.50)

☐ **THE SELECTED POETRY OF POPE.** Edited by Martin
Price   (#CW853—$1.50)

☐ **THE SELECTED POETRY AND PROSE OF SIDNEY.**
Edited by David Kalstone   (#CY498—$1.25)

☐ **THE SELECTED POETRY OF SHELLEY.** Edited by Harold
Bloom   (#CW832—$1.50)

☐ **THE SELECTED POETRY AND PROSE OF WORDS-
WORTH.** Edited by G. H. Hartman   (#CJ854—$1.95)